DISCOVERY & EXPLORATION

Opening Up North America
1497–1800

CAROLINE COX
KEN ALBALA

JOHN S. BOWMAN and MAURICE ISSERMAN
General Editors

Facts On File, Inc.

Opening Up North America, 1497–1800

Facts On File, Inc.
132 West 31st Street
New York NY 10001

Library of Congress Cataloging-in-Publication Data

Cox, Caroline.
  Discovery and exploration : opening up North America, 1497–1800 / Caroline Cox and Ken Albala.
     p. cm.
   Includes bibliographical references and index.
    ISBN 0-8160-5261-1 (hc.)
    1. North America—Discovery and exploration—Juvenile literature. 2. Explorers—North America—History—Juvenile literature. I. Albala, Ken, 1964– II. Title.
  E45.C67 2005
  917.04—dc22   2004010500

Text design by Erika K. Arroyo
Cover design by Pehrsson Design
Maps by Dale Williams

Printed in the United States of America

VB FOF 10 9 8 7 6 5 4 3 2 1

This book is printed on acid-free paper.

CONTENTS

Note on Photos

Many of the illustrations and photographs used in this book are old, historical images. The quality of the prints is not always up to current standards, as in some cases the originals are from old or poor-quality negatives or are damaged. The content of the illustrations, however, made their inclusion important despite problems in reproduction.

ACKNOWLEDGMENTS

 The authors would like to extend their deepest gratitude to Robyn Potts who did amazing bibliographic work for us and whose skills proved to be a great reassurance of our role as teachers. The best of luck in graduate school. Holly Levison and Victor Ninov deserve special thanks for their help as do all those friends and family who tolerated our brief stint as armchair explorers.

PREFACE

The story of the exploration of the northern tier of North America between 1497 and 1800 is not often told in one complete narrative. Studies of individual explorers, the exploits of one European nation, or the history of a single region are more typical of recent textbooks and curricula. The separation in studying what would become Canada from the United States, although understandable given the limitations of class time, makes even less sense. Explorers from England, France, Portugal, Spain, and the Netherlands traversed the length of the Atlantic coastline in search of a northwest passage to the Pacific, among other motives. Their rivalry, and the fact that none had initially carved out a definitive sphere of influence, makes coverage of all these nations together absolutely crucial. Thus, this volume seeks to integrate all voyages chronologically into one story stretching from Florida to Newfoundland, covering the first recorded contact of the Englishman John Cabot in 1497 through to Scottish-born Alexander Mackenzie's journey across the Rocky Mountains to the Pacific in 1793.

The story of these many expeditions that steadily pieced together the geography of northeastern North America is also less well known than the epochal voyages of Genoan explorer Christopher Columbus and the conquests by the Spanish that happened in his wake. Even though the exploration of North America began only a few years after Columbus, settlement took a good century or more. Voyages were more sporadic and the information gathered was often carefully guarded to prevent it from falling into enemy hands.

This means that, not only is the historical record less complete for northeastern North America, but the lives of many of the explorers themselves are shrouded in mystery. The fact that so many diverse individuals were involved, both European and Native American, and so many of the voyages ended in disaster, also makes this a less straightforward account. No nation sustained a continuous program of exploration either. Political events back in Europe often held back exploration for whole generations, so that both geographical knowledge as well as a firm foothold on the continent remained elusive well into the 17th century. Furthermore, many explorers were really searching for a navigable route to Asia and the spice trade and only incidentally found profitable trade in furs or fishing on the Atlantic coast.

THE MOTIVES BEHIND EXPLORATION

It is important to recognize that few, if any, of these voyages were made purely for the sake of exploration. Profit was the primary motive, and finding the shortest route to Asia was the surest way to find it in the minds of early modern Europeans. Explorers and European rulers had a vested interest in beating rival nations, both for their own glory and to spread their form of Christian faith, but most important, to raise money with which they could wage war. Each nation wanted to do what it could to protect its trading interests, and that included controlling trade routes and territories that might add to their wealth. This is why European nations directly sponsored, financed, or issued licenses for Atlantic exploration. It also explains why encounters among explorers from rival nations often turned violent.

In the course of the 16th century, the English, Portuguese, Spanish, and French sponsored their own voyages. They also began to carve out their own spheres of influence, although the ownership of some regions, especially those that remained uncharted, was still in dispute. Some regions, such as Newfoundland, were visited by fishermen and fur traders from many nations, but by the 17th century, British, Dutch, Swedish, and French colonists had begun to settle permanently in northeastern North America to exploit its fur trade, rich farmland, lumber, and fisheries. Even though there was money to be made in all these ventures, many merchants still dreamed of finding a northwest passage. Some continued to look for a sea route in icy waters around the north of the continent. Others continued to search for what they called an inland northwest passage. This was a river they believed could be easily navigated and would allow traders to travel from the Atlantic to the Pacific Ocean across the middle of the continent.

As exploration moved from the coastline into the interior, the fur trade grew increasingly important. Europeans quickly discovered that the continent was a source of luxurious pelts. Beaver pelts were especially important, but furs from martens and wolves were in demand too. This new source of pelts became available just as Europeans were exhausting their own supplies from overhunting. To make money in the North American fur trade, traders needed to contact American Indian hunters and arrange with them to bring their furs to European trading posts to sell them. Consequently, journeys of exploration often went hand in hand with a desire to find new groups of Native peoples who would be a source of furs and a desire to gain an advantage over a competing trader.

International competition also continued to be a critical factor driving exploration. A European nation could lay claim to a territory only by having a presence there, which often meant building a fort and protecting it with force. Thus, not only were individual fur traders in competition with each other, but the nations from which they came also had a vested interest in their success and would often help pay for the costs of the expedition. European powers also frequently allied with rival Native American peoples, drawing them into their conflicts.

Explorers, then, were not just engaged in discovery for the sake of the adventure. Whether exploring across the North Atlantic or across North America, trading profits and international power were critical factors setting these great journeys in motion.

NEW APPROACHES TO HISTORY

The great individuals of discovery and exploration have long been a favorite subject for historians. Within a few years of the first discoveries, European historians were collecting journals and firsthand accounts, which they then edited and published. One of the most important of these editors was Englishman Richard Hakluyt (ca. 1552–1616), whose monumental effort to record these achievements forms the basis of much subsequent coverage of the topic. Accounts of explorers' adventures and the great personal risks they took have consistently captured the public imagination too. However, the way scholars have written about explorers and their goals has changed significantly in the past 30 years.

In keeping with the move toward social history—that is, examining what ordinary people were doing rather than just focusing on the famous names of history—there has been a greater realization that the famous explorers rarely acted alone. Whether on land or at sea, significant groups of people were usually involved in expeditions. Historians such as Barry Gough, in his book entitled *First Across the Continent: Sir Alexander Mackenzie,* and John Mack Faragher, in his biography *Daniel Boone: The Life and Legend of an American Pioneer,* have included a more complete picture. While they keep the legendary figures in a central place in their narratives, the other members of the parties and their significant contributions to the expeditions' successes receive a full treatment.

Ethnohistorians—those who study the history and culture from the perspective of a particular group of people—have also shifted the perspective in the story of exploration to see and understand it from the American Indian point of view. Even the very concept of "discovery" has been seriously questioned: How can anyone claim to have "discovered" land where people are already living? In place of discovery, recent scholarship has focused on "encounters" and explores not only the impact of the arrival of Europeans on Native Americans but how contact altered the European world-outlook. It has become intellectually difficult to reconcile the European view that primitive peoples, or "savages" as they called them, would benefit from the imposition of European culture and religion with the plain fact that such people were thriving on their terms, and in fact, some were not really "primitive" at all. And despite their assumed superiority, Europeans absolutely depended on Native Americans not only for trade but often for their very survival.

Through their research, historians such as Colin Calloway, in his book *New Worlds for All: Indians, Europeans, and the Remaking of Early America,* and Daniel Richter, in *Facing East from Indian Country: A Native History of Early America,* have shown that as soon as European explorers reached the shores of northeastern North America, Native peoples were actively engaged in trade with the new arrivals. Native peoples readily shared geographic information and provided guides for exploring parties. Few expeditions moved without such guides or a plan to recruit them as soon as possible. Explorers in their journals frequently acknowledged their indebtedness to the critical information they received from Native guides. However, that critical role was written out of many history books as writers focused on dynamic European leaders and a triumphal view of European expansion. Ethnohistorians have helped refocus people's understanding of events that is more true to the experience of those men—and women—who were involved in exploration.

As historians' attention turned to Native peoples, they also became increasingly aware that Native women were sometimes participants in expeditions. A number of fur traders established relationships with Native women. These were sometimes entered into for trading or diplomatic reasons, but the relationships were sometimes long lasting. Historian Sylvia Van Kirk, in *Many Tender Ties: Women in Fur Trade Society, 1670–1870,* has shown that Native women brought many skills to the relationship and were able to show the traders how to survive in a country that was unfamiliar to them. Native women were often able to act as a bridge between European and Native cultures.

This new attention by historians has enabled them to take a fresh look at the impact of exploration on Native society and the dramatic economic changes that took place as a result of European exploration. Historians such as William Swagerty, in his article "Indian Trade in the Trans-Mississippi West to 1870," have shown the wide-reaching scale of Native trading activity long before the arrival of Europeans. Through studies such as his, people now have a better understanding of how European explorers were able to use these well-worn trading routes as they moved across the continent.

THE COLUMBIAN EXCHANGE

By far the most sweeping change in the way discovery and exploration is now studied has come about through an understanding of what historians call "The Columbian Exchange," a term coined by Alfred Crosby in 1972 in a book of this title. Since that time, historians have focused on what might be called the more sinister side of transcontinental encounters. In the original discussion, the emphasis was on the exchange that involved plants and animals: Europeans brought wheat, horses, and cattle to North America and brought back tomatoes, potatoes, maize (Indian corn), and a variety of other species to Europe. But the explorers also brought with them firearms, alcohol, and, above all, European diseases such as smallpox and measles. For Europeans, these were still dangerous diseases that sometimes killed. However, having had continual contact with these diseases, Europeans had built up some immunity—that is, resistance to these diseases had been genetically selected over the generations as a positive trait.

Native Americans had no such immunity. In the several millennia since Native Americans had left the Eurasian continent, they had not been exposed to these diseases and so had never built up immunities to them. In the long run, these diseases proved devastating. Some Native American groups disappeared from the face of the earth forever. One historian, David E. Stannard, has even called these events an "American Holocaust" in his book of the same name. Recent research has focused on trying to quantify the catastrophe and calculate what the precontact population of North America for the region above the Rio Grande—the territories of the modern United States and Canada—might have been. Some scholars put the number as high as 10 million. Scholars also estimate that by the end of the 17th century, that total had dropped perhaps as low as 2 million.

SUPPORTING ELEMENTS

Ironically, even though explorers were the unwitting agents of this tragedy and ecological transformation, their books, journals, and letters provide some of the best records about ocean travel, Native cultures, and the landscape through which they traveled. These records often have to be read with caution. Explorers writing about an expedition afterward were often self-promoting or trying to raise money for future journeys. Books sold better if they told exciting stories rather than about days of tedium. Still, with that screen of caution in place, the records can provide a window onto the explorers' world and that of their teams and the people they encountered. One of the special features of this book is its generous quoting from these original texts.

The reading list at the end of this volume includes some of these works along with some of the great classics of discovery and exploration, as well as works that reflect the most recent scholarship. These books are all accessible to a general audience interested in further reading on this subject. To help teachers and students alike, the suggested reading list also includes quality Internet sites that have rich resources. Additionally, there is a list of movies that are generally available either in a local video store or for purchase online. These movies, which include both documentaries and drama, have been selected for their faithfulness to historical events.

Throughout the book itself, two other elements enlarge and enhance the main narrative. Sidebar essays explore topics that, if sometimes of secondary relevance, are no less interesting for creating a fuller picture of life during this era. The many illustrations provide still more graphic views of the subject matter, while the numerous maps provide the means to see where everything is taking place, a vital need when discovery and exploration are being discussed. Finally, the glossary provides definitions of the many unfamiliar and more technical words or terms that appear in the course of the work.

THE LESSONS OF HISTORY

Although this book has taken into account recent research, it is for the most part written from the primary sources themselves—that is, from individuals who actually experienced these events or wrote about them at the time. This naturally means that the bulk of the narrative contained here consists of the facts, as much as can be ascertained, of exactly who went where, when, and why. This may give the impression that this is merely another triumphant account of the discovery of North America by great explorers, but nothing could be further from the truth. There has been a consistent attempt to balance these dazzling figures. There is also an awareness throughout that these events were not always glorious or even beneficial for the parties involved, and that plain greed and cruelty motivated many of these figures to act. Furthermore, much of the so-called exploration described here was purely accidental, and it can be refreshing to note how hopelessly confused and ill-prepared many of these explorers were. Many of the expeditions described here were abysmal failures.

Despite their mixed motives, the great national interests at stake, and the fact that teams of people were necessary, expedition leaders were still pivotal figures. Their drive and energy brought expeditions into being. When expeditions were successful, it was often because of careful planning and the ability to anticipate a variety of possible setbacks. Exploring parties and crews were often nervous and fearful, and there were times when the leader had to cajole and encourage people to carry on. Thus, heroic individuals get their due in this account, for without understanding them, this entire age of exploration becomes meaningless.

1

TRIUMPH AND DISAPPOINTMENT

1789–1793

In July 1793, the young Scot, Alexander Mackenzie, who was leading a party of nine men and a friendly dog, noted in his later book about their adventures that they had "come in sight of the sea." The sea they were looking out on was the Pacific Ocean. His party had fulfilled the hopes of European explorers for more than two centuries: They had found a route across the North American continent in its northern latitudes. Slowly over the years, explorers and fur traders had steadily extended their knowledge of the waterways of the continent farther and farther into the west. Now Mackenzie had completed the last part of the puzzle.

Mackenzie had crossed the Continental Divide and found a route down the western side of the Rocky Mountains and found himself gazing out at the Pacific Ocean. He had set off on the journey out of a sense of adventure, a desire to extend his knowledge of the region,

and a need to satisfy his own ambitions and interests. He had embarked on the journey on behalf of his fur trading company, the North West Company, in which he was a partner. He had also done it for his nation, Great Britain, which rewarded him a few years later by making him a knight, and he became Sir Alexander Mackenzie.

Reward and international recognition would be his, but if Mackenzie felt any excitement as he gazed out on the Pacific, the statement in his book showed no hint of it. There was still a lot of work to be done. The group was only at the mouth of the river they had traveled down, and he wanted to get out to the open sea. They headed out into the channel and, in the strong wind, they were buffeted so much that they had to shelter in a small cove. There, perilously low on food supplies, Mackenzie and his men celebrated with a dinner of boiled porcupine. Mackenzie was anx-

Alexander Mackenzie painted the inscription shown on this rock near present-day Bella Coola, British Columbia. *(National Archives of Canada)*

ious to find a safe spot from which he could calculate his exact latitude, and he moved the group to a small rocky island to do it.

On that island, amid a bustle of trade with Native peoples in furs and sea otter pelts, Mackenzie made his calculations that would prove to the world that his party had reached the Pacific Ocean. As the group was packing up to leave later that morning, Mackenzie, on impulse, decided to leave what he called a "brief memorial" of their visit. Using a mixture of bear grease and ver-million, a red dye, he wrote the following inscription on the face of a rock: "Alex Mackenzie from Canada by land 22d July 1793."

MACKENZIE'S FIRST EXPEDITION

For Mackenzie, this was the culmination of years of dreaming and planning. He had been born in Scotland in 1762 to a prosperous fam-ily and had emigrated to North America with some relatives when he was 12 years old. Few details are known about his early life. When he wrote his book of his expeditions in 1801, a wealthy man and publicly honored for his accomplishments, he chose to say little about his childhood, focusing instead on the journeys themselves. However, he did reveal that he had always had "an inquisitive mind and an enterprising spirit" matched with "a body equal to the most arduous undertakings." He revealed he had been ambitious too and so, shortly after his arrival in North America, he headed to the territory northwest of Lake Superior to enter the fur trade. He was successful and led many expeditions, steadily extending European knowledge of the continent and the scope of the fur trade. He was sure it was possible to get to the Pacific Ocean across the continent and felt he had the skills to find the route. So he embarked on what he called "the perilous enterprise."

This journey in 1793 was not his first attempt to reach the Pacific. The first had been in June 1789, when he led an expedition that set off down the Slave River from Fort Chipewyan on Lake Athabasca, in what is today northern Alberta. That journey resembled many such expeditions that had taken place before. It involved careful planning and gathering together all the most recent information from others who traveled in the region, European and Native. Just as with other exploring parties, his would trade for furs as it went and pay for the costs of the expedition by the profits they made.

As with many journeys of exploration, Native diplomacy played an important role in it. Consequently, Mackenzie's party included a number of French Canadian traders and the Native wives of two of them. It also included the Chipewyan leader, whom Mackenzie called either Nestabeck or the English Chief; Nestabeck's two wives; and other young Native men. Nestabeck's role as an intermedi-

Alexander Mackenzie attempted to reach the Pacific Ocean many times before succeeding in 1793. *(National Archives of Canada)*

ary was critical even though they were traveling into territory unknown to him. Guides and interpreters would have to be recruited along the way and, while Mackenzie would do what he could, much would depend on Nestabeck, whom Mackenzie described in his account as "a principal leader of his countrymen."

The journey confronted them with moments of great hope, great fear, delays, frustrations, and lots of hard work. At the high latitudes in which they were traveling, summer comes late. Even though it was June, the ice was just breaking up on the rivers and lakes as they headed to the Great Slave Lake. European traders who had visited that lake before had heard from Native peoples of a great river that flowed from it, and that was what Mackenzie was hoping to find. It took a long time. Even their local guide from the Yellowknife people got lost. Nestabeck was furious with the guide and, according to Mackenzie, flew into "a great passion." After searching through inlets, coves, ice, and rocks, they eventually found the entrance to the great river. On maps today, it bears Mackenzie's name and, at more than 1,100 miles long and often more than half a mile wide, it is one of the great rivers of the world.

Unfortunately for Mackenzie, it did not lead to the Pacific. High mountains were

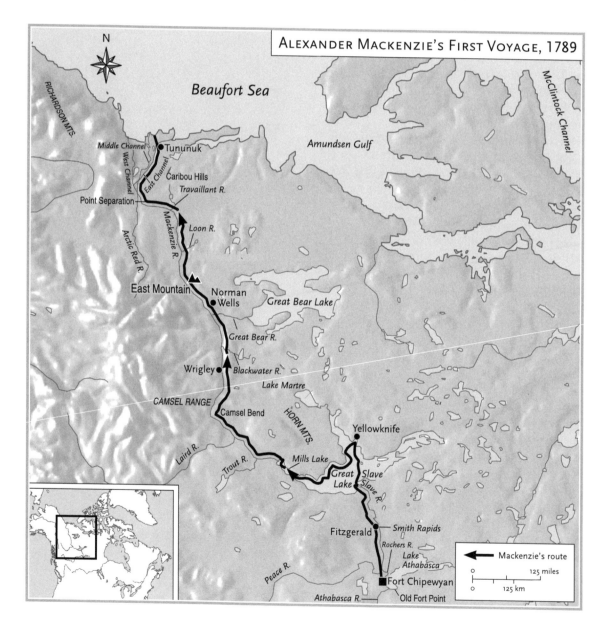

ALEXANDER MACKENZIE'S FIRST VOYAGE, 1789

always to their west, and there was no sign of a break in them through which the river might wind. Ice was forming on the river at night even though it was July and information they picked up from local people was not encouraging. They had met small groups of Slave and Dogrib people, who had been nervous as the strangers approached. However, Nestabeck found some among them who spoke Chipewyan and was able to smooth the path. These people were emphatic that the sea was a long way off and the journey filled with danger. This news made Mackenzie's own party anxious to turn back, but once they had a local guide with them, they agreed to press on.

Still, the river flowed northwest and made no sharp turn to the west. They traveled through a great gorge where the river spilled out into a broad channel with many islands. Mackenzie's calculations showed they were at latitude 67°N, there was ice on the riverbanks, and the weather was steadily colder. Mackenzie again had to talk his party into pressing onward. They met the Inuit peoples of the Arctic region, whom Mackenzie called "Eskmeaux," who told them they were not far from the sea. A few days later, when he and Nestabeck climbed a hill for a better view, they looked down on a huge body of water filled with ice floes. The ice and the whales they later saw convinced Mackenzie they were at the Arctic Sea. (They were at what is today called Beaufort Sea.)

Mackenzie was disappointed. He had mapped a great river to an ocean while making detailed observations of the landscape, the peoples he encountered, and their way of life. He had opened the door to future traders, advanced the understanding of the great waterways of the sub-Arctic, and, when they returned to Fort Chipewyan, had traveled a journey of nearly 3,000 miles without mishap. But he had not found the route to the Pacific.

MACKENZIE'S SECOND EXPEDITION

However, he was even more certain that such a route existed. After visiting England to improve his skills in navigation and mapping and to acquire some new instruments, in 1792 he was ready to try again. Now 30 years old, he was convinced he was the man with the skill and experience to lead another expedition to find it. Preparation was critical to success, and he carefully planned his next attempt, which, Mackenzie decided, would take place in two stages. The first would take his expedition high into the Rockies, where an advance party would already have prepared the ground to build a fort. The fort would be the expedition's winter quarters and a future trading post. After waiting through the winter, trading and preparing equipment, the second stage would take place as soon as the snow melted the following spring. Then they would cross the Rockies and try to find a river that would lead to the Pacific.

Mackenzie knew that having a good team was critical to success. Earlier experience taught him to keep the expedition as lean and efficient as possible, so, on the second stage of the expedition, he only took nine men with him. Among these, the leading figure was the 22-year-old Alexander MacKay (sometimes spelled McKay). Mackenzie had particularly wanted MacKay, a seasoned backwoodsman, to join the group. MacKay had been born in New York to a Loyalist family, just before the American Revolution. Loyalists were those who stayed loyal to the British during the Revolution. The MacKay family and many other Loyalists left the United States during and after the war and went to live in what was known as Upper Canada, now Ontario. As a young man, MacKay went west to enter the fur trade. Now, on this expedition, MacKay

Birch-Bark Canoes

Canoes were the principal means of transportation on the waterways of North America when the first Europeans arrived, and European explorers and fur traders quickly copied Native construction techniques. Materials varied from region to region, but in northern latitudes, travelers used birchbark. Despite the name "birch-bark canoe," the frame of the canoe was usually made of white cedar. Only its outer skin would be birch bark. The roots of a spruce tree would be used to sew the sections of bark together; the resin of the spruce was used to glue it to make it watertight.

The Indians had developed a technique whereby they could take the bark from a birch tree without killing the tree. They simply cut a vertical incision down the length of the tree trunk, but they cut through only the outer bark. The outer bark could then be peeled off in huge strips, leaving the inner layer, the living layer, intact and the tree alive. One fur trader from the end of the 18th century, David Thompson, noted in his narrative about his experiences that it was common to see single strips of bark up to two and a half feet wide and up to 15 feet long. Pieces this size minimized the amount of stitching and gluing that needed to be done and made the canoe stronger. An experienced canoe builder could look at a tree and tell where the thickest bark was and use that for the bottom of the canoe, where it would bear the most weight. The largest canoes used by the fur traders were 36 feet in length and could carry a load up to 6,000 pounds.

As an excellent way to travel along rivers, birch-bark canoes, such as the one shown here, were first made by American Indians and later adopted by the European explorers. *(National Archives of Canada)*

quickly became Mackenzie's right-hand man. Mackenzie always referred to MacKay as his "assistant," and it was frequently MacKay's assistance that was critical to success in difficult situations. Of the others, two men, Joseph Landry and Charles Ducette, had traveled with Mackenzie on the 1789 expedition to the Arctic. Of the remaining six men in the party, four were French Canadian and two were young Native men.

One thing they all had in common was lots of experience as canoe men on the rivers of the West. It was experience that was critical. Much of the journey would involve paddling on rivers, and the pace would be grueling. The group was traveling in a specially built, lightweight canoe that was 25 feet long and just under five feet at the beam, its widest part. The weight of the canoe was important because the trip would certainly involve many *portages*—that is, the times when the canoe

and all the baggage and supplies have to be carried around obstacles such as rapids or waterfalls or moved across land to another river. Consequently, Mackenzie wanted a canoe that two men could carry "three or four miles without resting." No other men could be spared for the task because this expedition was carrying more than 3,000 pounds of supplies that would also have to be carried.

THE EXPEDITION SETS OFF

On October 10, 1792, the expedition, at this time probably about 12 men total, set off on the first stage from Fort Chipewyan on Lake Athabasca. They followed the Peace River to the west and by late October reached the fork of the Peace and Smoky Rivers, on the eastern side of the Rocky Mountains. Here they met up with the advance party and completed building what they called Fort Fork, in which

Fort Chipewyan, located in present-day Alberta, Canada, was founded in 1788. *(National Archives of Canada)*

Linking Lake Superior and Montreal with the western lakes and rivers and ultimately the Pacific Ocean, Grand Portage, headquarters of the North West Company, served as one of the most vital fur trading posts in North America after its establishment in the 1780s. Since being designated a national monument, the Grand Portage buildings, shown here, were reconstructed in the early 1970s. *(Library of Congress, Prints and Photographs Division [HABS, MINN,16-GRAMA,1-2])*

they spent the winter. Even though they now needed to work on the construction of their winter shelter, the men were probably glad to do work other than paddling. Mackenzie wrote that they had been exhausted when they arrived, which was hardly surprising. Not

only had they just completed the first stage of this journey, most of the men who were with him had also, earlier that year, taken furs from Fort Chipewyan to Rainy Lake, just west of Lake Superior, and come back with supplies. All these miles would have been logged in

with furs back to Fort Chipewyan as soon as spring came. He was pleased. The profits on these furs would help pay for the expedition.

The group set off in May 1793, as soon as the ground thawed. It was only just as they were leaving that Mackenzie was able to recruit the two young Native men to come with them. He had trouble convincing the young men to come, as they had been worried about the journey, but Mackenzie persuaded them. He did not need them as guides; they did not know the terrain where the party was going either. Nevertheless, Mackenzie needed them to help recruit guides as they went along. He also needed them as hunters to augment the party's food supply and to be interpreters. Indeed, as Mackenzie observed, "without Indians I have very little hopes of succeeding."

The second stage of the expedition traveled along the Peace River with the hope of finding a pass through the Rocky Mountains and then, on the western side, to find a river that would take them to the Pacific. They had to portage many times around rapids and falls. With the help of the Sekani people, who provided advice and a guide, they were able to find a portage over a series of mountain lakes. Finally, they crossed the Continental Divide, which separated the eastward-flowing watershed from the westward, Pacific-flowing one. They then followed the MacGregor River and briefly the Fraser River before being forced by its raging waters to seek an alternate route over land. Finally, they reached the Bella Coola River, which took them to the coast. On their journey, they met many different groups of Native peoples, heard unfamiliar languages, and observed different cultures. Sometimes they had feared for their lives from the people they met or from the rivers, but they arrived at the coast safely. Satisfied with their accomplishments, the group now began

canoes on the rivers and lakes that were the highways of the fur trade.

During the winter at Fort Fork, Mackenzie was restless and anxious to be on his way, but the wait was profitable. He spent it trading with Native peoples and sent a canoe laden its arduous return journey over the Rockies and arrived back at Fort Fork on August 24.

To round out the expedition, they had taken along a dog, which Mackenzie never named in his account but simply referred to as "our dog." The dog had traveled with them until they were within a few days journey of the coast, and then, during a stay in a village, it wandered off and they were forced to go on without it. This, Mackenzie remembered, was "a circumstance of no small regret to me." However, on their journey home by the same route, when they came near that village again, they found the dog wretched, confused, and hungry. Mackenzie remembered they all felt as if they had "found a lost friend," and "our dog" rejoined them. Men and beast made it safely home to Fort Chipewyan, having become the first known party to cross the continent north of Mexico.

Mackenzie had shown that a well-chosen group, good preparation, diplomacy, the support of Native peoples, and skilled leadership were the keys to success in exploration.

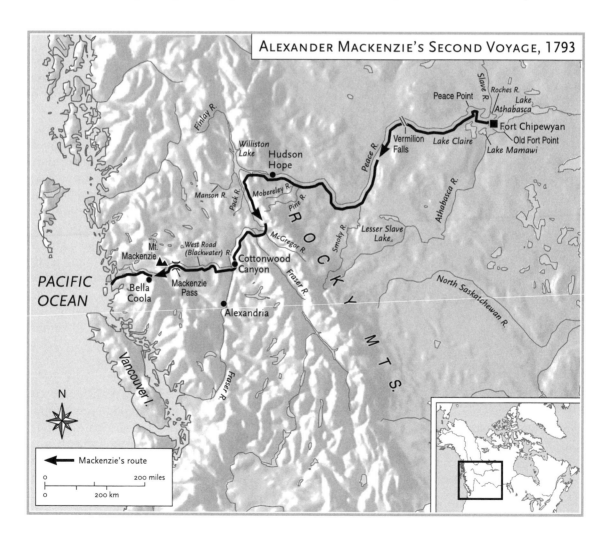

ALEXANDER MACKENZIE'S SECOND VOYAGE, 1793

Mackenzie and others who had gone before him were motivated to lead expeditions by a desire for adventure and by financial ambition. Their personal ambitions fit hand in glove with competition among merchants and traders and among nations and kings. It had been nearly 300 years since Europeans had landed on the coast of northeastern North America. When John Cabot first arrived on the shores of Newfoundland in 1497, little did he know that he would be initiating a quest that would involve several European nations and hundreds of Native American peoples. Nor could he have surmised that it would take three centuries, countless disasters, battles, and loss of life finally to reach the Pacific.

2

THE RACE FOR SPICES AND THE LAND OF CODFISH

1497–1509

On the fifth day of March 1496, King Henry VII of England personally witnessed scribes carefully draft a wide horizontal document in Latin bearing the name "John Kabotto." These were letters patent, an official document granting exclusive rights to conquer and trade with any newly discovered land. John Cabot, as he has come to be known, was given control over a route across the North Atlantic Ocean all the way to China. Although Henry VII may have been thinking only about all the gold coins he would be counting after England got its share of the lucrative spice trade with Asia, with these letters patent he had started England on the path of exploration and empire building.

The great era of European exploration began well before 1496 or 1492, and it could have happened much earlier. Asians might have been the first to reach Europe and the Americas had they been motivated to do so. But certain factors made it easier for Europeans: the development of seaworthy ships and favorable currents; improved navigational techniques; and, most important, money, which was provided by powerful kings or private investors who were granted charters and monopolies. There were also many reasons for Europeans to set forth. Profit was usually the most obvious motive, but explorers often had a desire to gain new converts to Christianity, as well as a lust for personal glory. Kings and queens became interested in exploration so they could finance their growing administrations and wage war, and rulers wanted to cash in on the anticipated riches of new lands before their neighbors. So the development of the nation-state, a country with well-defined borders and a unified administration, was itself a crucial factor in European exploration.

What may seem surprising is that exploration was rarely a goal in itself. Many explorers had a fascination with strange and exotic peoples, and fabled Englishman John Mandeville's mostly fictional 14th-century accounts of monstrosities throughout the world were well known by many travelers. But curiosity alone was not a sufficient motive. What Europeans of the 15th century wanted to reach first and foremost was Asia. From India and the Moluccas—the island group also known as the Spice Islands and today part of Indonesia—came rare and exotic spices, perfumes, and dyes. These were the ultimate luxury goods of the late Middle Ages. Only the wealthiest people could afford to pay the enormously inflated costs of transport and passage through the hands of dozens of middlemen. A cargo of cloves, for example, would travel from the Spice Islands either overland via the silk route from China or in small boats called *dhows* by Arab merchants around India and to ports in the Middle East such as Aleppo, Syria; Beirut, Lebanon; or Alexandria, Egypt. From there they would be picked up by Venetian middlemen, who would in turn pass them on to the rest of Europe. Imported spices such as pepper, cinnamon, cloves, ginger, and nutmeg were extraordinarily expensive and thus perfect status symbols. Anyone who

Decorating the Hôtel de Ville, an administrative building in Montreal, this sculptural relief depicts King Henry VII granting John Cabot his letters patent. *(National Archives of Canada)*

could afford to heap huge amounts of spice on his or her food must have been fantastically rich. Spices were even believed to have wonderful medicinal virtues. It is no wonder that the cost of spices, and the profit made by merchants who supplied them, was astronomical.

Although they had stiff competition through much of the Middle Ages, by the 15th century Venice, at the top of the Adriatic Sea, had almost complete control of the spice trade. Its only real competitors were the merchants of Genoa, on the other side of Italy. The success of the Venetians owed a lot to the way they had set up their mercantile empire. The Republic of Venice not only sponsored construction of galleys in a huge arsenal, but they also protected shipping to the eastern Mediterranean by conquering territory along the Dalmatian coast of the Adriatic Sea all the way to Greece and also the islands of Crete and Cyprus. By controlling many ports along the trade route, they could easily pick up food and fresh water, or reinforcements if necessary. The galleys themselves were huge flat-bottomed vessels rigged with square sails and manned with oars for maneuverability and mobility in case the wind gave out. They had been used for centuries, and although they were sometimes taken into the Atlantic, they were not particularly stable among large waves, strong wind gusts, and ocean currents. They were ideally suited for the Mediterranean, though.

THE CHALLENGES OF NAVIGATION

Navigators in the 15th century typically either hugged the coasts or hopped from one island to another, being sure never to lose sight of land for too long. Although they could measure latitude with a quadrant or astrolabe— that is, by sighting the North Star, they could

calculate how far north or south they had traveled—the distance west to east could only be figured by "dead reckoning." With this method, one person would count or turn an hourglass while the other dropped a bob, a small floating object, at the bow of the ship. By counting how long it took the bob to reach the stern, one could guess speed and distance. A "log and line" was another useful method; this was essentially a small log of wood tied to the end of a rope with knots along it. The log was dropped overboard and the knots counted as the ship moved. This would give a rough estimate of nautical miles per hour—hence the origin of the term *knots* for speed. Equipped with charts crisscrossed with rhumb lines— lines showing the most direct route for a

This astrolabe, an instrument used to determine latitude, belonged to Samuel de Champlain. *(National Archives of Canada)*

Shipbuilding

To gain a full appreciation for shipbuilding in this era, one must first imagine the sounds and smells of the shipyard. Naturally, the smell of the sea would be pervasive, but there would also be the scents of freshly sawn oak and pine, cauldrons of bubbling pitch giving off a smoky resinous perfume, and the dry astringent smell of hemp cordage and canvas sails. There would also be the sounds of axes and adzes shaping beams, and hammers pounding in nails, huge planks being swathed in tar, and everywhere men barking out orders. Shipbuilding by the 16th and 17th centuries was an enormous undertaking. Full-size replicas of many ships of this era have been rebuilt, from Christopher Columbus's *Santa Maria* and John Cabot's *Mathew* to the *Mayflower* of the Pilgrims. But no replica is quite so arresting as the *Vasa,* a warship that sank on its maiden voyage from Stockholm, Sweden, in 1628 and was actually dragged up again 333 years later. Today it is housed in its own museum, and its size is absolutely staggering. Several stories high, able to carry several hundred men and several hundred tons of cargo, the huge floating wooden behemoth sat in the water only 20 feet or so, with tons of cannon and rigging above. It was also delicately carved with lions' heads and painted human figures, a sublime example of pride but also a perfect example of shipbuilding techniques of the era.

The shipbuilding process was quite intricate. First the keel or lower edge of the ship would be propped into place with supports, and then the ribs mortised into place: A *mortise* is a square hole into which the notched ends of a frame could be secured. Then the ribs would be joined across by beams that formed a base for the decks, creating a skeletal structure. Only after the skeleton was complete would the hull be bolted into place and the seams would be caulked with pitch-soaked hemp fibers and waterproofed with tar. Lastly, the masts and rigging would be secured into place.

ship—a compass, and various weights and ropes to gauge depth, a seasoned captain of the late 15th century would have been fairly expert at navigation, and, of course, his profits depended on his skills.

These techniques were well known to the Portuguese. Their position on the Atlantic, however, demanded that they develop seaworthy ships, and in the course of the latter Middle Ages they used the *caravel*—a small tublike vessel with high fore and aft structures known as *castles,* three masts, and *lateen,* or triangular, sails good for sailing into the wind. They later built larger ships such as the *naō,* which had a combination of square and triangular rigging and several sails per mast, which added to maneuverability. Portugal's Prince Henry, although he himself did not sail on any voyage, earned the name "the Navigator" because he sponsored voyages down the coast of West Africa. The Portuguese also had a long tradition of mapmaking, using what is called a *portolan* (port guide), a chart to measure distance and direction between ports. From the west coast of Africa, they picked up gold, ivory, and slaves, all of which fetched high prices in Europe. The Portuguese also decided to use these slaves in a way that foreshadowed developments of the next century. On islands such as Madeira, their possession off the northwest coast of Africa, they used slave labor to grow and process sugar cane, then classified among the most sought-after of spices. In other words, they cut out the middlemen who supplied sugar from Asia by growing it themselves. It then occurred to them that they might find a direct route to Asia by going around the tip of Africa and from there directly to India, Indonesia, and China.

The only major difficulty with this plan was that the Atlantic currents and winds in the Northern Hemisphere run clockwise, which was fine as long as one was heading for the ivory or gold coast of Africa down to the equator. But in the Southern Hemisphere the currents run counterclockwise. This meant that a ship hugging the coastline would be pushed northward. It took a great leap of imagination and courage to follow the currents far out into the ocean—toward modern-day Brazil, which they would later bump into—in order to come back to South Africa. It was Bartholomeu Dias who first performed this feat in 1488, reaching the tip of South Africa, which he named the Cape of Storms but was later renamed the Cape of Good Hope by the King of Portugal in expectation of finding a direct sea route to India.

COMPETITION FOR NEW LANDS

News of Dias's feat set in motion the European competition for new lands. If the Portuguese could establish a direct trade route to Asia, they could effectively cut out all competition, import a much greater supply of spices, and

control prices. This is precisely what they did in the next few decades after Vasco da Gama rounded the cape and landed in Calicut on the west coast of India in 1498. The Portuguese subsequently established posts in Goa (India), Malacca, elsewhere in Indonesia, and as far as China and Japan, building *feitoria,* or trading posts, much as the Venetians had done. This direct trade route did not enable the Portuguese to immediately replace the Venetians as the premier spice merchants of Europe. That would take another century, but by the 1480s the race was under way.

Only one among several figures in this contest was Genoese merchant-mariner Christopher Columbus, and it is no wonder that he first took his project to discover a route to Asia by sailing west to the Portuguese. He also sent his brother, Bartholomew, to seek the support of England and France, which were probably good choices, considering these were wealthy nations. In the end it was Spain that accepted his plan to find this alternate route to Asia. For the moment, however, the rulers of Spain, Ferdinand of Aragon and Isabella of Castile, were busy with their own problems of unifying their nation, something they accomplished with the conquest of the last remaining outpost of Muslim control, the Kingdom of Granada, and with the expulsion of the Jews. Both these events took place in 1492, and only then could Ferdinand and Isabella turn their attention to overseas voyages.

Their initial reluctance to support Columbus had nothing to do with their ideas about the shape of the earth. Most Europeans at that time knew that the earth is a sphere, something that had been accepted as fact since antiquity. What the king and queen feared was the great distance and unlikely chances of success. In the end what prompted them to finance him was precisely the fear of a Portuguese monopoly and possibly becoming a poor neighbor. Another factor is that Spain, or more properly Ferdinand of Aragon, had ambitions to control the entire western Mediterranean, and he had a serious claim to Sicily and the Kingdom of Naples. By the 1490s this would drag Spain into a major war against France, fought mostly on Italian soil, which would last through half of the next century. What might have ended as a brief episode was extended into a major program of exploration and conquest. This was driven to a large extent by the Spanish Crown's constant need for money to pay for this and other wars. To ensure this income, they demanded 20 percent of all profits from overseas voyages.

The great irony of Columbus's achievement, the so-called discovery of America, is that he was convinced until the day he died that he had found a route to Asia. (He did, however, realize that he had discovered what he himself called "an other world.") His journals record his almost desperate search for spices and gold and his assurance to the Spanish monarchs that he had found what he was seeking. Neither he nor they could even begin to suspect the sheer size and riches of the New World that he had come upon. Columbus's discovery was publicized throughout Europe almost immediately after his return to Spain, and the fact that he returned with Native Americans, parrots, and promises of gold only made other nations all the more envious and soon fearful that Spain would become the most powerful nation in Europe.

In particular, Spain's advantage did not escape the attention of two other emerging nation-states, England and France, and it was at this point that North America finally entered the picture. Portugal controlled the eastward route to Asia, and Spain, following Columbus's voyages, hoped to dominate the westerly route. Their claims to these two

routes were formally sanctioned in 1494 by the Treaty of Tordesillas (named after a city in northern Spain), by which Pope Alexander VI basically divided the known world between the two powers. But perhaps there was another route to Asia, a passage via the northwest, far from Spanish control. The English and French were perfectly positioned to attempt to find it, and by 1505 Basque and French fishermen were already sailing as far as the shores of North America in search of cod, which when salted and dried was an important food throughout Europe. None of these fishermen had established permanent settlements or even charted their course, but it was not inconceivable to do so.

DEVELOPMENTS IN EUROPE

The rivalry between European nations had a long history, beginning long before the era of exploration. The kingdoms of Spain, Portugal, France, and England had each gradually changed in the course of the late Middle Ages and early modern period in ways that made each country's Crown—as the ruling monarchs of a nation are often known—far more powerful and pervasive. Before then, medieval states were highly decentralized. That is, within any given kingdom, there were administrative subdivisions, often virtually autonomous, ruled by dukes, counts, and various lesser nobles or even churchmen. These people not only had their own legislative powers but the power to tax their subjects and even wage war against each other. They owed allegiance to the Crown and could be expected to supply soldiers as vassals of the king if he demanded, but they were essentially small rulers with their own small budgets, and kings were just one among many small rulers. Sometimes even towns were granted autonomous charters and would thus be beyond any royal control. (This would remain the pattern in Germany and Italy for several more centuries.)

In Western Europe there was a trend, particularly in the wake of violent civil wars in the 15th century, toward increasing the power of the Crown at the expense of nobles. Many states also developed solid and definite borders at this time. For example, France had begun as little more than a patchwork of petty states surrounding the royal "Isle de France," the region adjacent to Paris. Gradually, a nation-state was built through marriage, diplomacy, and conquest, so that by the early 1500s a state looking something like the modern nation of France was recognizable. The

importance of this was that the Crown could now tax its subjects more efficiently and build an administration with more rigorous control from the center. The Crown could finance large armies and ultimately sponsor profitable ventures that would, in turn, support the machine of state. Exploration at this time was intimately connected with the growth and competition among these larger and more powerful states.

Related to this was dramatic growth of the European population in the 16th century. This made labor cheaper because there were so many people looking for jobs and willing to do anything for pay. Agriculture also gradually changed, becoming more market oriented. Many peasants who had been providing food

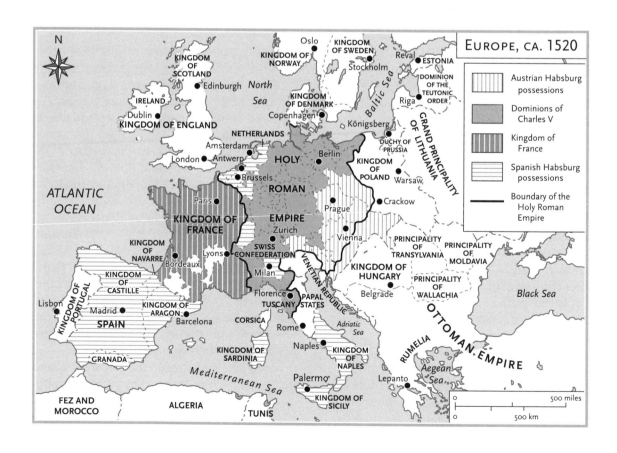

Discipline Aboard Ships

Ships' logs of the early modern era are filed with accounts of insubordination and mutiny. Maintaining strict discipline on board was an absolute necessity, and captains had little recourse beyond physical punishment. People of this time would already have been fairly conversant with branding and physical mutilation for such crimes as stealing, and there was hanging for more serious crimes, but at sea sailors were exposed to some unique opportunities for punishment. Walking the plank, normally reserved for boarding enemy ships for hand-to-hand combat, was one way to dispose conveniently of an insubordinate type. Marooning—simply abandoning a person on an island—was another equally effective means, only one step from actual capital punishment. (The word *marooning* is derived from the Spanish word *cimarrón*, meaning "wild" or "savage," and was applied to the Maroons, fugitive African slaves in the West Indies.) Whipping, particularly with the cat-o'-nine-tails—a short but effective instrument made of nine knotted cords—would leave painful welts on the back. For lesser crimes, a prisoner might be tied up in the bottom of the ship where he might drown in the bilge water.

But without doubt the most gruesome form of punishment was keelhauling, in which the man would be tied up and dragged underneath the ship at a full clip. If he managed not to drown, he might nonetheless have his head or limbs torn from his body, by the force of the currents. Anyone who survived this procedure was accounted lucky indeed.

for themselves became landless wage laborers producing food to be sold to rapidly growing towns and cities. This situation, compounded with a demand for goods such as cloth and the growth of manufacturing, meant that landowners and manufacturers were getting quite wealthy. There was now a critical mass of people with enough spare money to invest. It was this development, plus an entrepreneurial spirit among merchants, that made overseas ventures and exploration so appealing. In other words, it was the changes in the European economy and competition among individuals and companies as well as states that prompted Europeans to begin expanding their trade, which in turn led to the discovery of new lands.

JOHN CABOT'S VOYAGES

The merchants of Bristol, on the southwest coast of England, were one such group of investors, and they had already begun to send out voyages into the Atlantic in search of islands that might provide a base for further exploration and trade. It was to them that the Italian merchant Giovanni Cabotto (who became "John Kabotto" in the letters patent referred to at the outset of this chapter) turned with the idea of plotting his own route to Asia across a northwest passage. News had recently reached Europe that Columbus had succeeded in reaching islands adjacent to Asia, so John Cabot, as he came to be called in England, thought he could match Columbus's

In this painting, John Cabot prepares to leave Bristol, England, for North America in his ship *Mathew*. *(National Archives of Canada)*

discovery. And, Cabot figured that the distance across the Atlantic would be much shorter at a northerly latitude than around the middle of the earth.

News of Cabot's plan reached England's King Henry VII, himself a shrewd engineer of a centralized monarchy who had managed to put his own country's finances in order. Expansion of English trade and the potential customs duties due the Crown were certainly a prime reason he decided to give Cabot an official charter. Cabot himself, though probably born in Genoa, gained his experience working for Venice in the lucrative spice trade to Mecca in Arabia. Cabot should have known where spices came from, but he believed they

grew in northern Asia, a fatal mistake as it turned out.

With letters patent granting exclusive rights, Cabot set out in May 1497, sailing under the English flag, although he had actually financed the voyage himself with some support from the merchants of Bristol. The Crown would take 20 percent of his profits, but Cabot could govern whatever territory he discovered and keep the remainder of the earnings. With one small boat, the *Mathew*, of about 50 tuns (a tun was a large barrel, so 50 tuns meant a ship could hold 50 large barrels) and a tiny crew of 18, Cabot set out across the Atlantic. In only 35 days Cabot managed to make the voyage from Bristol to North America, landing on June 24, 1497. Although a replica of the *Mathew* retraced the voyage in 1997 for the 500th anniversary, there is really no way of knowing for sure exactly where Cabot landed, and there is still a great deal of dispute among historians whether he landed on Cape Breton Island or way to the north on the tip of Newfoundland. Near contemporary maps such as that of Juan de la Cosa of 1500 record landfall more to the south and show five English flags with the words *"Mar descubierta por Inglese"* ("Sea discovered by the English") beneath them. One of the few surviving letters describing the voyage claimed that Cabot landed at the same latitude as Bordeaux at 45°N, which would confirm that he landed down along the coast of Nova Scotia.

But, if Cabot rounded the south coast of England and headed due west from the tip of Ireland—and staying on one latitude was the typical way to navigate—that would mean that he must have landed far to the north, around 51°N.

Wherever Cabot actually landed, he did sail around the area for about a month, presumably charting the waters in preparation for his next visit. Although Cabot and his crew did not meet any Native Americans, they did find evidence of them. A letter from an Italian merchant in London, Lorenzo Pasqualigo, to his brothers back in Venice says that Cabot brought back snares and a needle for making nets and some kind of notched stick. Cabot did not waste time exploring the land or

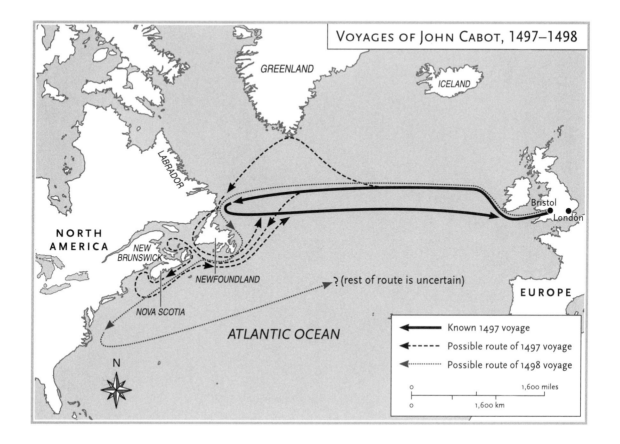

VOYAGES OF JOHN CABOT, 1497–1498

This model of John Cabot's ship *Mathew* is housed in the Government House in St. John's, Newfoundland. *(National Archives of Canada)*

searching for inhabitants, but he did recognize that this was a new land—somewhere east of Japan, or Cipangu as it was called at that time. The region came to be called New Isle or Newfoundland, and it was formally claimed for England. If Cabot did actually touch on the mainland of North America, then this was the first recorded voyage to do so since the Vikings and predates even Columbus's setting foot on the mainland of South America.

Upon his return to England, Cabot could not dazzle the court with gold, slaves, or parrots as had his competitor Columbus to the Spanish court. But his voyage did cause a brief sensation, and Cabot was seen swaggering about the streets of Bristol as a hero. Henry VII even granted him an annuity. Plans were laid for a second voyage to set up a permanent colony and a trading post—much along the same lines as the Portuguese were building on the other side of Asia. A dispatch to the duke of Milan from his envoy in London, Raimondo di Soncino, one of the only pieces of contemporary evidence regarding these events, even claims that Henry intended to "give him all the malefactors to go to that country and form a colony." In other words, this was to be a penal colony to dump off prisoners, presumably the only people willing to go. Whoever populated it, Cabot was firmly convinced that, with a trading post, he could make England a major competitor in the spice trade. By gaining direct access to the wealth of Asia, London would become, as Soncino claimed, "a greater depot of spices . . . than there is in Alexandria."

Cabot's second voyage was well outfitted with a year's provisions, five vessels, and about 200 men; one of the vessels actually had to turn around quickly for repairs. The remaining four vessels were never heard from again. It is conjectured that Cabot got as far as

Chesapeake Bay on this voyage. There is also still a lot of controversy over what became of him, some suggesting that he may even have returned home. Chances are that he was either lost at sea or remained in America.

THE PORTUGUESE PRESENCE

In these years England also had some direct competition from the Portuguese in the northern Atlantic, and, in fact, the two could have learned directly from each other via the lucrative trade between Bristol and Lisbon in wine. The first official Portuguese ship to sail to the North Atlantic was captained by a small landholder (a *lavrador* in Portuguese) named João Fernandes, from the island of Terceira in the Azores well out in the Atlantic. Although little is known about this voyage in 1500, he and his partner, the aristocrat Pedro de Barcelos, reached Greenland and called it *Tiera del Lavrador,* which is how it appeared in early maps. This name later transferred to an island to the west that still bears that name: Labrador. By the Treaty of Tordesillas, Portugal had a claim to Newfoundland, which lay on their side of the line.

Nothing came of this voyage of Fernandes, but the Portuguese effort was picked up by a family of explorers who also sought to find a northwestern route to Asia. Some claim that João Vaz Corte Real, governor of the island of Terceira in the Azores—an ideal navigational outpost—may even have visited Newfoundland, or the "Land of Codfish" as he called it, in 1474, but this is not accepted by most scholars. His two sons, Gaspar and Miguel Corte Real, certainly did make the voyage in the early 1500s in successive attempts. Each was granted an official charter by King Manuel of Portugal, but otherwise the details of their trips were kept a secret so as not to provide clues to competing

HISTOIRE
VNIVERSELLE
DES INDES
OCCIDENTALES,

*Diuisée en deux liures, faicte en latin
par Monsieur* WYTFLIET:

Nouuellement traduicte.

*Où il est traicté de leur descouuerte, description,
& conqueste faicte tant par les Castillans que
Portugais, ensemble de leurs mœurs, religion,
gouuernemens, & loix.*

A DOVAY,
Chez FRANÇOIS FABRI,
L'AN 1607.

An account of the Corte Real voyages by Corneille Wytfliet was published in 1607. The book's title page is shown here. *(National Archives of Canada)* nations. There were, however, Italian spies in Lisbon, and one named Alberto Cantino wrote back letters to Duke Ercole d'Este in Ferrara describing the voyages and how they encountered and forcefully kidnapped Native Americans with facial tattoos and long hair. The author claims they were brought back to Lisbon, and he described them:

> They kidnapped nearly 50 of the men and women of that land by force, and brought them to the king. I have seen them, touched and examined them. Beginning with their size, I say they are bigger than our people, with well-formed limbs to correspond. The hair of the men is long, as we wear it, letting it hang in plaited rings. They have faces marked with great signs, like those of the Indians. Their eyes incline to green, and when they look from them it gives a great fierceness to the whole countenance. Their speech cannot be understood, but, however, there is no sharpness in it, and it is altogether human. Their behavior and gestures are very gentle; they laugh a good deal, and show great delight. So much for the men. The women have small breasts and very beautiful bodies. They have very gentle faces, and their color may be said to be more white than any other tint, but that of the men is much darker. In the end, except for the fierce look of the men, they are very much like ourselves. They are naked except for a small covering made of deerskin. They have no weapons or iron, but for working or fashioning any thing, they use a very hard and sharp stone, with which there is nothing so hard that they cannot cut it.

Despite the great promise of these two Corte Real brothers, both were lost at sea and never returned. Legend has it that Miguel died as an Indian chief in what is now Massachusetts. Although the Portuguese maintained their claim to what is today part of eastern Canada, it was the English who would settle it, but not for a century after these first voyages in the late 15th and early 16th century.

CHANGING ROLES AND GOALS

The race across the North Atlantic was, however, taken up by John Cabot's son Sebastian soon after his father's disappearance. Although there is no certain evidence that he accompanied his father on any voyages, he and his brothers were named in the original charter, and Sebastian did carry on with his father's plans. He was given two ships by the Bristol merchants in 1508 or 1509, again to find a northwest route to Asia. He probably knew by this point that the New World was not part of Asia, but there might still be a way to sail through. Searching any major waterway, he probably entered what is now Hudson Strait, north of Labrador, but after encountering ice was forced to turn around. Searching other inlets may have taken him as far south as Delaware Bay, and according to his own account he went as far as Florida. None of these waterways, of course, proved to be the passage to Asia.

The long-term effect of these profitless voyages was that England quickly got out of the spice trade. The next English king, Henry VIII, had no interest in overseas voyages; he was more interested in reviving ancient English claims to the Kingdom of France and subduing the Scots. He was also seriously preoccupied with his own dynastic and religious problems for much of his reign. So while his neighbors were busy building empires, he was off fighting dynastic battles. The English would be out of the race to new lands until the middle of the 16th century. Sebastian Cabot left to serve the Crown of Spain, and he returned only after Henry's death, in the late

When the English discovered the abundance of Atlantic cod along the coast of the New World, many of them set up temporary settlements in which they could dry the fish to transport and then sell them. Detail of a 1715 map by Herman Moll, this illustration shows the process off the coast of Newfoundland. *(Library of Congress)*

1540s, this time to seek a Northeast Passage to Asia across the top of Russia.

In the meantime, although these explorers had found no spices, it became apparent that North Atlantic waters were teeming with cod and its coasts were covered in timber. Soon Portuguese, Spanish, and French sailors would be visiting the shores of the Grand Banks off Newfoundland and returning with enough fish to warrant taxation by their respective rulers. As Cabot had claimed, one need only drop a bucket into the water and it would be filled with fish. Cod provided one of the great imperishable staples in the European diet—either salted as *bacalao* or dried as stockfish. During the period of Lent imposed by the Catholic Church, people were not allowed to eat meat, and cod thus provided an affordable form of sustenance. Fishing did not provide the great wealth envisioned by the spice trade, but it was lucrative nonetheless and would at least keep North America on the mind of Europeans for some time to come. By the following decade, France would be the next major competitor in the race to chart the waters and territory of North America.

3

FRANCE AND SPAIN ALONG THE MID-ATLANTIC COAST

1504–1536

The first known voyages of Frenchmen to Newfoundland took place between 1504 and 1508. At that time these people identified themselves as either Normans or Bretons—that is, inhabitants of Normandy or Brittany—or Basques, inhabitants of the region along the border of France and Spain, rather than French. The earliest reference to these voyages date from 1539, so there is no way of confirming any specific details about them. The document does name one Jean Denys as captain and Gamart de Rouen as the pilot of a voyage in 1506. In 1508, the ship *La Pensée,* owned by Thomas Aubert, also made the voyage.

There is other evidence that in 1509 this ship brought back to Rouen seven tattooed "savage men" along with a boat—evidently a kind of canoe—and weapons. What the French remarked upon, which was no doubt their primary measure of being civilized, was the fact that these men "do not use bread, wine or money." When the 16th-century Italian scholar Pietro Bembo repeated the Frenchmen's story, he added that the captives ate raw meat and drank blood, perhaps to add some scandalous embellishments to an otherwise tame account.

These were not specifically voyages of exploration. Their primary goal was to catch codfish, a trade in which the Bretons, as well as the Basques, were well accomplished. Cape Breton is, in fact, named for these fishermen. These men did not describe the geography or attempt to chart the shores they encountered. Even if they had done so for their own personal use, they probably would not have published such information for fear of revealing the location of the best fishing banks to competitors.

Well into the 16th century and long after Christopher Columbus, there was still nothing approaching accurate geographical knowledge of the New World in the Western Hemisphere. Part of the mental conception of even the most well-educated Europeans, and pictured on the maps they drafted, were mythical places such as Brasil, Antilia, and the Fortunate Isles, or Hesperides. These places were dreamed up by medieval chroniclers or were mentioned centuries before by ancient authorities. It is no wonder that such places still figured prominently in the planning of overseas ventures, especially when explorers sought out the as yet uncharted shores of North America in search of a westerly passage to Asia.

In particular, it was the publication of Peter Martyr's *De orbe novo decades* (Decades of the New World) in 1516 that supplied what was believed to be incontrovertible evidence that waters flow from Asia to the Atlantic. Martyr (1457–1526) was an Italian-born historian of the early Spanish discoveries and drew on accounts such as those of Sebastian Cabot's voyages of 1508–09 that reported the existence of such a passage that would provide a direct route to Asia. It was this single geographical feature and the promise of fabulous profits that spurred on the discovery of North America.

THE VOYAGE OF VERRAZANO

Finding a direct route to Asia was the motivation for the voyages led by Giovanni da Verrazano, who was the first to explore the shores of North America from the Carolinas to Newfoundland. Verrazano was an Italian by birth and was given the finest education available in Florence at a time when it was the cultural vanguard of all Europe. His family had a castle in the hills of Chianti to the south of Florence in the area of Greve, and it is supposed that Verrazano was born there around 1485. Like

Giovanni da Verrazano (Verrazzano) sailed to America in 1524 in search of a passageway to China. *(National Archives of Canada)*

many of his contemporaries, such as the artist Leonardo da Vinci, he was lured to France by business opportunities and the dazzling court of Francis I, leader of what had become one of the most powerful and wealthy nation-states in Europe. France was a relative latecomer to the business of exploration, having been mostly preoccupied with wars in Italy against Charles V, king of Spain (as Charles I) and Holy Roman Emperor. But by 1523 Francis was intent on profiting from trade with Asia and hired Verrazano, then living in the French port town of Dieppe and experienced in the Middle East spice trade, to find the passage. Francis provided a flagship and Verrazano also received considerable financial backing from a group of Florentine silk merchants living in

Lyon, France, who were looking for a source for cheap raw silk. Again, the ultimate goal was reaching Asia.

Verrazano was equipped with more precise geographical knowledge than his English and Portuguese predecessors. Although the North American coast remained unexplored, the existence of a separate ocean, the Pacific, had been known since Vasco Núñez de Balboa crossed the Isthmus of Panama in 1513. The existence of a passage connecting the Atlantic and Pacific Oceans was also reconfirmed by reports of Ferdinand Magellan's rounding the southernmost tip of South America in 1519. It is possible that Verrazano knew Magellan and went with him to Spain before the circumnavigation in 1517. Although Verrazano did not accompany him on this voyage, and Magellan himself never made it home, the sparse remains of Magellan's crew, led by Sebastian Elcano on one remaining ship, did bring back to Spain a huge load of cloves in 1522. This proved once and for all that one could sail west to reach the riches of the Spice Islands, as

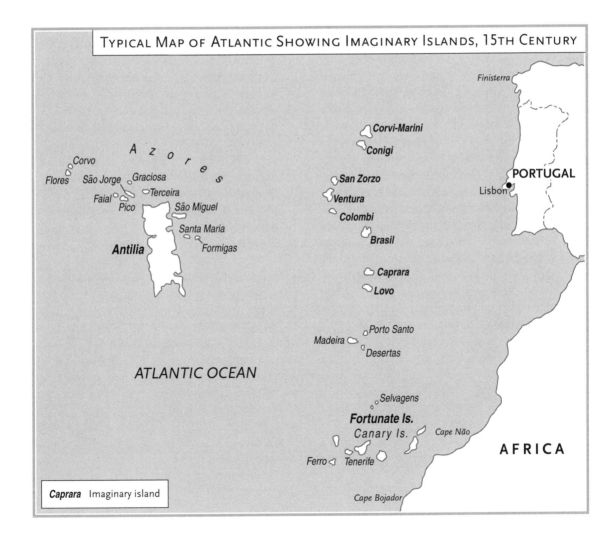

TYPICAL MAP OF ATLANTIC SHOWING IMAGINARY ISLANDS, 15TH CENTURY

Finisterra

Corvi-Marini

Conigi

A z o r e s

Corvo

Flores São Jorge Graciosa

San Zorzo

PORTUGAL

Faial Terceira

Ventura

Lisbon

Pico São Miguel

Colombi

Santa Maria

Brasil

Antilia Formigas

Caprara

Lovo

Porto Santo

Madeira

Desertas

ATLANTIC OCEAN

Selvagens

Fortunate Is.

Canary Is. Cape Não

Ferro Tenerife

AFRICA

Caprara Imaginary island

Cape Bojador

the East Indies were then known. Still the passage around the southern tip of the Americas was long and difficult. A northerly route would be much easier for Europeans. In any case, Verrazano's belief in a northwest passage was absolutely firm, and it was this alone that he sought when the idea was presented to the French king.

His voyage commenced in January 1524, after a previous attempt to launch was thwarted by storms in which he lost two ships. But finally leaving from Dieppe aboard a single ship, *La Dauphine,* he proceeded to a barren rock near the Madeiras, islands off the northwest coast of Africa. From there he crossed the Atlantic with 50 men, provisions for eight months, and munitions in the event of hostile encounters. Verrazano made the crossing far to the north of typical Spanish routes and thus landed on the shores of North America at 34°N latitude, somewhere near Cape Fear at the lowest point of present-day North Carolina. The numerous rivers and sounds flowing through these swampy lowlands can only have confirmed his belief that one of these waterways must lead to the other side. In fact, as he gazed over the outer banks toward Pamlico Sound without seeing land on the other side, he believed he was looking at the Pacific Ocean and the water that "bathes the shores of India and Cathay," as he wrote in his letter to Francis I. Presumably he thought this thin strip of land (from Cape Lookout to Cape Hatteras and all the way up to Virginia) was actually an isthmus like the one Balboa crossed in Panama. The idea actually took hold, and for many years navigators and mapmakers drew the same conclusion.

Although no logbook survives detailing these discoveries, Verrazano's remarkable letter to Francis I describes North America and his interaction with the Native populations. It would color European perceptions of Native Americans for decades to come. In describing the natural landscape, Verrazano wrote:

> The seashore is completely covered with sand 15 feet deep, which rises in the form of small hills about fifty paces wide. After climbing farther, we found other streams and inlets from the sea which come in by several mouths, and follow the ins and outs of the shoreline. Nearby we could see a stretch of country much higher than the sandy shore, with many beautiful fields full of great forests, some sparse and some dense; and the trees have so many colors, and are so beautiful and delightful that they defy description. . . . And these trees emit a sweet fragrance over a large area. . . . We think that they belong to the Orient by virtue of the surroundings, and that they are not without some kind of narcotic or aromatic liquor. There are other riches, like gold, which ground of such a color usually denotes. There is an abundance of animals, stags, deer, hares; and also of lakes and pools of running water with various types of bird, perfect for the delights and pleasures of the hunt.

These comments were carefully calculated to pique the king's interest. Not only did they promise wealth and spices that could adorn the meals Francis served, but they seemed to offer a potential playground, much like the Loire Valley where Francis had his châteaux and beautiful parks and animals to hunt, not to mention gorgeous weather. Verrazano even claimed that the wild grapes "would doubtless produce excellent wines if they were properly cultivated." Coming from Chianti, a region of Italy famous for its wine, Verrazano would certainly have been well informed on this topic. The mid-Atlantic coastal region certainly did strike him as beautiful, and it is

Sailors' Diets

The seaman's diet was coarse and monotonous, consisting almost entirely of dried provisions. Hardtack, biscuits consisting of little more than flour and water, were the universal staple. Salted beef, pickled beef or pork, stockfish (dried cod), or herring, perhaps beans, and wine or beer were the usual accompaniment to the hardtack. Europeans' ships were also usually provisioned with olive oil. Some ships carried other foods. Englishman Hugh Plat published a little broadside pamphlet in 1607 entitled *Certaine Philosophical Preparations of Foode and Beverage for Sea-men,* which recommended dried macaroni. Apparently he furnished Elizabethan privateers Francis Drake and John Hawkins with it. Physicians frequently recommended garlic for sailors, for they believed it would act as a preservative against eating foul meats and smelling bilge water. Lemons, although not standard issue until the 18th century, were also sometimes carried on board to prevent scurvy. Fresh vegetables were almost unheard of as rations.

Most ships carried along live animals, usually pigs or chickens that would be slaughtered and cooked on board. One can easily imagine not only the difficulty but also the extraordinary danger of cooking with open flame on a wooden ship rigged with rope soaked in pitch, a flammable tar. At sea the sailors' diet could be supplemented by fresh fish, and naturally one of the first things the crew would do when reaching land was to hunt for fresh game. Perhaps most important of all, though, was fresh water, which was needed to prevent dehydration at sea but also to soak the hardtack. A voyage whose water had gone bad was in grave peril. Even still, the sailors would not have begun drinking water until the beer or wine ran out, which must have happened frequently given the gallon per day of beer each seaman enjoyed every day.

perhaps not surprising that much of this very ground is today covered with resorts and golf courses.

Proceeding up the coast, Verrazano appears to have missed the Chesapeake and Delaware Bays, but he did explore what is now the harbor of New York (hence the name of the Verrazano-Narrows Bridge, which spans the bay from Staten Island to Brooklyn today). Not until the early 1600s would another explorer set eyes on the mouth of the Hudson and what would later become Manhattan. Verrazano named the region the Land of Angoulême in tribute to Francis's having been count of Angoulême before he became king. Why he did not proceed up the Hudson as a candidate for his passage is not known, though it seems he feared navigating beyond the bay in bad weather.

Verrazano then proceeded along the south shore of Long Island and explored Block Island (which he called Aloysia after French queen Louise) and Rhode Island (whose name he contrived because it reminded him of the island of Rhodes off of Greece). It was here that his crew rested and made direct contact with

Native Americans. Verrazano's account was obviously colored by his expectation, inspired by classical authorities, that the Native people would be living in a blissful age of innocence and purity. He did encounter more savage tribes around what is today Maine, people who had perhaps already experienced unpleasant encounters with Europeans. But his account on the whole depicts Native Americans as a happy unspoiled people living in a Golden Age. This is what he had to say in his letter about one tribe he encountered:

> These people are the most beautiful and have the most civil customs that we have found on this voyage. They are taller than we are; they are a bronze color, some tending more toward whiteness, others to a tawny color; the face is clear-cut; the hair is long and black, and they take great pains to decorate it; the eyes are black and alert, and their manner is sweet and gentle, very like the manner of the ancients. I shall not speak to Your Majesty of the other parts of the body, since they have all the proportions belonging to any well-built man. Their women are just as shapely and beautiful, very gracious of attractive manner and pleasant appearance.

The very fact that the Native peoples did not value gold but preferred bells and other

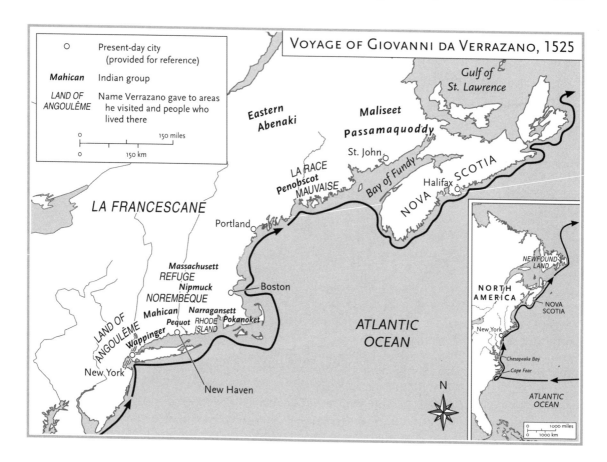

trinkets implies that not only did Verrazano believe he could easily take whatever gold he might find, but also that these were a simple people unspoiled by the trappings of corrupt civilization. They were apparently unimpressed with European weapons as well. They also freely gave away whatever they had, seemingly unconcerned with material possessions. Verrazano's description sounds very much like those of classical authorities on the mythical Golden Age, and not coincidentally like that of English scholar Thomas More in his depiction of the fictional land of Utopia.

In his progress to the north, Verrazano gave a detailed description of Narragansett Bay and may have journeyed as far as Newfoundland before returning to France in July 1524. The significance of these discoveries was not only that they filled in the gap between Spanish discoveries to the South and English and Portuguese discoveries to the North, they also bolstered the conception of North America as a separate continent, entirely distinct and unconnected to Asia. Clearly, his failure to find a quick and easy passage to Asia by the end of his journey had convinced Verrazano that this was a separate continent, which he named *La Francescane*—again to honor the king—and would soon appear on maps as New France, long before there was a New Amsterdam or New York.

Verrazano probably would have followed up this voyage with another had not Francis needed ships to protect northern ports from a supposed English invasion. That the king was himself taken prisoner by the Spanish at the battle of Pavia in 1525 only further delayed any further exploration for the next few years. But Verrazano did eventually make other voyages. In 1527 he went to Brazil and returned with a hefty cargo of dyewood. And in 1528 he went with his brother Girolamo to Florida, the Bahamas, and the Lesser Antilles, where he

met his untimely end. On what is now the Island of Guadaloupe he disembarked, was captured by Native peoples, and was killed and eaten while his brother and other crew members looked on in horror.

AYLLÓN AND FLORIDA

Even before the demise of Verrazano, the Spanish were intent on preventing the French from establishing a permanent presence on the Atlantic seaboard so close to their own possessions in the Caribbean and even as far north as Florida. The Spanish had claimed Florida as early as 1514, when Juan Ponce de León was installed as *adelantado,* or military governor, of Florida. Several voyages were thereafter sponsored by Lucas Vásquez de Ayllón, a prominent judge back on the island of Hispaniola, which held jurisdiction over this entire area. In 1520, on Ayllón's first voyage, to trade or steal from the Native Americans whatever they could, they made their way up to 32° N latitude. There they traded and picked up some Native peoples who it was said "died of sorrow and hunger, for they would not eat what the Spaniards gave them," although they would eat dogs and other beasts found dead on a dung heap, according to the commentator Francisco López de Gómera in his *General History of the Indies.* In 1525, with an official charter from King Charles of Spain in hand, Ayllón set out again. The charter gave him exclusive rights and remarkable latitude to trade for gold, silver, and pearls or to exploit the region however he saw fit and rendering to the Crown only a tenth of his profits. The charter also agreed that Ayllón might start a silk industry there, using free Native labor, naturally.

By 1526 Ayllón had embarked on a major colonization effort somewhere in the vicinity of the Savannah River with 500 men in six ships. They named the new region Gualdape. The project met with disaster from the very start. The flagship sank, and when they finally found a spot to build houses, it grew very cold and many men fell sick and died, including Ayllón himself. The Spaniards appeared to have contracted some kind of horrific infectious disease. According to Spanish historian and naturalist Gonzalo Fernandez de Oviedo's *General and Natural History of the Indies,* one man among the sick "wanted to take his breeches off and all the flesh came away from both legs from the knees downwards, leaving his bones bare, and he died that night." Leaderless in the midst of this calamity, the colony was soon taken over by a pair of cruel soldiers and quickly descended into turmoil. It was finally abandoned—with only 150 of the settlers able to make it back to Hispaniola alive.

GOMES AND NEW ENGLAND

At about the same time as Verrazano's voyage, a Spanish expedition was planned specifically to find the Northwest Passage. This one was led by Estevão Gomes, a Portuguese navigator who had served under Magellan and like him was now working for Spain. His instructions from the Spanish Crown, dating from 1523, specified that he should explore Eastern Cathay (China) and venture as far as the Moluccas in the East Indies, where he should find gold, silver, spices, and medicinal drugs. He was also told in no uncertain terms not to encroach on the possessions of the king of Portugal, on the eastern side of the demarcation line set out in the Treaty of Tordesillas (1494), although exactly what islands that would entitle him to exploit was not entirely clear.

Having built a new caravel for this voyage, it did not get underway until September 1524,

a few months after Verrazano had returned. Gomes covered much of the same ground as Verrazano, although it is still a matter of debate whether he sailed southward from Newfoundland or northward from Florida. He did manage to travel and survey the region around Cape Cod (which he called San Pedro) and as far north as the Penobscot River in Maine (which he called Río de los Gamos, or Deer River), but naturally found no passage to Asia. Gomes did, however, return with 58 Algonkin Indians taken as slaves in August 1525, an act that was explicitly against the orders he had been given. No doubt, he did not want to return to Spain empty-handed. And, as Peter Martyr told the story, when he returned someone misunderstood that he had brought home slaves (*esclavos*) and announced that he had brought back cloves (*clavos*), which could only have come from the Orient. The mistake was particularly embarrassing for Gomes. Despite his monumental failure to find a passage as promised, navigators would continue to search for it through the next century.

For the Spanish, however, the North American continent provided an effective barrier preventing the French and English from reaching Asia, and it is probably for this reason that no further attempts to explore or settle this region were made. Gomes's journey did, in the end, provide valuable information, though. He was the first to provide geographical information on Cape Cod and the coast up to Maine and the Penobscot River. Contemporary maps, like that of 16th-century Spanish cartographer Diego Ribeiro, depict Gomes's discoveries.

EARLY ENGLISH VOYAGERS

In the 1520s one final attempt to seek out a northwest passage, on the part of the English,

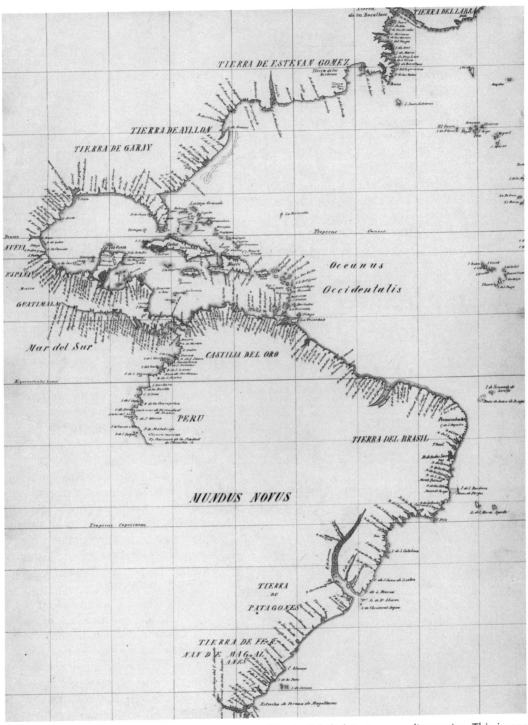

Diego Ribeiro completed a world map in 1529 on which he labeled Portuguese discoveries. This image is the Western Hemisphere portion of Ribeiro's map as traced by 19th-century geographer Johann Georg Kohl. *(Library of Congress)*

Richard Hakluyt
(CA. 1552–1616)

Perhaps as much as any single individual, Richard Hakluyt (ca. 1552–1616) was responsible for goading the English into taking a major role in the exploration and settlement of North America. Hakluyt studied at Oxford and by 1580 was ordained a priest in the Church of England. Apparently his main interest was in geography, on which he lectured at Oxford, and he collected documents about anything to do with trade and travel. As early as 1582, in his book *Divers Voyage,* he was writing about John Cabot and the promising beginnings of English exploration, as well as the voyages of Giovanni da Verrazano and others. This led to his being named chaplain to the English ambassador to France. In 1589 he published the first parts of his monumental collection of primary documents entitled *The Principall Navigations, Voiages and Discoveries of the English Nation.* Further volumes followed, and it remains to this day the most extensive source of information about the subject.

Beyond being an editor of others' texts, he believed that North America would not only provide markets for trade but could also be a base for launching attacks on Spanish colonies to the south and might contain a northwest passage to Asia. Hakluyt was also directly connected with Sir Walter Raleigh's Virginia projects, serving as its propagandist. Hakluyt is regarded as the premier historian of the era of exploration, and the Hakluyt Society, organized in England in 1846, has continued to this day his goal of making widely available accounts of discovery and exploration.

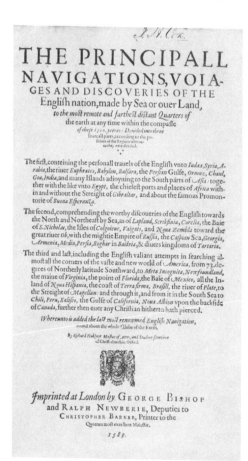

Shown here is the title page from Richard Hakluyt's multivolume publication, part of the National Library of Canada's Rare Book Collection. *(National Archives of Canada)*

was made, led by John Rut, a wine merchant, in 1527. The stated intention of this voyage according to Robert Thorne, a Bristol merchant who initiated the venture, was to sail directly over the North Pole. He understood that the distance to Asia would be much shorter this way than the route taken by the Spanish and Portuguese. Airplane routes today affirm this idea. Thorne also understood that the days are much longer at these latitudes during the summer and much safer sailing could take place by sunlight. What these merchants could not have anticipated was solid ice. In a letter to King Henry VIII, Thorne tried to appeal to the king's innate sense of rivalry. He noted that since Portugal had already exploited the east, and Spain the west, "So that now rest to be discovered the said North parts, the which it seemeth to mee, is onely your charge and dutie. Because the situation of this your Realme is thereunto neerest and aptest of all other." These were, of course, prophetic words.

With two ships, the *Mary Guildford* and the *Samson,* Rut followed the route of the fishing fleets across the Atlantic to Newfoundland; encountering storms and icebergs, the latter ship was lost. Rut then decided, rather than strike ice, to follow the coastline southward toward Norumbega, as New England was then called. En route he encountered several foreign fishing vessels from France and Portugal and took the time to write a letter to King Henry VIII, the very first letter to be "mailed" from North America to Europe. One of the fishing boats took the letter back for him. In it he says, "the third day of August we entered a good haven, called Saint John, and there we founde eleven saile of Normans, and one Brittaine, and two Portugall Barkes, and all a fishing." This is a good reminder that extensive and unrecorded voyages were made throughout these years by several competing nations, which at least for the purposes of fishing

could overlook their national rivalries—and even carry mail.

Rut proceeded down the coast and made it all the way to Florida and into the Spanish West Indies, still with the intention of continuing to meet the Great Khan in China. On Mona Island he spoke with Spaniards and decided to pick up dyewood in Puerto Rico. Before this, Rut tried to harbor in Santo Domingo to trade. But he feared Spanish betrayal, especially after stray cannon fire, shot perhaps only as a welcome, nearly hit his ship. The warden who fired the shot had apparently not been informed of the English arrival and afterward claimed he was only following orders—to protect the fortress. In any case, Rut decided to leave quickly and trade discretely elsewhere, then head home. By the next season he was back in Europe, once again carrying wine. Following Rut's voyage, which in the end accomplished nothing, the English would express no interest in North America, apart from codfishing, for many decades.

There was only one curious exception— the fishing venture and pleasure cruise of Richard Hore in 1536. Some 30 gentlemen came along on this cruise just to see Newfoundland. They did not, however, expect to run out of food, which was what occurred. Several men died of starvation, and some apparently resorted to cannibalism. As Richard Hakluyt related the story:

> such was the famine that increased among them from day to day, that they were forced to seeke to relieve themselves of herbes being to little purpose to satisfie their insatiable hunger, in the fields and deserts here and there, the fellowe killed his mate while hee stouped to take up a roote for his reliefe, and cutting out pieces of his body whome hee had murthered, broyled the same on coles and greedily devoured them. . . .

[When accosted by his fellows] he that had the broyled meate, burst out into these wordes, If thou wouldest needes knowe, the broyled meate I had, was such a piece of a mans buttocke.

As luck would have it, a well-laden French ship soon appeared, which they promptly plundered. Several months later King Henry VIII, embarrassed by the whole affair, actually reimbursed the French out of his own pocket.

It is no wonder that the English gave up exploring North America. King Henry VIII at that time was preoccupied with internal politics, several wives, and structuring the now reformed English church. This explains why it was only private ventures such as Hore's that sailed across, with the limited objective of catching fish. Only the French continued their efforts to follow up Verrazano's voyages and, in doing so, would be the first to make a solid claim of the northern Atlantic coast as a French possession. By a quirk of fate they were also given official permission to do so. In 1533 French king Francis I arranged for the marriage of his son to Florentine Catherine de' Medici. He also had her uncle, Medici pope Clement VII, officially alter the Treaty of 1494, which divided the world between the Spanish and Portuguese. The French were then allowed to explore and claim regions unoccupied by Christians. For whatever it was worth, with official papal sanction the French immediately planned to capitalize on Verrazano's voyage by sending Jacques Cartier to the New World.

4

JACQUES CARTIER'S VOYAGES

1534–1543

Nearly a decade after Giovanni da Verrazano's voyage, the French resumed their exploration of North America. An explorer named Jacques Cartier made three separate voyages, the last of which was to be commanded by Jean-François de La Roque, sieur de Roberval, but in fact became a fourth voyage by Roberval. These would be the first expeditions to penetrate the St. Lawrence River and explore a good thousand miles into the North American interior. They also provided a remarkably detailed account of this region, both of its people and geography.

Little is known about Jacques Cartier except that he was born in Saint-Malo, Brittany, in 1491, that he married into a prosperous Breton ship-owning family, and that he had sailed to Brazil and perhaps Newfoundland as a young man. There are no authentic contemporary portraits of Cartier nor any contemporary descriptions of his personality. Many consider Cartier to be probably the most skilled navigator and cartographer in

Jacques Cartier, in a portrait that imagines how he might have looked, explored the St. Lawrence River in 1535. *(National Archives of Canada)*

France at the time. His discoveries would also provide a solid claim to the future colony of New France, and that people in the province of Quebec still speak French is only the most obvious legacy of his accomplishments.

CARTIER'S FIRST VOYAGE

Two ships under the command of Cartier left the port of Saint-Malo in Brittany on the northwest coast of France on April 20, 1534. Brittany had only been formally linked to the Kingdom of France in 1514 with the marriage of Francis I, king of France, to Claude of France, daughter and heir of the duke of Brittany. This added significantly to France's seaworthy fleet, for the Bretons had long been experienced sailors, by this time having already sent fishing fleets as far as Newfoundland. The ships Cartier took on this voyage bore about 60 tons manned by a crew of 61 each. His orders from the king were primarily to discover a passage to China, but also to find a source of gold and silver, and clearly it was international rivalry with Spain that prompted this part of the expedition. They reached Newfoundland in a remarkably swift 20 days, heading straight across the Atlantic at about 48°N. The account Cartier composed, probably later copied and altered by someone else, offers remarkable descriptions of the native wildlife. For example, at the Isle of Birds, as he called it (it is known as Funk Island today and is located just off Newfoundland), he encountered the great auk, which is now extinct.

> Some of these birds are as large as geese, being black and white with a beak as big as a crow's. They are always in the water, not being able to fly in the air, inasmuch as they have only small wings about the size of one's hand, with which however they move

as quickly along the water as other birds fly through the air. And these birds are so fat that it is marvellous. We call them apponats and our two long-boats were laden with them as with stones, in less than a half an hour. Of these, each of our ships salted four or five casks, not counting those we were able to eat fresh.

His crew also managed to capture and eat a polar bear that was swimming out to the island from the mainland. They found "his flesh was as good to eat as that of a two year old heifer [cow]." On another island they found puffins with red beaks and feet and later in the trip they saw a walrus, which Cartier described as a great beast; they are "large like oxen, have two tusks in their jaw like elephant's tusks and swim about in the water." Fortunately, the walrus did not share the Frenchmen's curiosity, or it would probably have ended up on their plates.

Cartier's account also gives detailed and precise geographical descriptions and fairly accurate measurements of distance and latitude. He also had no delusions about the promise of these first islands for future exploitation—nearly everywhere all he could see were barren rocks. He admitted, "I did not see one cart-load of earth and yet I landed in many places. Except at Mont Sablon [in Labrador] there is nothing but moss and short stunted shrub. In fine I am rather inclined to believe that this is the land God gave to Cain." Whether he meant this literally or not is impossible to say, but Cain was sent to the barren land of Nod, to the East of Eden, which by Cartier's reckoning would have been somewhere in Asia. At this point, Cartier met some Native Americans wrapped in furs and painted skin. Cartier believed that they had come from the interior with their birch-bark canoes to hunt seals.

That Cartier had a cross set up at one point and mentions that he and his men had the mass sung suggests he was a fairly devout Catholic. It is also recorded that he objected to swearing. Although missionary efforts were not part of the original instructions, it would become a major component of French voyages to come. Certainly, Cartier's descriptions of Native Americans would have inspired his fellow Frenchmen with the idea that these people would welcome conversion, and Cartier himself frequently alludes to his belief that "civilization" (European) could be easily impressed on the Native peoples. He refers to them as "savages," but this implied humans in the state of nature, without religion,

The Language of the Sea

As with any profession, sailors developed a unique language, sometimes official and sometimes slang, to refer to parts of the ship and various onboard activities. Many of these terms originated in this era or slightly earlier. For example, the word *starboard* derives from the steering paddle or rudder that was always located on the right side of the ship. *Port* derives from the fact that goods would be unloaded from the left. The *poopdeck,* the raised deck at the stern (or rear) of the ship derives from the ancient practice of placing a protective idol at the rear of the ship, in Latin called a *puppin.* When the captain or mate shouts out *avast,* he was using an English corruption of the Italian *basta,* meaning "enough" or "stop." *Jetsam* (derived from "jettison," to throw away) was the term for goods washed up from a shipwreck, which were legally the property of whoever gathered them at shore. Food referred to as *mess* comes from the Latin *missum,* which referred to a meal or something brought forth to the table. To *rummage* (derived from the same word as "room") meant to empty and clean out the ballast of the ship. Many of these terms have come to have non-nautical meanings, as with *scuttlebutt,* which comes from the water casks or butts that, when scuttled—that is, tapped with a small hole—would be a good place to exchange gossip.

Sailors were also proverbially fond of swearing. Technically this should be distinguished from the simple use of obscenities—words that are indecent and lewd. It literally means to swear or take an oath invoking the name of God or a saint, promising to do something if supernatural aid is forthcoming. At sea there were, of course, ample opportunities to call on divine aid to quell a storm or deliver the ship from danger. *'Swounds* and *'Sblood* (meaning "By God's Wounds" or "By God's Blood") were typical Elizabethan oaths. They are also blasphemous if one follows the second of the Ten Commandments—"Thou shalt not take the name of thy Lord your God in vain." Cursing is slightly different, as it seeks to use supernatural powers to bring someone harm, as when saying "Damn!" Though, sailors were also known for cursing and using obscenities.

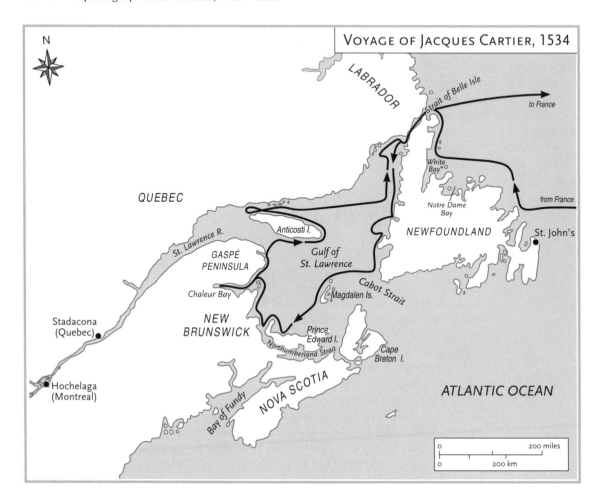

VOYAGE OF JACQUES CARTIER, 1534

"courteous" customs, or possessions. Although he observed that they "eat their meat almost raw," it would be wrong to assume that he considered these Native Americans to be sub-human. Because they were as yet unaccustomed to European customs, Cartier believed it his right, if not his duty, to subjugate them and impose French rule.

As Cartier made his way south toward Prince Edward Island, he began to find more fertile land covered with wild peas and berries. He believed the region would not only provide good farmland but also that the cedars and spruce could be made into sturdy masts for ships more than 300 tons, which was about as large as the French built them in this period. This area was also more heavily populated, and at one point his ship met a fleet of some 40 or 50 canoes. Presumably wanting to trade, the Indians in the canoes pursued Cartier, displaying their furs and entreating the French to come forth in their own language, which obviously the Frenchmen could not understand. Cartier seems to have panicked, because he ended up firing a cannon to frighten them away. He did eventually trade with them, though, exchanging knives and iron goods for furs. Unwittingly, Cartier stumbled on what would become one of the most important resources of the future colony, and a pattern of interaction with Native peoples that would last for centuries.

The people the French encountered at this point are according to current scholarship identified as Laurentian Iroquois, or Stadaconans, after their city, present-day Quebec. (Some scholars today prefer the term Saint Lawrence Iroquoian, and in older sources these people were sometimes identified as Huron. There is still disagreement among experts as to who these people actually were.)

By the beginning of the 17th century, these people had completely disappeared, either through disease, warfare, or migration, so there is still a good deal of controversy over their specific background. Cartier's description of their customs and diet can be considered one of the earliest ethnographic studies of a North American First Nation—as they are called in Canada. He describes shaven heads adorned with a long tuft of hair at the top tied up with leather, their custom of rubbing someone's arms and chest as a way to express thanks, as well as their methods of fishing for

As they traveled the St. Lawrence River, Jacques Cartier and his fellow explorers encountered American Indians, who are known as Stadaconans, inhabiting what would later become Quebec. This drawing depicts Cartier and the Stadaconans holding a conference. *(National Archives of Canada)*

mackerel, growing corn, and drying figs and other fruits as well as beans.

Cartier also describes what is one of the most vivid examples of misunderstanding between these two cultures. As he had done before, Cartier set up a cross, with a shield bearing the fleur-de-lys (the lily) from the French flag and a motto saying *Vive Le Roy de France* (Long Live the King of France). These crosses probably served many purposes—a directional marker, a way of thanking God for a safe journey, but most important a territorial claim for French sovereignty. This is certainly how the Native leaders of the Iroquois interpreted it. One figure, who we learn later in the account is Chief Donnaconna, made a vociferous protest before the cross; Cartier interpreted this to mean that the land belonged to him and that the French were not welcome. The very fact that Cartier recorded this at least shows he had some misgivings over appropriating the land without the permission of the inhabitants. His giving them some shirts, red caps, and brass chains, which he assumed satisfied them, only reveals the great misunderstanding that existed between these peoples when it came to the ownership of land. It also seems very unlikely that two of the chief's sons who were taken aboard understood that they were being taken to France. For within a week of this encounter, Cartier was heading back across the Atlantic, arriving at Saint-Malo on September 5.

Although there exists only Cartier's account of the initial interaction of the chieftain's sons with the French, Donnaconna may have believed he was sealing an alliance with the French. He may have thought this would guarantee exclusive trading privileges or perhaps that the French would help fend off other, hostile tribes. The two Iroquois youths, who came to be called Domagaya and Taignoaguy, once brought to France, dressed like Frenchmen and learned a bit of the language.

Someone back in France—it has been suggested the great French writer François Rabelais—even made a vocabulary of their native language.

Somehow they were able to communicate to Cartier that, on the next trip, they wished to be returned home to Stadacona rather than where they were picked up some distance away. It was their information, and Cartier's effort to return them home, that ultimately lead to the discovery of the St. Lawrence River and his futile search for the mythical land of Saguenay, a kingdom thought to be rich beyond measure.

CARTIER'S SECOND VOYAGE

Cartier's second voyage was planned and financed with remarkable speed with a worthy patron, Philippe Chabot de Brion, an admiral of France. He was given three ships: *La Grande Hermine* of more than 100 tons, *La Petite Hermine* of about 60 tons, and *L'Émerillon,* the smallest at about 40 tons. This expedition was recorded by Cartier and was published in 1545 as *Brief recit.* Cartier and his crew left in May 1535, reaching the other side of the Atlantic in about two months. After negotiating some bays and islands, on August 10 they entered St. Lawrence Bay, named for the early Christian martyr St. Lawrence, who was burned on a grill for his faith in A.D. 258. It was along this great highway of water, his Native American captives informed him, that he would find the great Kingdom of Saguenay. They also told him that farther on they would come to "Canada"—after which the entire nation would eventually take its name.

For some reason Cartier did not trust Domagaya and Taignoaguy, and instead of proceeding along the St. Lawrence River, he ordered his boats to continue searching the

La Grande Hermine was one of three ships Jacques Cartier's patron Phillipe Chabot de Brion gave Cartier for his second voyage. *(Library of Congress, Prints and Photographs Division [LC-USZ62-105525])*

gulf for a passage. They did eventually make their way upriver toward the region called Canada, after marveling at the beluga whales and walruses, and met up with Donnaconna. It was there that the chief saw again his two sons after their long absence. With all parties convinced of each other's goodwill, Cartier then proceeded to Stadacona. Donnaconna, however, seems to have believed that if Cartier proceeded on to the next large settlement, Hochelaga, he might prefer to have those Indians as allies, and so Donnaconna sought to forestall Cartier. To this end, he presented Cartier with what he considered a rare and precious gift: a young girl, his own niece, and two young boys, one of which was his son. In return for this present Cartier was entreated not to visit Hochelaga. Ending his exploration

here was not an option, so Cartier refused, but had nonetheless taken the children on board and made what he believed was a reciprocal gift of swords and a wash basin. Clearly there was some serious miscommunication here.

To impress his guests and at the instigation of Donnaconna's sons who had been to France, Cartier had some artillery fired off, which so frightened the local inhabitants that, as Cartier put it, they "began to shriek and howl in such a very loud manner that one would have thought hell had emptied itself there." What can only be described as mayhem followed, still with the intention of preventing Cartier from going on to Hochelaga. Painted black and dressed as horned devils, three men appeared as emissaries from the local god Cudouagny, who had predicted that if they went all would meet their doom in the ice and snow. To this dire threat Cartier and his men could only laugh, assured that their own god would protect them, and that Jesus had promised good weather. According to Cartier's accounts, realizing that this scheme had also failed, Donnaconna suggested that Cartier leave behind some men in good faith and only then would he let his sons act as guides. Whatever then transpired, Cartier—at this point thoroughly fed up with what he considered to be their treachery—decided to press on without his Native guides.

Relations with Native Americans improved dramatically as the French proceeded up the St. Lawrence. Cartier wrote: "These people came toward our boats in as friendly and familiar a manner as if we had been natives of the country, bringing us great store of fish and of whatever else they possessed, in order to obtain our wares, stretching forth their hands toward heaven and making many gestures and signs of joy." They were once again offered children, a girl of about 8 or 9, and they refused a little boy of two or three as too young. When they reached Hochelaga at the current site of Montreal, they met with an equally happy and welcoming population and were happy to make presents of knives, beads, and other trifles. In turn the locals filled the French boats with fish and bread made of cornmeal. These were probably the first white men the Hochelagans had ever set eyes upon, and from what followed historians conjecture that they may have thought of them as super-human. Only Cartier's account of these events survive though, so what actually happened must remain conjectural.

In an elaborate ceremony within the city palisades on the slopes of what the French called "Mount Royal," after women had rushed up to rub the strangers arms and present their babies for them to touch, Cartier and

his men were seated on mats. Then the chief was carried in by nine or 10 men, and set down next to Cartier, at which point Cartier

Native Americans wave to Jacques Cartier as he and his crew continue to traverse the St. Lawrence River. Cartier and the Native Americans living along the St. Lawrence River generally had positive encounters. *(National Archives of Canada)*

realized that the chief was paralyzed. Presumably the Hochelagans expected Cartier to cure the man. Cartier obliged by rubbing the chief's arms and legs. Then a whole procession of afflicted people came forward for which Cartier could only read out the gospel

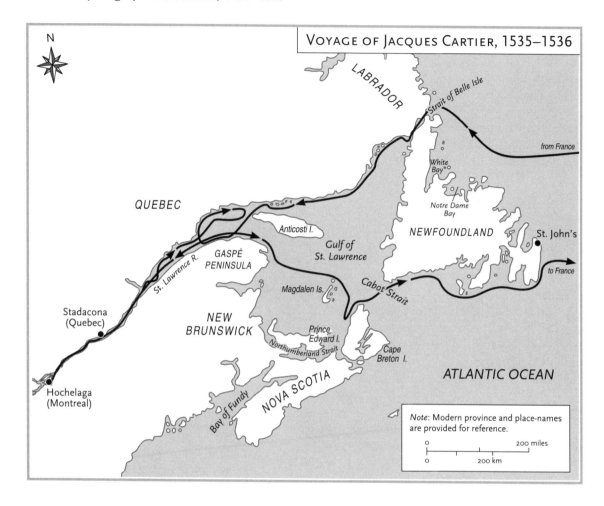

VOYAGE OF JACQUES CARTIER, 1535–1536

N

LABRADOR

Strait of Belle Isle

from France

White Bay

QUEBEC

Notre Dame Bay

Anticosti I.

NEWFOUNDLAND

St. John's

Gulf of St. Lawrence

St. Lawrence R.

GASPÉ PENINSULA

Magdalen Is.

Cabot Strait

to France

Stadacona (Quebec)

NEW BRUNSWICK

Prince Edward I.

Northumberland Strait

Cape Breton I.

Hochelaga (Montreal)

Bay of Fundy

NOVA SCOTIA

ATLANTIC OCEAN

Note: Modern province and place-names are provided for reference.

0   200 miles
0   200 km

and pray. It is not surprising that Cartier did not wait around long enough to have his healing powers put to the test of time. Most important, he had realized by this point that the rapids upriver from the settlement were not navigable.

Cartier also realized he would not be able to make the passage back to France in the winter and so decided he would spend the winter in Stadacona and from there search for the fabled Saguenay. In a small fort on the shoreline, they chose to brave their first Canadian winter. In this time Cartier had ample opportunity to witness the customs of the Laurentian Iroquois in detail, and he recorded many remarkable things. He noted their almost complete lack of private property, their communal living, and their custom of men taking several wives. He marveled at their way of marrying off young girls as well: "as soon as they reach the age of puberty [they] are all placed in a brothel open to everyone, until the girls have made a match." It was also here that Cartier took his first puffs of tobacco—which he found so hot that it reminded him of ground pepper.

But their winter stay was not to be a pleasant one. Not only did the snow begin to fall and their casks freeze solid, but a disease struck both Native people and Frenchmen alike, whose symptoms appear to have been scurvy, brought on by severe vitamin C deficiency. Gums bled, teeth fell out, and swollen and blackened limbs appeared on practically the entire crew, 25 of whom died. All Cartier could do was pray to the Virgin Mother and vow to go on a pilgrimage. It was not until the Iroquois offered them a concoction of bark from the *arborvitae* ("tree of life" in Latin) that they were cured.

Meanwhile, probably to get rid of Cartier, Chief Donnaconna fabricated a fantastic story of the wealthy kingdom of Saguenay to the north of Stadacona. It may be that Cartier merely heard what he wanted, and the lure of gold and jewels was enough to make him believe anything. In his account he even repeated a story about people who never eat solid food and have no anus, and another people who have only one leg. These were actually standard fables back in Europe, pretty good evidence that Cartier consistently misinterpreted the Native people's words. Cartier also knew that to finance another trip and convince the French at home that Saguenay really existed he would have to bring the chief and his sons back with him. Cartier kidnapped them and brought them back to France with a handful of children he had been given as presents.

Donnaconna's people exchanged gifts with Cartier. According to Cartier's account, as translated by Richard Hakluyt and published in London in 1580:

> [Understanding] that their Lorde was taken to be caryed into France, they were all amazed, yet for all that, they would not leave to come to our Shippes, to speake to Donnaconna, who told them, that after twelve monethes, he should come agayne, and that he shoulde be very well used, with the Captayne, Gentlemen, and Mariners. Which when they hearde, they greately thanked our Captayne . . .

CARTIER'S THIRD VOYAGE

Cartier had arrived back in France in summer 1536, ready to make preparations for another voyage. It might have happened had not King Francis I once again become preoccupied with war against Spain. Donnaconna was presented at court, where he further expanded on the catalog of riches that could be found at Saguenay—now adding spices. Cartier probably had intended to bring him home, but in the next few years Donnaconna and all but one girl among the Native Americans died. Without any previous contact with European diseases for countless generations, Native Americans were particularly susceptible to smallpox and measles. Although the precise circumstances of their deaths are unknown, this was the fate of most Native Americans brought to Europe, willingly or otherwise.

Cartier set out on his third voyage in May 1541 after five years' delay. Unfortunately, there survives no detailed account of this voyage as there was with the first two. By this time the French had abandoned hope of reaching China, but plans were laid for establishing a permanent settlement from which they could subdue and exploit Saguenay—which the French hoped would prove as rich as Mexico or Peru, both of which had been conquered by the Spanish. To ensure a fitting and noble ruler of the future colony, Jean-François de La Roque, sieur de Roberval, a wealthy French nobleman, was appointed leader of the entire venture. Presumably his experience as a soldier would come in handy, although why King

Francis allowed a Protestant to take charge is not very clear, especially when converting the Native to Catholicism was one of Francis I's explicit goals. Fortunately for Cartier, Roberval's contingent did not leave until a year after he did, by which time efforts to find Saguenay had failed miserably.

Cartier's third voyage was perhaps ill-fated from the start. It did not help that the crew included a large contingent of freed criminals, including women, because hiring men proved too difficult, especially when fishing fleets proved so profitable. There were also a handful of noblemen eager to carve out little fief-

doms in the new colony. Cartier's ships left in 1541, with Roberval still in France waiting for cannon and supplies. It took about three months before they made it back to Stadacona, where Cartier informed the people that their chief, Donnaconna, had died in France. To quell the locals, however, he made up a lie that the other Iroquois had married, were living happily and would not return. About eight miles from the Native settlement, he then proceeded to build his colony, a fort surrounded by gardens and animals brought from Europe. They also began to mine for metals in earnest. They named the settlement Charlesbourg-

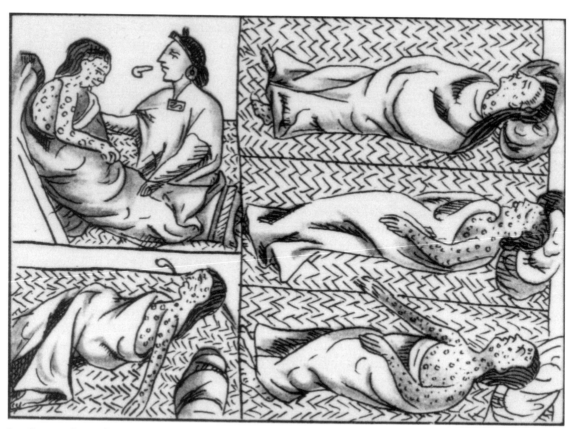

Smallpox and measles, among other diseases that European explorers brought to North America, killed numerous American Indians. In this detail of a drawing from *Historia general de las cosas de Nueva España*, Aztec people of Mesoamerica are infected with smallpox. *(Library of Congress, Prints and Photographs Division)*

Royal after the son of King Francis I and intended it to be a base for launching their conquest of Saguenay. Two small ships were also sent to France with samples of diamonds and gold—which in the end proved to be quartz crystals and fool's gold (pyrite, a compound of iron and sulfur).

The story of Cartier's attempts to reach Saguenay exists only in bits and pieces as translated by Hakluyt. Cartier spent about a month searching upstream of Montreal trying to figure out how to get past the waterfalls and rapids. Native guides picked up in villages along the way were of no help. After having to carry the boats overland twice, he finally just gave up. Relations with the Native Americans back at the fort also turned sour, and the French were attacked, leading to several fatalities. Scurvy hit once again, and while waiting for Roberval to arrive with reinforcements, the food began to run out. It became apparent to Cartier that to linger in his fort would mean losing everything, including his life. In June 1542 he finally decided to head home in his three remaining ships containing not only all the surviving colonists but barrels of what he believed to be gold and precious jewels. Nothing could have been worse than returning home emptyhanded.

On the return voyage Cartier's ships met up with Roberval's around Newfoundland. He had apparently been busy the past year privateering—that is, seizing Portuguese and English ships to finance his voyage—and was now well stocked and well armed. Cartier tried in vain to convince Roberval to give up and return home, but naturally, as his subordinate, he was constrained to obey the nobleman's orders. Roberval ordered him to stay. Rather than do so, and face further disaster, Cartier's ships escaped by cover of night and left Canada and his dreams of fabulous wealth behind for good.

Jacques Cartier returned to Stadacona, present-day Quebec, during his third voyage, without bringing back any of the Native people he had taken to Europe. All of them, except one girl, had died. *(National Archives of Canada)*

Roberval, however, would not give up so easily. In the account left by his pilot Jean Alfonce, he was called The General, a good indication not only of his plans for Canada but also how his methods would contrast with Cartier's. The nobles who accompanied him were also there primarily for conquest and profit, and hoped to receive estates once the

An Extraordinary Young Woman ⟋

One of the most fantastic—although not necessarily true—stories in the era of exploration involves a particular couple on Jean-François de La Roque, sieur de Roberval's ship. The young woman, Marguerite, a relative of Roberval's, was accompanying him with the goal of marrying a suitable husband when she arrived in New France. She fell in love, though, with one of the crew and began to carry on secretly with her new lover. Their passion was concealed by Marguerite's old handmaid, a peasant women named Damienne, but apparently was not concealed well enough. The general found out and, given his puritanical frame of mind, decided to maroon the girl and her maid on a tiny, desolate island in the Gulf of St. Lawrence. The girl's lover managed to escape and join them. By winter they were growing weak and sick. The sailor soon died. After some months Marguerite gave birth. The newborn infant promptly died, and soon after the handmaid also died. Somehow Marguerite managed to survive another two years—living on polar bears—and was then miraculously picked up by French fishermen and taken home. This exemplary story of courage and fortitude was passed on to the king's sister, Marguerite de Navarre, who used it in her collection of stories titled *The Heptameron*. Unfortunately, given her own Protestant sympathies, she could not resist making the couple married, marooned for some unmentioned treason, and even fending off lions. The baby and maid were also conveniently excised from the story.

job was complete. They even brought along their wives with the intention of raising families comfortably in their new possessions.

Roberval and his contingent continued the search for Saguenay, faring no better than Cartier had. Near the site of Cartier's Charlesbourg-Royal, he built an extensive and well-defended fort on a high mountain, named France-Roy, and began preparations to plant vegetables for the winter. The food in the end proved insufficient, and the group also suffered from scurvy, some 50 dying from it. By spring the remains of his men set off to find Saguenay, but they too were stopped by rapids and powerful currents. By summer 1543 they abandoned the fort and sailed back to France.

That would be the last of France's exploration of Canada until the 17th century. Their claim remained on the maps, as did the imaginary Saguenay. France itself would be torn by violent wars of religion for many decades. The last thing anyone had the energy or effort to search for was fabulous wealth, let alone a passage to China. As for the Laurentian Iroquois, in the intervening years they disappeared entirely and were replaced by Huron in the course of the 16th century and other tribes whom the French encountered when they returned to Canada with Samuel Champlain.

5

SPANISH, FRENCH, AND ENGLISH FAILURES
Mid-16th Century

Despite the failure of the Spanish to gain a foothold in North America along its southern coast, news of an incredible fortune made by Spaniard Hernán Cortés in his conquest of the Aztec Empire in Mexico spurred on many other individuals to explore the interior with the intention of finding their own kingdoms to conquer. Florida was one possibility. Spanish explorer Juan Ponce de León had made an attempt to found a colony there in 1521, and Lucas Vásquez de Ayllón failed miserably along the Atlantic coast later that decade. There was another attempt by Pánfilo de Narváez in 1528 to establish a colony on the Gulf side of Florida near Tampa Bay, but this too ended in disaster.

Still the Spanish continued to explore in hope of finding another great empire, particularly after Francisco Pizarro spectacularly defeated the Inca of Peru in the 1530s. The most incredible venture inspired by this was a search conducted by Francisco Vásquez de Coronado for the mythical Seven Cities of Cíbola from 1539 to 1542, trekking across New Mexico, Texas, and Kansas. At the same time, Francisco de Ulloa explored lower California, to be followed up by voyages by Juan Rodríguez Cabrillo as far north as Bodega Bay. All these were part of a concerted and carefully timed Spanish effort between the late 1530s and early 1540s to extend their possessions to the north from the Atlantic to the Pacific. What lay in between was still a mystery.

Hernando de Soto was another Spaniard who took to exploring the southeastern flank of North America. Having made a nice fortune for himself in Peru, he was now anxious to find his own empire. He set out in 1539, landing in Tampa Bay, on Florida's Gulf coast, and proceeded north from there. He encountered many Native peoples in his journey through what is now Georgia, South Carolina, over the Blue Ridge Mountains, and into Alabama, and fought with several of them. His expedition went as far as Mississippi and Arkansas, his army growing weaker and shrinking every day. Finally, de Soto died of a fever along the Mississippi River. The entire venture only proved that there was no great kingdom in North America and only the vaguest hope of finding precious metals. These ceased to be attractive motives for the Spanish to explore North America.

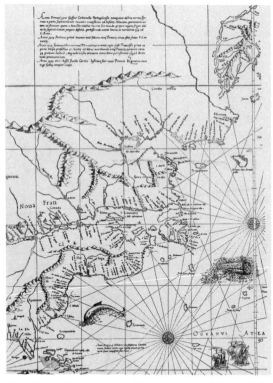

Gerardius Mercator's well-known map of the world was first published in 1569. In the portion shown here, the cartographer's use of what would become known as Mercator projection, in which longitude is drawn as parallel lines meeting latitudinal lines at right angles, is evident. *(Library of Congress, Prints and Photographs Division [LC-USZ62-92883])*

But international rivalry once again provided the impetus for further exploration. The French had by this point charted the Atlantic coast under Giovanni da Verrazano, and Jacques Cartier had already laid claim to a good portion of North America. Furthermore, the French had proved that they were interested in colonization, even if not yet successful at it. In the course of the 1550s the French were also engaging in privateering ventures against the Spanish. These were essentially officially licensed voyages, privately financed, permitting the forceful seizure of enemy vessels. It was a way for early modern states to strike at their enemy without spending money on navies. Private French expeditions had even sacked and burned several Spanish cities in the Caribbean. Spain's decision to found further colonies was primarily a tactical one: to prevent the French from settling North America. Even a small base could be used to launch attacks on Spanish possessions, so the Spanish would have to get there first, despite the lack of fabulous profits.

The viceroy of New Spain (modern-day Mexico) sent Tristán de Luna y Arellano in June 1559 with the intention of founding settlements on the interior that could be linked by roads to the coast. Despite a hurricane that destroyed most of his ships, his expedition proceeded north from modern-day Pensacola to the Alabama River. Food shortages were a serious problem and the local inhabitants avoided the Spanish, probably the result of having experienced disastrous encounters with de Soto years before. Luna y Arellano's men basically followed de Soto's route at this point, and met with equally disastrous results. They got as far as the border of present-day Tennessee before giving up.

At the same time, Spanish efforts to found a settlement on the Atlantic coast continued. The site of Santa Elena, in present-day South

Carolina, was chosen as best calculated to thwart French efforts. Angel de Villafañe was instructed to take about 70 colonists to a point at 33°N, but they found that the site was poor, and after a hurricane destroyed some of their ships, they abandoned the effort. Before the Spanish could find a suitable site, the French beat them to it.

The rivalry between France and Spain also took an unexpected twist after 1559, one that would not only influence exploration for the next century but also change European politics entirely. First, the half-century-long war (the Habsburg-Valois Wars) fought between these nations, mostly on Italian soil but spilling out elsewhere, finally came to an end in 1559 with the Peace of Câteau-Cambrésis. Moreover, there were new rulers on several thrones. Philip II soon became king of Spain. He was a fervent Catholic who would not hesitate to spend any amount of money to ensure the orthodoxy of his possessions, the Netherlands in particular. Elizabeth I, a committed although not as strident Protestant, had become queen of England after the death of her Catholic half-sister, Mary. And France came under the sway of the Queen Mother Catherine de' Medici, a fervent Catholic trying to control a nation divided in religion and that would soon plunge into bloody civil wars over it. Not surprisingly, these European religious controversies spilled over into the quest to control North America.

RIBAUT AND LAUDONNIÈRE

Religious competition among European nation-states influenced the first French attempt to found a colony along the southern coast of North America—all of which was then called Florida—under the leadership of Jean Ribaut in 1562. The venture was sponsored by

French admiral Gaspard de Coligny, a Protestant. Ribaut and most of his future colonists, 150 in number, were also Huguenots, as French Protestants were known. The thought was that, if the Huguenots' situation became unbearable in France, such a colony might provide a religious haven for exiles. Second in command of the voyage was René de Laudonnière, whose account of this and subsequent trips provides a full picture of this remarkable episode.

At what is today the southern tip of Parris Island in the Port Royal Sound of South Carolina, they built a fort called Charlesfort for the new French king Charles IX. Ribaut himself returned to France for supplies and reinforcements but apparently did not leave enough food for the 26 men left behind to survive the winter. A return voyage was forestalled by the outbreak of civil war in France in which Ribaut himself had become caught up in the Protestant defense of the port city of Dieppe. Ribaut was forced to flee to England, where he tried to convince Queen Elizabeth to back his Protestant colony but was soon thrown into jail as a spy when relations between England and France fell apart.

The abandoned colonists were in a desperate situation, and the Native Americans by this point had no intention of helping them. Their commander tried to maintain discipline by hanging one rabble-rouser and exiling another, but the men ended up mutinying and killing their leader, Albert de La Pierria. Eventually, the French decided to leave on their own in a small boat they managed to put together (except one man, Guillaume Rouffin, who stayed behind). Still with no food, aboard their boat the colonists resorted to drinking their own urine and even killed and cannibalized one of the crew to stay alive. They were eventually rescued by an English ship off the coast of Brittany and returned to France.

Engraved by Theodor de Bry from a painting by Jacques Le Moyne, this map shows the French expedition reaching Port Royal Sound in South Carolina. *(Library of Congress, Prints and Photographs Division [LC-USZ62-380])*

Meanwhile the Spanish had heard word of this colonization attempt; an expedition of Hernando Manrique de Rojas found the fort abandoned except for Rouffin and were convinced that the French posed a real threat.

Little did they know that Admiral Coligny was planning a second colonization attempt and this time put Laudonnière in charge. Three ships and about 300 colonists set off in 1564, among them the artist Jacques Le Moyne, who both charted the coasts and made remarkably sensitive paintings of the Native Americans they encountered. His record of the Timucua is one of the prime sources for the study of Native Americans of this era, though most of his original paintings have been lost. What survives are the engravings made by Flemish copper-plate engraver Theodor de Bry based on them. They were probably altered significantly as well. The colonists chose a site farther south than the first attempt and began to build a fort, named La Caroline, at the St. Johns River in what is now South Carolina. It was actually a very poor site, being fairly swampy, but relations with the Native Americans were very good. The French traded gifts and dealt with them fairly, assuming they would be there to stay.

But among the colonists, many had come merely for profit. This became painfully apparent when, after food began running low and times became more difficult, several men escaped in boats to seek booty by preying on Spanish ships. Eventually, the entire colony mutinied and locked up Laudonnière. Sixty men took two of the ships to go privateering in the Caribbean, and their very presence would only further irritate the Spanish. With the mutineers gone, Laudonnière managed to restore order among the remaining colonists but soon fell afoul of the Native Americans whom he had pledged to help in warfare in return for food. As it turned out, the French became caught up in intertribal rivalries, making alliances with several mutually hostile groups. The Frenchmen were also keenly interested in finding the source of the Native peoples' gold trinkets, assuming it was local. In fact, it had come from Mexico via the Spanish. In the end, the Native Americans grew to mistrust the French, especially after a chieftain was kidnapped, and they stopped providing them with food altogether. Laudonnière was left with no choice but to make plans to go home.

While living among the Timucua villages, Laudonnière wrote a detailed account of their customs. He described their finely crafted bows and arrows with fish teeth or stone points. His description of scalping, here in Hakluyt's translation, was clearly calculated to give an impression of savagery to European readers. As with all such observations by outsiders, its true significance was probably misunderstood:

> The kings of the Countrey make great warre one against the other, which is not executed but by surprise, and they kill all the men they can take: afterward they cut of their heads to have their haire, which returning home they carry away, to make thereof their triumph when they come to their houses. . . . Being returned home from the warre, they assemble all their subjects, and for joy three days and three nights they make good cheare, they daunce & sing, likewise they make the most ancient women of the Countrey to dance, holding the haires of their enemies in their hands. . . .

Laudonnière also described Native foods and methods of planting corn, beans, and pumpkins. He explained how Native Americans smoke fish, gather oysters, and hunt for deer, crocodiles, and turkeys: "They eate all their meat broyled on coals, and dressed in the smoake, which in their language they call Boucaned." (The word "buccaneer" is derived from this term, which refers specifically to the rack on which meat was roasted.)

The situation was growing desperate, and a few men starved to death. More would have followed had not English captain John Hawkins stumbled across the colony and left behind some provisions and a boat in which to return home. Before they could, however, Ribaut arrived with more food and reinforcements. The French colony might survive after all. What the Frenchmen did not know, though, was that Spaniard Pedro Menéndez de Avilés, captain general of the West Indian Fleet, was a short distance to the south with a large fleet and had explicit instructions from Philip II to destroy the French settlement. Menéndez, it is believed, thought the French, as heretics, would help Native American slaves rebel, so there was much at stake in destroying their settlement.

When the Spanish approached they encountered the as yet unarmed French ships, which were able to outrun them. But it was also clear to the French that they would have to launch a preemptive strike on the Spanish

North American Native Foods

Many of the most important foods eaten around the world are native to the Americas. Corn, sweet potatoes, and most species of beans and squash come from what is today Mexico and were widely cultivated in the upper parts of North America when Europeans arrived. Native Americans typically planted corn, beans, and squash together in the same plot; the beans were allowed to climb up the corn stalks and the squash vines trailed on the ground. This proved to be an extremely efficient way to grow these crops. Native peoples also made extensive use of wild game and seafood either from the sea or from inland rivers and lakes. Turkey is perhaps the greatest contribution North America has made to world cuisine. Surprisingly, there are few plant species of importance globally that are actually native to what is now the eastern United States and Canada. The sunflower is one. From it are derived seeds and oil, and a certain species yields an edible tuber that is known today as the jerusalem artichoke. This name is actually a corruption of the Italian word *girasole*—meaning "turn toward the sun," which is exactly what the flower does. The French in North America called them *topinambours* after the name of a tribe in Brazil, where they supposed, incorrectly, the tubers originated. The French still use this term. Other foods originating in the upper parts of North America include maple syrup and wild rice—actually a species of grass—and modern strawberries, blueberries, and cranberries. Many nuts are also native to this region: the black walnut, hickory nuts, and pecans.

This engraving by Theodor de Bry based on a painting by John White records the Algonquian village of Secotan, including its crops and homes. *(Library of Congress, Prints and Photographs Division [LC-USZ62-52444])*

at St. Augustine or wait like sitting ducks to be attacked themselves. Ribaut took his ships, now well-armed with guns from the fort, and headed south. Foul weather should have advised caution, but urgency demanded swift action. The storm eventually grew into a full-scale hurricane of the kind that still periodically devastates this area. The French ships were all destroyed. Those who managed to survive the wrecks were eventually captured by the Spanish and killed, including Ribaut.

Soon thereafter Menéndez arrived at La Caroline with 500 men who marched overland and attacked the remnants of colonists left behind with Laudonnière. They put to the sword every single one, with the exception of a

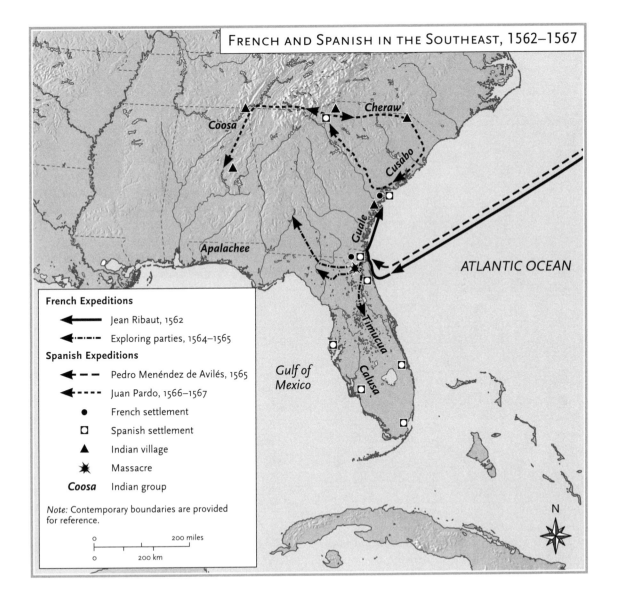

FRENCH AND SPANISH IN THE SOUTHEAST, 1562–1567

French Expeditions

◀━━━ Jean Ribaut, 1562

◀━·━·━ Exploring parties, 1564–1565

Spanish Expeditions

◀━ ━ ━ Pedro Menéndez de Avilés, 1565

◀━ ━ ━ ━ Juan Pardo, 1566–1567

● French settlement

▢ Spanish settlement

▲ Indian village

✸ Massacre

Coosa Indian group

Note: Contemporary boundaries are provided for reference.

0 ———————— 200 miles

0 ———————— 200 km

few who were able to scatter into the woods, including Laudonnière, and the women and children whose lives were spared. The Spanish then occupied the fort, rebuilding and strengthening it, and renaming it San Mateo. For three years they maintained it as a northern outpost, until they themselves were attacked by a French fleet bent on revenge. In 1568 Dominique de Gourgues, a French soldier returning to the area with three ships, somehow gained the support of Native Americans, reclaimed the fort, and put to death all the Spanish captives. Satisfied with revenge,

On behalf of Spain, Pedro Menéndez de Avilés and his crew attacked and defeated the French settlement established by René de Laudonnière at La Caroline. *(Library of Congress, Prints and Photographs Division [LC-USZ62-102263])*

the French ships returned home, and the French hereafter abandoned all their projects for this region.

A SPANISH FOOTHOLD IN FLORIDA

The Spanish fort 30 miles to the south of San Mateo survived despite European competition, and St. Augustine properly claims its title as the oldest continuously occupied city in what is now the United States, founded on August 28, 1565. The fine stone fort that remains there today, the Castillo San Marcos, was built in the late 17th century. From this site there were further Spanish voyages of exploration up the coast. Menéndez had the idea that the Chesapeake Bay, or Bahía de Santa María as the Spanish called it, extended 1,200 miles inland, and he believed it could be used to transport silver from the mines in Mexico. It might even connect with the Pacific Ocean. He was also given the right to exploit this region as its future ruler, which meant he could enslave the Native populations to work on plantations. He would also set up missions and proceed with the conversion of anyone encountered. At the center of his colony would be the city of Santa Elena, located near Port Royal Sound, South Carolina. He also commanded Spanish explorer Juan Pardo to investigate the interior with the intention of finding a road to Zacatecas, a Spanish city located in northern Mexico.

Pardo's first expedition took place in 1566–67 and included 125 soldiers. Because they did not bring much food, they were told to take what they could from the Native populations as tribute—that is, by force. Pardo was thus forced to go from settlement to settlement, which he did, traveling north through North Carolina and Tennessee. He also built several forts and left men behind to deal with the Native Americans, peoples who would later come to form the Catawba, Cherokee, and Creek chiefdoms. On occasion, they would help one group fight against their enemies. This voyage was cut short when Pardo was ordered back to defend Santa Elena from possible French attack. A second voyage was organized; this one was well-documented by a member of the expedition, Juan de la Bandera. Pardo was given orders to establish friendly relations with the Natives peoples, to inform them that they were now Spanish subjects, and to leave behind monks who could instruct them in Catholic dogma. Pardo's men once again headed north through the Carolinas and Tennessee. The forts they left behind, however, were never well manned, and they were never able to control the Native populations the way Menéndez had planned. In the end only St. Augustine and Florida proper remained as a legacy of Spain's efforts to control the Southeast.

THE ENGLISH:
Newfoundland, Norumbega, and the Northwest Passage

During much of this time the Spanish were also engaged in trying to put down the Protestant rebels in the Netherlands. The English tried to help the Dutch by lending money and sending troops but also by engaging in privateering that preyed on Spanish shipping, and this led to the English once again becoming interested in overseas ventures. As early as the 1560s English privateer John Hawkins began selling African slaves illegally in the Spanish West Indies, as well as seizing merchant ships. By the end of the decade, trade between England and Spain was officially suspended, and engagements at sea became violent. It was in the wake of this that Sir Francis Drake began a spectacular run of raiding voyages against

Spanish colonies, one of which, starting in 1577, succeeded in circumnavigating the globe.

While this was happening, plans were once again being made to explore the northern Atlantic. In 1576 Humphrey Gilbert's book *Discourse of a Discoverie for a New Passage to Cataia* was published. It was a promotional piece intended to muster support for a voyage through the Northwest Passage across the Sierra Nevada Mountains, out the Strait of Anian, and all the way to China. Such a voyage, though, was purely fictional; the Strait of Anian soon became a widely spread myth. The first voyages to attempt to find a "northwest passage" were led by English explorer Martin Frobisher. Having been to West Africa and having successfully led privateering voyages against the Spanish, he was a logical choice for the job. But the plan met with misfortune from the very start. There were bad storms and a collision early in the trip. A passage was eventually found extending 150 miles inland; it is still called Frobisher's Strait. Meeting up with Inuit, whom Frobisher and his men mistook as Asian Tartars, only confirmed their suspicion that they were on the right track. But bringing back a Native inhabitant alone would not satisfy investors. To succeed in impressing investors, they gathered up pyrite, a type of iron ore that they took to be gold, and for some reason no one disabused them of this idea. The excitement sparked off what might be considered the first gold rush.

With numerous wealthy investors, including Queen Elizabeth herself, a joint-stock company was formed and by 1577 was ready to make a second voyage. Apart from extensive contact with the Inuit, who were painted by John White, and the discovery of a narwhal whose tusk was presented to Elizabeth, the expedition mined 200 tons of pyrite. It was once again fool's gold, and once again no one back in England successfully tested it. By the time the third voyage was arranged in 1578, there were even more investors, and the greed for gold appears to have entirely supplanted the passage to China and promise of trade with Asia. This time they mined 1,350 tons of pyrite, and only after this was revealed to be fool's gold did the entire enterprise end in utter failure and bankruptcy. But the existence of a northwest passage remained tantalizingly real despite this fiasco.

Even before Frobisher's attempts had ended in failure, Sir Humphrey Gilbert entertained the idea of setting up his own colony. Having failed in colonization plans for Ireland, he managed to obtain the very first colonial charter from Queen Elizabeth to set-

tle in the New World. With four big ships and 365 gentlemen and soldiers, plans were laid for an extensive colony over which Gilbert would have vice-regal powers. The enterprise was underway by 1578. One possible site for the colony was the fabled city of Norumbega. As had been the case with Saguenay and Florida, rumors of a wealthy kingdom waiting to be conquered proved irresistible. It was placed on European maps on the Penobscot River in Maine, and although it means "quiet place between two rivers" in Algonquian, no such place existed outside Europeans' imagination. It was recorded as fact in several French accounts, and one English sailor, David Ingram, even claimed to have walked there from Florida in 1567. Ingram's descrip-

Saint Elmo's Fire

During severe thunderstorms, and usually toward the end of them, there sometimes appears a luminescent bluish glow on the masts of ships. It is actually a discharge of electricity, or corona, due to a buildup of electricity in the atmosphere, and although it has no heat, it is referred to as a "fire." Its appearance — and there are many recorded in the early days of exploration — was taken as a sign of heavenly intervention to protect sailors from the storm. Ancient peoples had many names for this phenomenon, but the one used by the English was "Saint Elmo's fire." St. Elmo is believed to be an Italian name derived from a Sant'Ermo or Saint Erasmus (who lived about A.D. 300), who was the patron saint of sailors in the Mediterranean. The phenomenon was also sometimes referred to as *corposante* ("holy body"), as though Elmo was himself appearing to signal deliverance. U.S. statesman and inventor Benjamin Franklin was one of the first to connect Saint Elmo's fire to atmospheric electricity. Although usually confined to one spot, these electric charges could also roll around the deck, which inspired English playwright William Shakespeare in his play *The Tempest* to write: "sometimes I'd divide / And burn in many places; on the topmast / The yards and bowsit, would I flame distinctly / Then meet and join." Today Saint Elmo's fire can sometimes be seen as a glow on airplanes' wing tips, propellers, and antennae. There is even a theory that the *Hindenburg* zeppelin disaster (the explosion of a dirigible airship in Lakehurst, New Jersey, in 1937) may have been sparked by Saint Elmo's fire igniting leaking hydrogen.

While exploring present-day Baffin Island and Hudson Bay in search of a "Northwest Passage" in 1576, Martin Frobisher encountered Inuit. This engraving depicts Inuit of nearby Greenland. *(National Archives of Canada)*

tion of the size and wealth of the city and the people adorned with gold and pearls inspired Gilbert.

The objectives of Gilbert's voyage were varied. The colony would provide a base for attacking Spanish shipping, as well as trade opportunities. Finding the Northwest Passage also remained a goal, and with remarkable foresight it was believed that America could absorb England's excess population and provide a market for English manufacturers. Unfortunately, the lure of booty was too great, and his ships abandoned him for privateering.

Gilbert would not give up, though. A second voyage was planned within a few years. Before leaving, Gilbert parceled out 22 million acres on paper but could not find many

investors apart from his friends. It was to be a model utopian community, with a governor and some 260 colonists who would enjoy full rights as Englishmen. The voyage, after a very difficult crossing, first reached Newfoundland, claiming it for England. But only disaster followed. Two ships had already abandoned him, one ship sank with all hands drowning. On the return voyage, Gilbert's own boat sank and the captain with it.

VIRGINIA

There were further attempts to find the Northwest Passage, most notably three voyages led by English explorer John Davis from 1585 to 1587. But in these years the emphasis shifted south to what would become Virginia, named for Elizabeth I, who was known as the Virgin Queen. The interest in this region first came to the queen's attention through one of her court favorites, Sir Walter Raleigh. As with his half brother Gilbert, he was issued official patents to found and rule over the colony. Raleigh chose two men to lead an expedition to choose a suitable site first, Philip Amadas and Arthur Barlowe. They left in two small ships in 1584, crossing to the West Indies before making their way north to the Carolina coast, which they promptly claimed for England. They then met the native Algonquian-speaking peoples in a place they called Windgandcon but would later be called Roanoke Island.

As with other first encounters, the two peoples were on friendly terms and exchanged gifts. Given the mild climate and ample opportunities for agriculture, the English naturally favored this site for their future colony. Given the happy and generous Native Americans, who shared their corn, pumpkins, fish, and game with them, they had little reason to look much farther. They quickly returned home with two Native Americans

Despite repeated failed attempts, Sir Walter Raleigh remained quite determined to establish a colony in present-day Virginia. *(Library of Congress, Prints and Photographs Division [LC-USZ62-111785])*

such as mastic and cinnamon, and medicines such as sassafras.

> This Island had many goodly woods, and full of Deere, Conies, Hares, and Fowle, even in the middest of Summer, in incredible aboundance. The woodes are not such as you find in Bohemia, Muscovia, or Hyrcania, barren and fruitless, but the highest, and reddest Cedars of the World, far bettering the Cedars of the Açores, of the Indias, or of Lybanus, Pynes, Cypres, Sassaphras, the Lentisk, or tree that beareth the Masticke, the tree that beareth the rinde of black Sinamon . . . and many other of excellent smell and quality.

By 1585 the English were ready to mount a major expedition to found a new colony. With a coterie of backers, some privateered vessels, and impressed men (that is, both ships and men forcefully seized and made to go)— though not with Raleigh himself, whom the queen wanted by her side—Sir Richard Grenville was put in charge of the voyage. Some 600 people in all went. The governor of the new colony was to be Ralph Lane. They also brought along a scientist, Thomas Hariot, to make an accurate assessment of the flora and fauna, as well as Native peoples, and to write a report, which he did (*Briefe and True Report of the New Found Land of Virginia,* 1588). John White came to illustrate their discoveries, which were later copied and printed by Theodor de Bry. These depictions constitute one of the principal ways Europeans learned about Native American culture of this region and period.

The ships made their way across the Atlantic in April 1585, reconnoitering on Puerto Rico, where they built a fort, built a small boat to replace one that had sunk off Portugal, and picked up fresh supplies. The

and glowing reports of the bounty this land afforded. "The soile is the most plentifull, sweete, fruitfull, and wholesome of all the world." Barlowe's account of Virginia, which first appeared in Raphael Holinshed's *Chronicles* in 1587 and later in Richard Hakluyt's *Voyages,* had the following to say about Roanoke. At this time, there was still a marked interest not only in food resources but also in spices

Spanish on the island were certainly outnumbered or they would have tried to oust the English. It may seem strange, especially being at war and after seizing Spanish vessels, that the English were later able to land on Hispaniola, where they entertained the local Spanish gentlemen with a sumptuous banquet. The king of Spain's war was apparently of little interest to these colonists, who were able to sell cattle and tobacco. Finally, along the Carolina coast, after running aground in the shallow shoals, they arrived at two Native villages, Pomeiooc and Secotan. Relations soon soured when a silver cup was stolen and Grenville decided to burn a village in retribution. Again, it may seem strange that the English colonists could be so cordial to their enemies, the Spanish, yet treat Native Americans with such disregard. Eventually, the colonists were set ashore at Roanoke, with Ralph Lane as governor. Grenville himself returned to England and captured a Spanish ship along the way.

Roanoke was not a particularly good site for a colony, primarily because the waters were so shallow and unapproachable in large ships. As with so many other colonial efforts, the English would have to depend on the good graces of the Native Americans, and at this

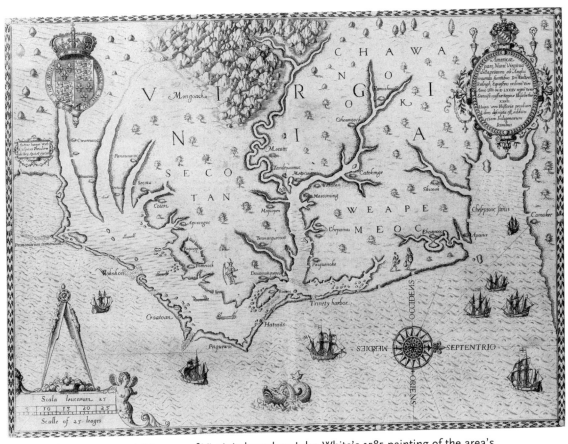

Theodor de Bry engraved this map of Virginia based on John White's 1585 painting of the area's coastline. *(Library of Congress, Prints and Photographs Division [LC-USZ62-54020])*

In this engraving by Theodor de Bry based on a painting by John White, the Algonquian village of Pomeiooc and its surrounding stockade, or perimeter made of tall timbers sharpened at one end and driven into the ground, is clearly visible. *(Library of Congress, Prints and Photographs Division [LC-USZ62-54018])*

Governor Lane was particularly inept. Fearing an attack, he decided to make a preemptive strike in which Wingina, the Native chieftain, was killed. What might have transpired next can only be guesswork, and the colony might have been destroyed then and there had not a relief mission under Sir Francis Drake accidentally arrived in 1586, fresh from successful raids in the West Indies and a sack of St. Augustine. Every one of the colonists begged to be taken home, and so they were. Soon thereafter Grenville arrived with his own relief and found the colony completely abandoned. He left 18 men behind to maintain the fort, all of whom had disappeared by the time the next colonial expedition had arrived.

Raleigh would simply not give up his plan to "plant" a colony in Virginia. The second attempt was financed by a joint-stock com-

pany, and this time John White was to be governor, a person more sensitive to relations with the Native Americans, the investors probably thought. This time whole families were sent, and there was even a baby born, White's grandchild, appropriately named Virginia. Obviously, they intended this colony to be permanent and much more than a trading depot or fort from which to launch attacks. Although the original plans were to settle along the Chesapeake Bay, which had much deeper harbors and where relations with the Native Americans had not yet gone sour, the ships landed once again at Roanoke and decided to stay there. This would prove a fatal mistake. All efforts to make peace failed, and

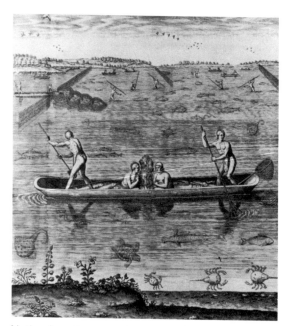

Native American people create a dugout canoe from a tree by burning the inside of the trunk and scraping it with seashells in this Theodor de Bry engraving. They developed dugout and birch-bark canoes, both of which Europeans adopted. *(Library of Congress, Prints and Photographs Division [LC-USZ62-52443])*

After Columbus's exploration of the Americas, the Spanish controlled the seas, largely because of their galleons, or large, heavy ships, that looked much like this model, until their defeat in 1588 by England's more maneuverable fleet. *(Library of Congress, Prints and Photographs Division [LC-USZ62-103297])*

even worse, no relief voyages could be arranged back in England, as every boat was needed to fend off the Spanish Armada, which had been sent to invade England in 1588.

By the time the English were able to return to Virginia in 1590, the colony had been destroyed, and all they found was the word CROATOAN carved in a tree. Either the English had been killed or they left this word to signify that they had melded with one of the Native peoples. There remains a tradition that this was indeed the colonists' fate, and apparently English surnames and even English words were later found among the Native tribes.

6

EUROPEANS COLONIZE AND CONTEST NORTHEASTERN AMERICA
Early 17th Century

After nearly a century of almost total failure, European efforts to settle North America would finally bear fruit in the 17th century. It is true that, in terms of exploration alone, much of the coastline had been accurately charted, as had some of the interior. But there was no fabulously wealthy empire to conquer like the Aztec or Inca. There was no gold or spices. Only sarsaparilla and sassafras briefly enjoyed a vogue as New World medicines to treat syphilis, a sexually transmitted disease believed to have originated in the New World. Tobacco was the only native crop to be cultivated widely, and it too was first used as a medicine for "phlegmatic" disorders—those like coughs and colds that brought up phlegm or mucus. No Northwest Passage was discovered, nor would one be, for

another few centuries. And most important, no permanent settlement, apart from tiny St. Augustine, was founded in the modern-day United States until the 17th century.

The success of the English and French, and even the Dutch who had newly entered the fray, is to some extent the result of changes in European politics. Once again there was a major change in rulers. King Philip II of Spain died in 1598 and was replaced by his less fervent son, Philip III. The long protracted Wars of Religion in France came to an end not long after 1589 with the accession of the Protestant leader Henry of Navarre, who, to maintain the peace and assure the French throne, converted to Catholicism in 1593 but also granted extensive toleration to Protestants. The Revolt of the Netherlands, although not officially over, was halted by a 12-year truce, the Spanish having finally exhausted their resources and energy. Lastly, Queen Elizabeth I of England died in 1603 and was succeeded by James I, who ruled Scotland as King James VI and who promptly ended hostilities with Spain. For the first time in decades there was peace among these nations.

That alone would not account for the colonization of North America. It was partly dogged determination, as well as a refocusing of motives from plunder to settlement, agriculture, and trade in beaver skins to supply the growing fashion for fur felt hats. Perhaps most important, and sadly, it was the slow disappearance of the Native population due to disease. The full impact of European diseases such as smallpox and measles was not felt for many years, but these diseases made the colonial experience of North America very different than elsewhere in the world. Settlers would, once they managed to feed themselves, have a much easier time maintaining their colonies and populating them. But their efforts were not at first so smoothly realized. It should also be recognized at the outset that the English, French, and Dutch voyages described in this chapter were practically contemporaneous, all taking place in the first decade of the 17th century.

ENGLISHMEN IN NEW ENGLAND

At the turn of the century there were attempts to explore in the familiar ways of previous generations. One such venture was led by Englishmen Bartholomew Gosnold and Bartholomew Gilbert in 1602 in one ship, the *Concord*. Their stated objective was to find the "Refugio," or Narragansett Bay, mentioned by Verrazano years before, and there to set up a station from which furs could be traded. Gos-

nold first landed on the coast of Maine and proceeded south around Cape Cod. He explored Martha's Vineyard, which was named for his daughter (although it has been suggested that it was a smaller island and not the present one that they so named).

Gosnold finally decided to begin building a trading post on another island, which they named Elizabeth—today Cuttyhunk, a small island to the west of Martha's Vineyard. There they gathered sassafras root, then a medicine but today familiar as one of the ingredients in root beer, and they cut cedar logs. Although they expected to leave behind a small number of men to guard the post, no one was willing to remain. It seems as if the large number of Native Americans visiting the area to fish in the summer frightened them, even though relations between the two groups at this point were still for the most part friendly. The English even found it very amusing when they offered *bacalao* (salted cod) with mustard to the Native Americans, "but the mustard nipping in their noses they could not endure," according to the account of John Brereton who witnessed it. Nonetheless all the Englishmen returned home with their cargo, and their accounts awakened great interest in the region. Sir Walter Raleigh considered "Northern Virginia," as it was still called, part of his New World jurisdiction, and directly promoted his own ventures.

The first of these expeditions left within a year in 1603. It was a similar voyage to Gosnold's, led by English merchant Martin Pring, with the same objective of collecting sassafras and trading. The English ships traversed much the same coastline as well, stopping somewhere on Cape Cod, or perhaps the very site that would later become Plymouth, Massachusetts. Here the relations with Native Americans appear to have been more guarded, if not antagonistic. The English brought with

American Indians used sassafras as a medicine and to add flavor to food. Europeans first harvested it for medicinal purposes, but later it became more popular as an ingredient in root beer. *(National Archives of Canada)*

them two mastiffs—huge vicious hunting dogs, which they enjoyed letting loose and using to frighten the Native peoples. Having collected their sassafras, the English departed, as their only motive was to make a profit. By the time of their return to England, however, Raleigh had been disgraced at court and lost his patent. Thereafter only the king could decide who would be allowed to go.

About this time there was a plan being concocted by English Catholic nobleman Sir Thomas Arundel to provide a refuge for English Catholics in this region. Now that there was peace with Spain, exiled Catholic Englishmen might choose to return to a colony held by the English Crown. English explorer George Waymouth was hired to lead the expedition, which would also seek to discover good fishing grounds to the north of the area explored by Gosnold. This is precisely what he accomplished along the coast of Maine. With only 29 men in a small ship named the *Archangel,* Waymouth successfully weathered a storm in the shoals around Nantucket and explored the coastline, trading with Native Americans. Waymouth and his crew also sailed up a river, as yet not positively identified, but either in Maine or most likely the St. John in New Brunswick, which they found to be an ideal site for a "plantation," owing to its deep harbor and lack of sandy shoals. "Here are more good harbors for ships of all burdens, than all England can afford, and far more secure from all winds and weathers, than any in England, Scotland, Ireland, France, Spain, or any other part hitherto discovered," claimed crew member James Rosier, who wrote a firsthand account of the voyage. He also described the land as fertile, ideal for farming and husbandry.

It was glowing accounts like Rosier's that prompted the English to immediately begin plans to settle. Within a year both the Virginia Company of London and the Virginia Company of Plymouth were granted royal charters, and in 1607 two separate colonies were organized, one to be based at Jamestown and the other in Maine and to be called Sagadahoc. The jurisdiction of the first company extended from Cape Fear in modern-day North Carolina north to the Hudson River; the second from Maine south to the Chesapeake. The overlap was intentional; whoever could settle the mid-Atlantic region first could claim it. Before either of these expeditions set out, however, Pring made one more voyage to fish and trade furs in 1606 in what became known as the Hanham-Pring expedition. Thomas Hanham was appointed commander. It was Hanham and Pring's report that ultimately persuaded the Plymouth Company to colonize Maine (then called Mawooshen after the

Abenaki name) and to locate their settlement along the Kennebec River.

The Plymouth Company's efforts were hampered by several factors. First, their patron, Sir John Popham, had recently died and the venture was never sufficiently financed. One of their ships was lost earlier that year, and probably most important they had not expected the winter in Maine to be so harsh, nor to run out of food. Even the trading opportunities were not as glowing as the printed accounts made them out to be. The colonists left at Sagadahoc in their makeshift fort were suffering from disease and malnutrition; many died or returned home with provision ships. Worse yet, the control of the company back in England kept passing hands, and no one it seems wanted to invest a lot of money in such a risky venture. By 1608 the settlers were ready to abandon their site along the Kennebec River, which they did.

JAMESTOWN

The other Virginia Company was organized along similar lines as a joint-stock company, which means that shares could be freely sold and investors would have only a limited risk depending on how many shares they held. It gained enormous financial backing from nobles and gentry who wanted to invest in land, as well as merchants who were hoping to carry colonial products back to Europe. Along with agricultural products, there would also be wood for shipbuilding, cabinetry, and dye woods. And there still remained the possibility

This detail of John Smith's 1624 map shows Jamestown and its surrounding Native American villages. *(Library of Congress)*

Cooperage

The success of any voyage depended on many factors, not least of which was the quality of wooden barrels intended to store provisions on board. The "cooperage" (originally from the Latin *cupa,* "cask") was the workshop where barrels were constructed, and the master cooper and his apprentices were the people who fashioned them. By the early modern period, barrels were the primary way of transporting liquids, having replaced earthenware jars (known by their Greek name, *amphorae*) some time in late antiquity. The ingenuity of the barrel's design consists in its shape: the broad bulging side touches the ground on only a tiny point, so a several hundred pound barrel can be turned or rolled on deck with ease. A well-made oak barrel would be used on ships to store water, wine or beer, hardtack biscuits, or even gunpowder. Ships were even measured not by length or square footage but by their barrel-carrying capacity or tonnage, the "tun" being a barrel of about 252 gallons, occupying roughly 40 cubic feet. There were also smaller barrels: hogsheads (63 gallons), butts (126 gallons), puncheons (72 to 120 gallons), and smaller wine barrels of about 50 to 60 liters, the size of a wine barrel most often used today. (Note that today a ship's tonnage refers to the number of tons of water it displaces.) Because they were stowed throughout the ship, barrels also had to be absolutely waterproof. This was accomplished by using oak or other woods such as pine, first split and slowly air-dried, then shaped and bent over an open fire. The staves—as these strips of wood are called—were then fitted into a hoop of willow saplings or iron, and skillfully hammered to fit together snugly. Then the interior of the barrel would be slowly toasted over the fire, caramelizing the sugars in the wood, but also making the inner surface watertight. The contents of a poorly made barrel would not only leak but spoil and be subject to infestation of weevils, maggots, or rats, so sailors across the centuries depended a great deal on well-made barrels.

of finding gold. Virginia would also stem the advance of the Spanish to the south and French to the north. Many trained soldiers were brought along, many of whom would not or could not become settled farmers.

The Jamestown colony of 105 settlers, lead by Christopher Newport, was founded in 1607, less than three weeks before Sagadahoc, but unlike it, Jamestown would succeed to become the first permanent English settlement in North America. The site they chose

was some 60 miles from the mouth of the Chesapeake Bay along the James River. When the colonists arrived, the region was densely populated by Algonquian peoples allied in a large confederacy led by Powhatan—their *werowance,* or big chief. For some reason many of the settlers did not intend to work hard and came to depend on the Native Americans for food, which they provided in expectation of profitable English trade as well as English help in fighting their enemies. Despite this help, the colony barely survived; there were only 38 men left when a relief ship arrived in 1608.

The company decided that stern measures were required and placed Captain John Smith in charge. He was an experienced but brash commander and forced the colonists to build houses and plant food while he maintained strict discipline. But even he was forced to plunder the Native American's food reserves, in retaliation for which Powhatan decided to starve them out. At this he nearly succeeded. In the winter of 1609–10, the majority of settlers starved to death, some resorting to cannibalism.

The investors back in England were nonetheless determined and sent out additional colonists, supplies, and weapons with the intention of occupying the entire region with force. Within the next few years they accomplished just that, and in the wake of

Native submission, Powhatan sent his daughter Pocahontas to come to friendly terms with the English. There is a famous episode in which Pocahontas saved John Smith's life by declaring her love for him moments before he was to be executed. If it actually happened at all, it was probably a staged reconciliation between the English and Native Americans. Modern scholars now believe that Smith invented the story to enhance his own reputation. Pocahontas, though, married tobacco farmer John Rolfe and went to England, where she became a celebrity but died before getting a chance to return to the Americas.

The long-term success of this colony was due primarily to their discovery of a cash crop with which they could make the venture profitable and self-sustaining. Pocahontas's husband, John Rolfe, had planted a tobacco that would ultimately seal the economic fate of this region for centuries. To set up large

In this illustration from an early 17th-century book about John Smith, he fights with Native Americans before being captured. *(Library of Congress, Prints and Photographs Division [LC-USZ62-99524])*

tobacco plantations, the colonists consistently moved the Native populations out as English families were brought in; eventually the two groups engaged in open warfare. In the end, this bankrupted the company, and the Crown was forced to take control. After a few decades the English prevailed as the Native population succumbed in alarming numbers to European diseases. In the coming years African slaves were brought in to work in the plantations; the first such slave actually arrived as early as 1619.

Jamestown was not the only English possession in North America. A relief fleet sent to Jamestown in 1609 led by Sir George Somers ran into a violent hurricane. The flagship *Sea Venture* was wrecked on Bermuda (named for Spaniard Juan Bermudez, who discovered the island in 1503). Several accounts were published by the survivors after their rescue. One of these inspired William Shakespeare to write a play about a similar shipwreck—*The Tempest*. In 1612 settlers arrived in Bermuda, and it has remained in English hands ever since.

There were also further attempts by the English to explore and settle the northern coastline of what was newly renamed New England. Captain John Smith made a voyage in the summer of 1614 and mapped the region between Cape Cod and the Penobscot Bay. His glowing account about the prospects of the region "Description of New England," was published in England in 1616 and was meant to attract investors. He also considered whaling in this area, but "We found this whale-fishing a costly conclusion. We saw many and spent much time in chasing them, but could not kill any." Little could Smith have guessed how important whaling would become to New England in later centuries. Instead of whale hunting, they fell back on fishing and fur trading, but neither was enough to impress investors at home, even though Smith

reminded them of how the Dutch had grown so fantastically wealthy on such a lowly business as fishing. In the next few years Smith made further attempts to settle New England, all of which met with failure. His dream of populating the region with small land-holding freemen, rather than aristocratic estates, would come to pass when the Pilgrims arrived seeking religious freedom in 1620.

THE FRENCH AND CHAMPLAIN

France too became interested again in overseas exploration around the turn of the 17th century. Even before this there were fishing fleets and fur-trading voyages making regular visits. An expedition of 1583 led by Étienne Bellinger, a merchant of Rouen, to set up a permanent trading station failed, but it did provide meticulous descriptions of the coast and a map of Nova Scotia up to the Bay of Fundy. The official right to rule new French settlements as viceroy was then granted to Troïlus du Mesgouez, marquis de La Roche. He had made two attempts in 1578 and 1584, but both were failures and never completed the passage across to North America. In 1598 a third venture was finally organized. This time he had the questionable idea of using convicts and beggars to trade for furs and seal pelts. He sent the men to Sable Island off the southeast coast of Nova Scotia and renamed it Ile de Bourbon for the king; as a precaution he placed them under military guard. The plan worked for a few years until the men killed their guards and were eventually brought back to France. La Roche's commission was eventually revoked.

The monopoly on trade in Canada was then transferred to the Protestant Pierre de Chauvin. Significantly, the Edict of Nantes, a grant of religious toleration, had just been

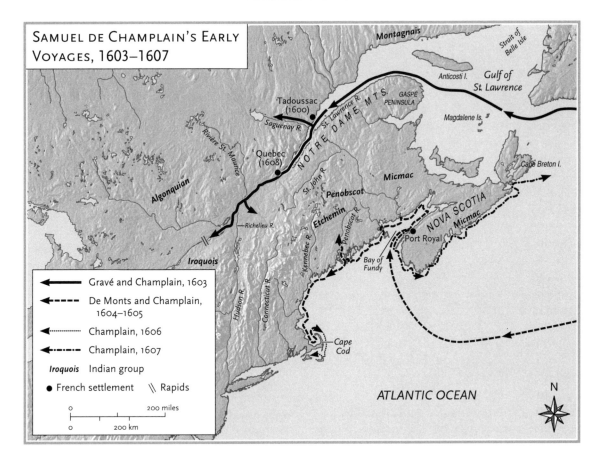

SAMUEL DE CHAMPLAIN'S EARLY
VOYAGES, 1603–1607

signed (1598), and peace with Spain had been achieved, so there was no longer fear of sending Protestants to the New World. Chauvin's fleet of four ships went up the St. Lawrence and arrived at the mouth of the Saguenay River in 1600, over a half-century after Cartier and Roberval had been there. The colony would be called Tadoussac. He left 16 men there in a makeshift cottage and returned to France. They barely made it through the winter, and despite a few further trading voyages, the site became nothing more than a trading post, occupied intermittently.

There was another voyage of exploration up the St. Lawrence led by François Gravé in 1603, that included the future French explorer

of this entire region Samuel de Champlain. It was Champlain's observations and report of further waterways in the interior learned from the Algonkin and Montagnais tribes that kept alive the idea of trade and colonization in this region. By this time, the Laurentian Iroquois whom Cartier had met earlier in the century had completely disappeared.

The next major French efforts at colonization were not along the St. Lawrence but to the south in what would be called Acadia (now Nova Scotia). It was lead by Pierre de Gua, sieur de Monts, who was granted a monopoly on exploitation of the region and fur trade in 1603. As lieutenant general it was also his job to populate the colony, and in 1604 he left

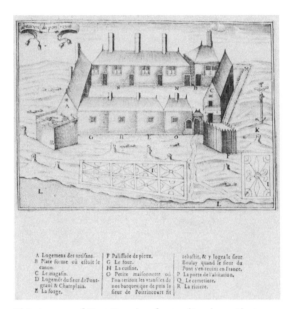

A Logemens des artifans.
B Place forme où eftoit le canon.
C Le magafin.
D Logemér du fieur de Pont-graué & Champlain.
E La forge.

F Paliffade de picux.
G Le four.
H La cuifine.
O Petite maifonnette où l'on retiroit les vtanfiles de nos barqzesqze de puis le fieur de Poitrincourt fit

rebaftir, & y logea le fieur Boulay quand le fieur du Pont s'en reuint en France.
P La porte de l'abitation.
Q Le cemetiere.
R La riuiere.

This image of Port Royal, a fur-trading base that Samuel de Champlain established in present-day Nova Scotia, was included in a 1613 book by him. *(National Archives of Canada)*

fect nature of converting the Native Americans. Many were perfectly willing to be baptized, presumably not understanding what the ceremony meant, for they soon forgot their baptized names. They also persisted in keeping several wives, and it is amazing that Biard could be so persistent in what seems to have been an impossible task, especially given the language barrier. In his letters, his missionary zeal is evident:

> Isaiah assures us that the kingdom of our Redeemer shall be recognized throughout the earth; and there shall be neither caves of dragons nor dens of cockatrices, not inaccessible rocks, nor abysses so deep, that his grace will not soften and his salvation cure, his abundance fertilize, his humility raise up, and over which his cross will not at last victoriously triumph. And why shall I not hope that the time has come when this prophecy is to be fulfilled in these lands.

France with 120 settlers. Champlain was also on this voyage and was given the task of finding a suitable site after their original location along the St. Croix River was found to be too harsh. Champlain explored the coast beyond Cape Cod in several successive voyages over the course of three years. In the end they chose a site, Port Royal, on Nova Scotia facing the Bay of Fundy. This colony might have been the seat of New France had not the sieur de Monts's patent been revoked in 1607. The settlement was then turned over to another nobleman, Jean de Biencourt, the sieur de Poutrincourt. He did not attempt to reoccupy the site for a few years, and when he did, Jesuit missionaries such as Father Pierre Biard were brought along to commence the conversion of the Native population.

In a letter back to his Jesuit superior in France, Biard related the curious and imper-

Port Royal and Father Biard struggled on for the next few years, and this might have claimed the title as the first permanent French settlement in the New World had not the English under Samuel Argall destroyed it in 1613.

Thereafter, however, attention again focused on the St. Lawrence under the guidance of Champlain. In 1608 he founded what would be the first permanent French settlement in the New World, Quebec, from which he could trade furs and continue the search for a passage to Asia. To this end he explored the interior, discovering the lake that bears his name, and in the next few years he penetrated the interior farther than any European before him. These voyages, as far as the Great Lakes, would result in scores of French trappers, missionaries, and explorers arriving in New France for the next century.

HENRY HUDSON, THE DUTCH, AND THE SWEDISH

While the French were preoccupied with the St. Lawrence, a new European power initiated its own exploration of North America—namely, the Dutch. It was not, however the Dutch government per se, nor did they even have a king or royal court that could sponsor such voyages. Rather, it was the Dutch East India Company, whose main efforts lay in Asia, where they did eventually wrest from the Portuguese a major maritime empire. Part of their plans for heading to North America also included searching for a northwest passage, and under the guidance of Englishman Henry Hudson, a trip was organized in 1609. Hudson had already, under the employ of the English Muscovy Company, made trips to find a northeast passage (above Russia). But he also thought there was a passage somewhere above Virginia; the explorations of John Smith, whom he knew, seemed to confirm his idea. This, Hudson's third voyage in his ship the *Halve Maen,* was also intended to go above and across Russia to reach Asia, but his crew would not press into the frozen Arctic. Instead they changed their plans and headed west. Hudson arrived at Newfoundland and explored the coast south, arriving at what is now New York Harbor on September 11, 1609. From there he sailed up a grand river as far as Albany—the river was later named after him.

Henry Hudson explored in 1609 what would become known as the Hudson River in present-day New York. In this painting, an American Indian family observes Hudson entering the river's bay. *(Library of Congress, Prints and Photographs Division [LC-USZ62-107822])*

According to the account left by Hudson's first mate, Robert Juet, the Native Americans they met here (Mahicans of the larger Lenni Lenape group) were eager to trade tobacco and corn for knives and other European wares. But the Dutchmen would not trust them, and although at times their relations seem to have been friendly, at others the Dutch merely plundered what the Native Americans would not willingly offer. On one occasion, after trading for beaver and otters, Hudson was determined to find out if the Native Americans were secretly plotting against him: "so they took them [the chiefs] down into the cabin, and gave them so much wine and aquavitae [alcohol] that they were all merry. . . . In the end one was drunk, which had been aboard of our ship all the time that we had been there." On this occasion, the Native American chief eventually passed out, and what the Dutch expected to learn from him by these means one can only guess.

Although Hudson considered this venture a failure, and though he was marooned in the Arctic by a mutinous crew on his fourth voyage, the Dutch remained interested in this as-of-yet unclaimed region of the mid-Atlantic coast. Another voyage was lead by Jan Corneliszoon May in 1611–12, and in the coming years the Dutch realized that the Iroquois had an extensive fur trading network upon which they could capitalize. In 1614 another Dutch explorer, Adriaen Block, went to chart the region. He was the first to map out Long Island as separate from the mainland. He also named Manhattan and explored the Connecticut River.

Soon thereafter a new company was formed, The New Netherland Company, which set up trading forts at New Amsterdam (present-day Manhattan) and Fort Nassau, later renamed Fort Orange (near the site of present-day Albany). Although they were later replaced by the Dutch West India Company,

Mermaids ⌒

Legends of mermaids—human females from about the navel up, fish from the navel down—stretch back to ancient times and through many cultures, and although often confused with sirens—who have the head of a woman and body of a bird—mermaids were also thought to lure sailors to their death. During the era of exploration, mermaids were taken to be symbols of illicit lust, considered a mortal sin by the Church. They were nonetheless taken seriously by many educated people. Christopher Columbus recorded in his log that he saw three in 1493. Over a century later, two of Henry Hudson's men reportedly spotted one. Hudson's log entry for June 15, 1608, relates: "From the navill upward her backe and breasts were like a womans . . . her skin was very white, and long haire hanging down behinde, of colour blacke; in her going downe they saw her tayle, which was like the tayle of a porposse, and speckeld like a mackerell." It is difficult today to know what to make of such claims. Presumably, these men were not mistaking a porpoise for a mermaid here, although it has often been theorized that the dugong or manatee in warmer waters were often mistaken for mermaids by delirious sailors.

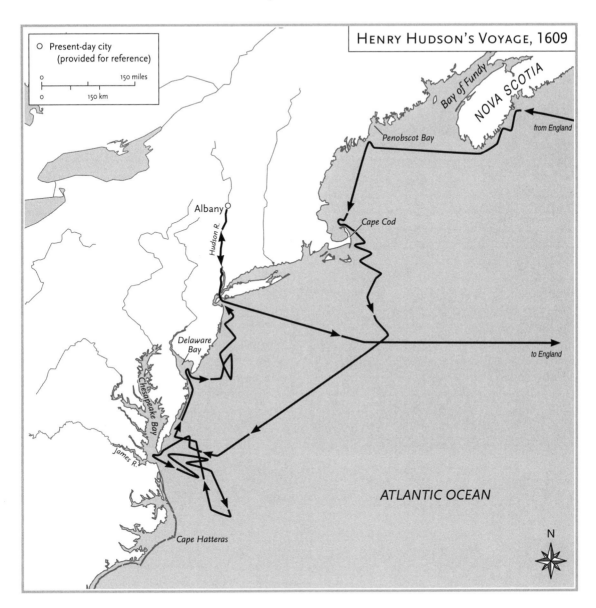

these Dutch traders made a considerable profit from their trade with the Iroquois. This was in direct competition with French trade among the Huron, and these alignments would have long-term historical significance in the control of the continent for the next few centuries. New Amsterdam did survive as a colony and was in fact the first multiethnic settlement that included Europeans of many nations, Africans, and Jews and that practiced religious toleration. It was ceded to the English after an Anglo-Dutch War in the late 17th century, when in 1677 the English agreed to relinquish claims to possessions in the East

Indian Spice Islands, but in return for which they were ceded New Amsterdam—which then became New York. The Dutch street plan of Lower Manhattan can still be discerned

Peter Stuyvesant served as director of New Netherland between 1647 and 1664, during which time he led the successful effort to conquer New Sweden. *(Delaware Public Archives)*

today, and many Dutch place names survive: The Bowery, Harlem, The Bronx, Brooklyn, Yonkers, and many others.

There was one other European colonial power that contributed to the opening up of this region. From 1638 the Swedes also set up posts along the Delaware Valley from which to trade fur. They were successful for nearly two decades, having set up forts like Fort Christina (present-day New Castle, Delaware) and small settlements throughout southern New Jersey. For a brief time the Atlantic seaboard was carved up by Spanish, French, English, Dutch, and Swedish colonies. It was only in 1655 that the Dutch, led by Peter Stuyvesant, marched down and forcefully annexed New Sweden to the New Netherlands colony.

In the first decades of the 17th century, five major European powers had footholds on the North American continent, and in the coming years their continued exploration and exploitation of the interior would not only lead to conflicts among themselves but also among various Native American tribes jockeying for survival as the colonists began to pour in. Through all the conflicts, however, Europeans from all lands would continue to rely on the Native Americans for knowledge of the unknown continent even as they displaced them from their native grounds.

7

THE FRENCH LEAD THE WAY
1607–1635

 In fall 1620, a group of English Puritans traveled on the ship the *Mayflower* to settle in New England. They landed on Cape Cod in early November and, from what is today Provincetown, began a brief exploration of the coast. By mid-December, they had identified a location with a natural harbor and a fresh water supply for their new settlement. Today the place they established is known as Plymouth Plantation. As the group's leader, William Bradford, recorded in his account of the settlement, the little community came to that place "and resolved where to pitch their dwelling."

Within a short time, however, the group was in serious trouble. They suffered from cold, scurvy (a deficiency of vitamin C), and other illnesses during the winter months. By summer 1621, only half the original 102 in the group were still alive. But the tide had already begun to turn. In March 1621, Bradford wrote that an Indian named Samoset "came boldly amongst them." He and another Indian called Squanto taught them how to grow local foods and gave them advice about where to fish. The Puritan settlers now had a secure food supply and cordial relations with local Native peoples. The colonists, Bradford wrote, considered the aid these two men gave them essential to their survival and saw Squanto as "a special instrument sent of God."

This is one of the most famous encounters between settlers and Native peoples in North American history, and it is commemorated across the United States through the annual Thanksgiving holiday. This simple story is often all that people know of the events of 1621. The full story is much more interesting and demonstrates several important aspects of the journeys of discovery and exploration that would take place in this part of North America.

THE ROLE OF FUR TRADE

In the full story, when Samoset met the Puritans, he greeted them in broken English, which he had learned from English fishermen

Beaver Hats

Although a beaver's fur was useful as warm protective covering, many Europeans wanted it more because of its soft underfur, which could be made into felt for hats. Beaver hats became fashionable at the end of the 16th century and stayed fashionable in a variety of styles for more than 200 years. In the 17th and 18th centuries, the fashion was for a three-cornered, or tricorner, hat, and it might be trimmed with ribbon, insignia, or a feather. (In the 19th century, a quite different style came into fashion—the stiff, upright cylindrical hats.) The best beaver furs that traders could buy were those that had been already worn by Native people as clothes or blankets. That was because the regular use had already taken off some of the outer fur and helped prepare the skin for feltmaking. Hatmakers cut the fur from the pelt, smoothed the hair, and used heat and pressure to make it into felt. Beaver felt held its shape better and lasted longer than any other material that was used in hatmaking, and hatmaking was a big business. Until quite recent times, few European men would ever have gone out in public without a hat. In fact, a beaver hat, which would have been expensive, held its shape so well over time that it could be handed down for generations.

when he lived in what is now Maine. Bradford remembered that the Puritans "marveled" at this. The colonists' wonder only increased

Beavers were plentiful in the New World, and the people of Massachusetts Bay Colony profited from trading the animals' pelts. *(U.S. Fish and Wildlife Service)*

when they met Squanto, who not only spoke English but had also been to Spain and England after being kidnapped by an English sea captain. Having such interpreters was a great advantage to both sides.

Their story also shows that settlers and explorers were not always separate people. In the early decades of settlement, a family or a group of families looking for fertile land to farm had to explore to find it. They needed to know an area well and where there was a supply of fresh water before they could make a good choice.

Additionally, as they explored, the Puritans depended heavily on local Native people for their knowledge and language skills. Bradford wrote that Squanto was "their pilot to bring them to unknown places." By fall 1621, Squanto was not only their guide, he was also their interpreter and purchasing agent as the colonists explored Massachusetts Bay and traded for beaver skins with local Native communities. Squanto had his own reasons for wanting to take on this role. He was a Wampanoag Indian, and his village of Patuxet had been virtually wiped out by disease in the years he had been away in Europe. Other Native communities had also been badly ravaged and were interested in making new alliances for protection against their enemies. Squanto was able to forge that alliance with the English.

The final revealing factor in the full story is the centrality of the fur trade. Even the Puritans, committed to settling in tightly knit farming communities, soon took up trading in beaver pelts, and that activity was, at least initially, critical to the economic survival of the colony. As the decades passed and the colony became prosperous from its agriculture, the fur trade continued to be a critical part of its relations with its Indian neighbors, and a number of colonists would still gain their livelihood from it.

Samuel de Champlain is known as the founder of Quebec. *(National Archives of Canada)*

CHAMPLAIN MOVES IN

The fur trade was the engine that was driving exploration in many parts of the northeastern region of North America. It was the fur trade that drew Samuel de Champlain to found a permanent trading post at Quebec in 1608 and to explore to the north and west. He already knew the St. Lawrence River valley well, through trading at Tadoussac, exploring the river as far as Montreal Island, and traveling up the Saguenay and Richelieu Rivers. His goals at Quebec were to establish a permanent settlement, trade furs, explore the region, introduce Christianity to the people, and still try to find a river route to the Pacific.

Before he could do any of these things, however, he had to secure his new community, as well as his trading and diplomatic relationships with the local Native peoples. These were the Huron, Algonkin, and Montagnais. These communities traded with the French and wove the French into their own diplomatic and military alliances. Consequently, in 1609, when the Huron were attacked by their old enemies, the Iroquois Confederacy, who occupied territory south of Lake Ontario, they expected and received Champlain's help. Although few in number, the French had gunpowder weapons and helped the Huron drive off their enemies.

The French and Huron victory at a battle near the southern tip of Lake Champlain in July 1609 had a profound impact. The French did indeed cement their relationship with the Huron but also cemented enmity with the Iroquois, whom they would intermittently fight for the better part of the next century. That battle and subsequent encounters showed the effectiveness of gunpowder weapons and gave

The French and the Huron defeated the Iroquois near Lake Champlain in 1609, as shown in this drawing by Samuel de Champlain. *(National Archives of Canada)*

the Iroquois a good reason to welcome the Dutch traders when they came. The Five Nations of the Iroquois Confederacy found the Dutch willing to trade weapons and other metal tools for furs.

Champlain understood that success in cornering the fur trade lay in finding routes and making friends, and he set out to do just that. For the rest of his life, until his death in 1635, he himself either traveled or sponsored the journeys of others to explore and map the region. He needed money to do this, and so he regularly published accounts of his journeys to promote the colony.

Another group who needed to raise money by publicizing their activities were the Jesuit missionaries. Following various brief missions

to Canada, priests from the Jesuit order, formally known as the Society of Jesus, arrived to stay permanently in the colony in 1632. They too wrote regular reports, published annually as the *Jesuit Relations,* in which accounts of all their activities in New France were gathered together. Champlain's books and the *Jesuit Relations* are the most important sources of information about exploration in this area during this period.

Despite Champlain's regular absences to raise money back in France, his own accomplishments as an explorer and those of his men were prodigious. By 1635, they had reached as far west as what is now Green Bay, Wisconsin. They had also gone as far south as the Susquehanna River, which has its source in what is today central New York, and they had perhaps followed it down to its mouth at Chesapeake Bay.

In May 1613, after securing the safety of the settlement of Quebec, Champlain's own next major journey of exploration took him up the Ottawa River, a major tributary of the St. Lawrence River. Champlain and his crew traveled as far north as what is now Allumette Island (opposite Pembroke, Ontario) on the Ottawa River. Even though this great journey is always associated with him, Champlain was not the first European to travel this route. A young Frenchman, Nicolas de Vignau, had already been there. As part of a diplomatic exchange with the Algonkin, Champlain had placed Vignau with them and had taken an Algonkin young man back to France. During his time among the Algonkin, Vignau had learned the language. Champlain had also "sent him on explorations," and on his return, Vignau told Champlain that he had paddled up the Ottawa to its source at a lake, which had a river to the "North Sea" (Hudson Bay) that he claimed to have seen. Champlain was later sure that Vignau had lied about that, but for the moment Champlain was eager to see for himself.

Champlain was traveling lightly with only two canoes, one Native guide, and four Frenchmen, one of whom was Vignau. They had to *portage,* that is, carry their canoes and all their supplies over land, around the La Chine rapids (near Montreal). These rapids had blocked Jacques Cartier's path when his expedition had sailed down the St. Lawrence in 1536. He named them La Chine Rapids (literally the "China rapids" in French) in the belief that the river was the route to Asia for which he had been looking.

Even traveling lightly, Champlain found the portage arduous and wryly noted in his later accounts that it was "no small matter for persons not accustomed to it." It was the first of many portages the party had to make. At another point, where the water moved against them with "great velocity," they could not portage, as the forest was too thick. So the party had to "get into the water and drag our canoes along the shore with a rope." Champlain almost lost his hand doing this. He had a tow rope wound around his wrist to pull his canoe when it was swept into particularly

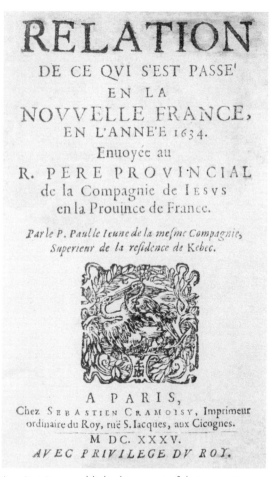

RELATION
DE CE QVI S'EST PASSE'
EN LA
NOVVELLE FRANCE,
EN L'ANNE'E 1634.
Enuoyée au
R. PERE PROVINCIAL
de la Compagnie de IESVS
en la Prouince de France.

Par le P. Paul le Ieune de la mefme Compagnie,
Superieur de la refidence de Kebec.

A PARIS,
Chez SEBASTIEN CRAMOISY, Imprimeur
ordinaire du Roy, ruë S. Iacques, aux Cicognes.
M DC. XXXV.
AVEC PRIVILEGE DV ROY.

Jesuit priests published a report of their activities in Canada under the title *Jesuit Relations* each year. This title page accompanies the volume covering 1634. *(National Archives of Canada)*

fierce waters. Only when the canoe became jammed between two rocks was he able to "undo quickly enough rope which was wound around my hand, and which hurt me severely and came near cutting it off."

The next day, they met a party of Algonkin going in the opposite direction, and the two groups visited for a while. The Algonkin told Champlain that the way ahead was harder than anything they had yet seen. Champlain offered to exchange one of his own party for one of the Algonkin to serve as a guide, which they agreed to. The new group now passed where the Gatineau River flows into the Ottawa—where the modern city of Ottawa is now located. Their Native guide offered them critical advice that saved days of arduous portages. The Ottawa River along which they were slogging was a south-flowing river, and the party was moving against its flow. Their guide directed them to make a

portage to what is now Coldingham Lake, which got them to a north-flowing watershed. The party was thus able to make their outward journey through a series of lakes and waterways; the return journey would be down the rapids of the south-flowing Ottawa River.

When he reached Allumette Island, Champlain discovered that he was living in a small world. He met Tessoüat, an Algonkin leader, whom he had met years before at the trading post at Tadoussac and who had met Vignau before. Tessoüat denied that his people had guided Vignau to the "North Sea," and Champlain realized that Vignau had lied to him. Tessoüat convinced Champlain that he could get no farther that season, and so Champlain began his return journey. Historians are undecided today about whether Vignau might indeed have reached Hudson Bay. They speculate that Tessoüat might have encouraged

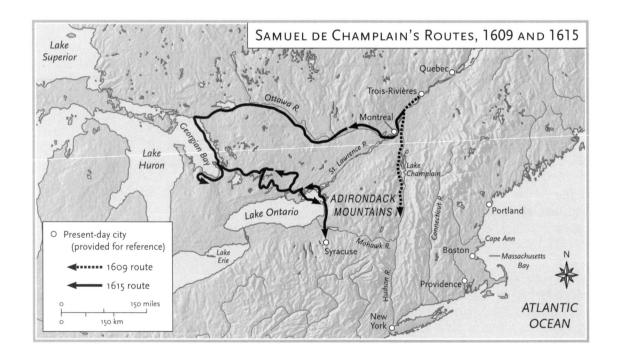

SAMUEL DE CHAMPLAIN'S ROUTES, 1609 AND 1615

Champlain to turn back in order to maintain his own power in the region.

On his return journey, 40 canoes accompanied Champlain as part of a celebratory farewell from the Indians, and they ran the rapids on the return journey without any accidents. He had successfully mapped parts of the region, having taken measurements of the latitude using an astrolabe. He had cemented diplomatic and trading relationships with Indian friends. He had a better idea of how the rivers might be used to head west. All this and the whole journey had taken only three weeks. Champlain returned to France with the news.

In 1615, he again returned to New France for another journey of exploration but this time was accompanied by four Récollet priests to be missionaries to the Indians and the small French community. The Récollets were the French branch of the Franciscan order of Catholic priests. With their arrival, the complex intertwining of missionary work and exploration in New France began. The Récollets were not trained for such rigorous work, and in the next decade the Jesuits would replace them. In the meantime, however, they set about their tasks, and one, Father Joseph Le Caron, set off to convert the Huron.

Backed by new money from investors, Champlain also set off, this time hoping to reach Huronia, the territory of the western Huron, and Lake Huron itself. His party quickly reached Allumette Island, the farthest point of his trip two years earlier. They now went farther up the Ottawa and then up the Mattawa River, reaching Lake Nipissing by late July 1615. From there, they followed the French River to Lake Huron. Champlain and his party explored the eastern shore of Georgian Bay of Lake Huron, enjoying the sight of what he called *"La Mer Douce,"* the sweet sea. He marveled at the fertile land around the lake and the huge trout that swam in it. So fertile was the land that thousands of Huron lived in the region in many villages and towns. However, Champlain was in for a surprise. A couple of miles inland on the Midland Peninsula (near Penetanguishene, Ontario), at a Huron village called Carhagoua, there was Father Le Caron already established. Le Caron was very surprised to see Champlain, and he celebrated mass to mark the occasion.

ÉTIENNE BRÛLÉ'S ROLE

In fact, neither of these men were the first Europeans to explore the region or see Lake Huron. That honor belongs to a young Frenchman named Étienne Brûlé, a protégé of Champlain's. Brûlé was probably about 16 when he came to Quebec with Champlain, in 1608. Champlain later sent him to live with the Huron so "he might ascertain the nature of their country, see the great lake, observe the rivers and tribes there, and also explore the mines and objects of special interest." Although very little is known about the specifics of Brûlé's journey, he did visit the Huron in the region and saw Lake Huron. He was traveling with Champlain on Champlain's 1615 expedition.

This journey of Champlain's had a purpose other than simply mapping the region. He intended to join with the Huron and together attack the Onondaga, one of the Five Nations of the Iroquois Confederacy. That goal inadvertently led to another great journey of exploration about which there is little record. Champlain and his Huron allies decided to draw in another ally, the Andastes, who lived south of the Onondaga on the Susquehanna River where the Chemung River joins it (present-day Elmira, New York). They hoped that a simultaneous attack from the north and south would defeat the Onondaga. Champlain

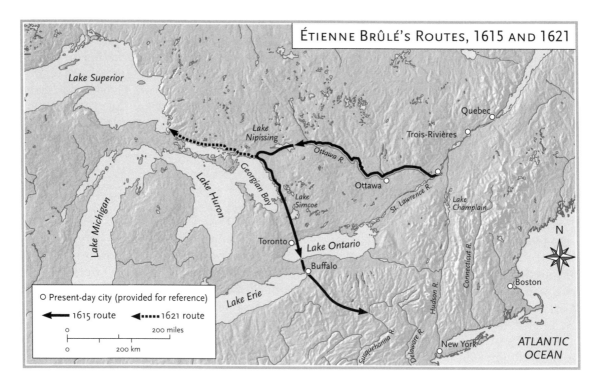

ÉTIENNE BRÛLÉ'S ROUTES, 1615 AND 1621

Lake Superior

Lake Nipissing

Quebec

Trois-Rivières

Ottawa R.

Ottawa

Georgian Bay

Lake Huron

Lake Michigan

Lake Simcoe

St. Lawrence R.

Lake Champlain

Toronto

Lake Ontario

N

Buffalo

Connecticut R.

O Present-day city (provided for reference)

◀—— 1615 route   ◀▪▪▪▪ 1621 route

Lake Erie

Boston

0   200 miles

0   200 km

Hudson R.

Susquehanna R.

Delaware R.

New York

ATLANTIC
OCEAN

chose Brûlé to undertake this journey to speak to the Andastes.

Brûlé set off with 12 Huron. Champlain later noted that Brûlé was delayed in his mission by "impenetrable forests, wood and brush, marshy bogs, frightful and unfrequented places." Between these hindrances and the fact that the Andastes's war council moved slowly, the group missed the attack on the Onondaga in which the French and Huron had been resoundingly defeated. Obliged to stay with the Andastes, Brûlé told Champlain he had been able to explore to the sea, which if true, was probably by way of the Susquehanna River to Chesapeake Bay. Later, as he made his way back to New France, he was captured and tortured by the Onondaga before being released. He finally met Champlain again three years after having left him.

Champlain was ultimately disgusted with his protégé. Brûlé returned to live with the Huron and continued to explore, but he did not see Champlain again until 1629. That year, when two English raiders briefly captured Quebec, Champlain was stunned to see Brûlé and another of his protégés from the earliest days in Quebec, Nicholas Marsolet, arrive with the attacking English, the two young Frenchmen apparently having decided that greater opportunity lay with France's old enemy. Even though Brûlé, in the previous decade, had probably discovered Lake Erie and Lake Superior, little is known about his exploits. Champlain only remembered him as "licentious and otherwise depraved." Brûlé was living with the Huron when they killed him in 1633 for some unknown reason, and few in the French community considered it a great loss. A Jesuit priest, Father Paul Le Jeune, wrote in his annual report that the Huron had been worried about coming to Quebec after they had killed Brûlé, fearing retaliation, but Le Jeune told them that the French did not care, as Brûlé "was not looked upon as a Frenchman."

NICOLET, COUREURS DE BOIS, AND THE JESUITS

Another protégé of Champlain's, Jean Nicolet, was also a successful explorer and had a more illustrious career. He had come to New France with Champlain in 1618, and Champlain had sent him to live among the Huron at Lake Allumette as a way of learning about the region. Nicolet lived a total of 11 years among the Huron and various other peoples of the Ottawa River. In 1634 he set off with a party of Huron on a journey of exploration to Mackinac Island, across Lake Michigan, and landed at the present site of Green Bay, Wisconsin. There he met the Winnebago people, a few of whom then traveled with him as he explored the Fox River. When he heard he was near a tributary of a large body of water, probably the Mississippi River, he thought this was a route to China. It is unclear why he chose not to pursue this information. Instead, he returned to the St. Lawrence River valley without having seen the Mississippi.

Nicolet's route through the Straits of Mackinac to Lake Michigan became the main French trading route to the west. It would be

Native Women and the Fur Trade

Native women played a vital role in the success of the fur trade. It was they who, through their relationships with French traders, taught men how to survive in an alien country and climate. They taught the men such things as how to make snowshoes and moccasins, how to store food for a long winter in isolation, and how to dress for the greatest warmth. They also acted as interpreters of language and culture. These relationships came about because coureurs de bois were often gone for long periods of time when they set off into the backcountry to trade furs. They used Native villages as their bases and, while there, many traders formed relationships with the Native women. (A few of these men may have had wives and families back in Quebec, but most spent their lives in the backcountry.) Some of these relationships were casual and short lived. Some were formed to cement a trading partnership with the host community. Others were long-lasting and were referred to by the French as marriages *à la façon du pays,* meaning "in the manner of the country." These were like "common law" marriages, which were recognized by many groups at that time. Eventually, these women and their children became known as *métis*—that is, people of "mixed" ancestry. It was not until the 19th century that European women joined their menfolk in the fur trade in the West. Until then, European fur traders married Native women *à la façon du pays,* and future generations of *métis* men and women would play a central role in the fur trade. They combined French with Native languages and developed a Métis language that is still spoken today.

followed over the next decades by westward-bound missionaries and coureurs de bois. Literally meaning "runners of the woods," *coureurs de bois* was the name given to the French who went into the interior to trade furs without a license. On these journeys, traders and missionaries accumulated a significant body of knowledge of the region that they exchanged with each other.

By the time of Nicolet's expedition, the missionaries were actively engaged in exploration. The work of the Jesuit missionaries and a last burst of activity by the Récollets added greatly to the store of geographic knowledge in the 1620s and 1630s. Gabriel Sagard, a member of the Récollet order but not a priest, spent 10 months on Georgian Bay on the east shore of Lake Huron in 1623–24 and later wrote extensively about the region and its people. He found that the hard journey out there was a test of his faith as he dealt with unpalatable food, "dark thick woods," and "swarms of mosquitoes and midges."

In the next decade, it was the Jesuit missionaries who roamed territory far from the small French settlement at Quebec. A central purpose of the Jesuit order was missionary work and, with its emphasis on language skills and its focus on discipline and self-sacrifice, Jesuit priests were well suited to the challenges of New France. Father Paul Le Jeune arrived in 1633 and immediately set off with a band of Montagnais Indians who were headed east of Quebec and south of the St. Lawrence

Jesuit missionaries spread their message throughout the area surrounding Quebec. In this Frederic Remington drawing, American Indians paddle a canoe carrying a Jesuit missionary. *(National Archives of Canada)*

Quite favorable to the Jesuits, this image in one of the first volumes covering Canadian history, written by François du Creux, depicts Native Americans as cruelly attacking the pious Jesuit priests trying to "save" them. *(National Archives of Canada)*

River to engage in a winter hunt for game. One of the Montagnais, Pastedechouan, had been to France and was able to act as an intermediary. The journey was one of great hardship. The Montagnais were continually on the move. Le Jeune lamented that "Sometimes we were in deep valleys, then upon lofty mountains, sometimes in the low flat country; but always in deep snow." He longed for a European village and the welcoming sight of an inn where "one can refresh and fortify oneself." Instead, "the only inn we encountered were brooks," and even then they "had to break the ice in order to get some water to drink." He was glad to get back to the familiar banks of the St. Lawrence.

THE DUTCH AND ENGLISH COMPETE

While French fur traders and missionaries were extending their knowledge of the region and making contact with peoples hundreds of miles inland, their European competitors, even those in the fur trade, were making little headway inland. The Dutch trading post of

Fort Nassau, founded in 1614 and renamed Fort Orange in 1624, was doing almost all its business with the Iroquois. They traded pelts for trade goods and weapons, which they used to dominate their enemies. For the most part, the Dutch traders, who had a government monopoly, left the business of collecting furs to the Iroquois and managed

The seal of Massachusetts Bay Colony features a Native American saying "Come over and help us," implying that the Native Americans needed to be "saved" from their way of life. *(Library of Congress, Prints and Photographs Division [LC-D4-71598])*

their extensive fur trading interests from the trading post.

Others were making inroads into the fur trade and learning the geography of New England as they went. Englishman John Oldham of Plymouth colony had traded with the coastal Indians in the 1620s and decided he would settle in Watertown, close to Boston, after the new colony of Massachusetts was founded in 1629. He and three others traveled some 100 miles overland west to the Connecticut River in 1633 and, along the way, noted suitable sites for future settlement. In 1632 William Holmes from Plymouth colony went up the Connecticut River to engage in the fur trade and set up a trading post at Windsor (Vermont). In 1637 traders from New Sweden were also traveling inland to trade, although these were mostly Dutch men trying to get around the monopoly of the post at Fort Orange.

Meanwhile, the population of Puritans and other English settlers in New England was growing rapidly even though many of their towns still hugged the coast. But the communities' appetite for farmland was bringing them into steadily greater conflict with their Native neighbors. In 1636 war broke out between the Puritans and the Pequot in the Connecticut River valley; although over in a year, it was a war in which the English and their Native allies decimated the Pequot.

During this period, settlers and explorers continued to be often the same individuals. Unlike the French, however, missionary work did not prompt the English to explore inland. The Puritans were a tightly knit religious community who saw their faith as exclusive, not inclusive. So, in this period, their faith kept them gathered together. Fur traders such as William Pynchon and Thomas Morton were also alert to the farming, lumbering, and trading opportunities of the places they visited.

Pynchon founded a community later called Springfield on the Connecticut River in 1636. Morton, who was based south of Boston (in present-day Quincy), wrote a book called *New English Canaan* on early Massachusetts that is one of the great records of the natural landscape and Native peoples that exist from the period.

In 1617 the Jamestown colony in Virginia exported its first tobacco crop, and the community was transformed. With a strong commercial basis, population soared, as did a need for land and men such as William Claiborne, who went out to explore Chesapeake Bay more thoroughly for potential sites for settlement. The result of the increased desire for land was a bloody conflict in 1622–23 and again in 1644 with the Powhatans, which ultimately left the English in control of the coastal lands.

Given these tensions and bloodshed, it is not surprising that the English did not explore inland. However, they were still jealously casting their eyes toward rival European settlements. In 1613 Captain Samuel Argall was sent from Virginia to break up a Jesuit settlement in Maine so the French would know that the English considered that part of the coast theirs. Argall also burned the small French post at Port Royal in Acadia (now Nova Scotia) just for good measure.

By the middle of the 1630s, the French had found a route to Lake Michigan and had established effective trading relationships with their Native allies, but their settlement at Quebec stayed small. The Dutch and the much more numerous English had secured their colonies in New England and on Chesapeake Bay. Whether they grew a variety of foods or tobacco, the English farming frontiers were creeping slowly inland. Neither the Dutch nor the English communities had any interest in missionary activity, in New England for religious reasons, and in Virginia and New Amsterdam because the settlements had little interest in organized religion at all. Both in New England and Virginia, the English had to fight bloody wars against Native communities for control of the land, which left them little opportunity for inland exploration. However, they were always aware of where their European rivals were operating and jealously guarded their own areas from others.

8

FURS, FRIARS, AND FRENCH EXPLORATION

1635–1673

 In late summer 1673, Father Jacques Marquette, a Jesuit priest, and Louis Jolliet, a French Canadian fur trader, had to make a big decision. They had spent the summer traveling where no European had gone before. They had led a party of men from the northern shores of Lake Michigan down to Green Bay, along the Fox River, and then by rivers and streams and occasionally on land to the Wisconsin River, and then gone down that as it flowed into the Mississippi. They had followed that great river down to where the Arkansas River flows into it, where the modern states of Arkansas and Louisiana now meet.

Marquette and Jolliet were not sure what their next move should be. Marquette wrote that he and Jolliet tried to decide "whether we should push on or remain content with the discovery which we had made." They had already learned "all the information that could be desired in regard to this discovery." Jolliet had made an extensive map of their travels, and they had closely observed the environment, the peoples, and the vegetation. Although they had some hair-raising moments, their encounters with Native peoples along the route were generally friendly. They guessed (correctly) that they were probably no more than a two- or three-day journey from the place where the great river flowed into the sea, although they were not sure if that was going to be the Atlantic Ocean or the Gulf of Mexico.

Even though they were so close, they decided to turn back. They were afraid of falling into the hands of the Spanish, and that the Native peoples ahead might be unfriendly, but most of all they hated to risk "losing the results of this voyage." Others would later get credit for being the first Europeans to travel down the Mississippi to where it flowed into the Gulf of Mexico.

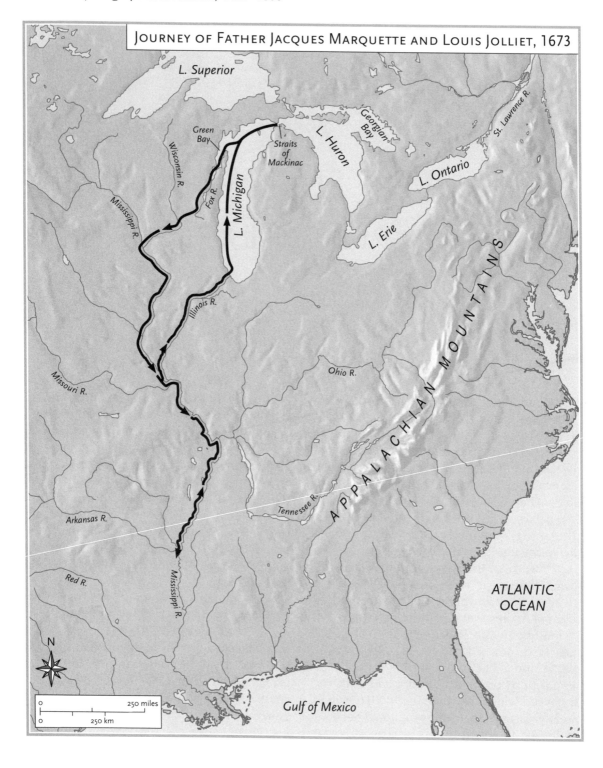

JOURNEY OF FATHER JACQUES MARQUETTE AND LOUIS JOLLIET, 1673

L. Superior

Green Bay

Straits of Mackinac

Georgian Bay

L. Huron

L. Ontario

St. Lawrence R.

L. Erie

Wisconsin R.

Fox R.

L. Michigan

Mississippi R.

Illinois R.

Missouri R.

Ohio R.

APPALACHIAN MOUNTAINS

Tennessee R.

Arkansas R.

Red R.

Mississippi R.

ATLANTIC OCEAN

N

Gulf of Mexico

250 miles

250 km

Jacques Marquette and Louis Jolliet explored much of the Mississippi River in 1673. In this painting, the two men and their crew, traveling in two canoes, observe an American Indian structure along the river. *(Library of Congress, Prints and Photographs Division [LC-USZ62-116498])*

Marquette and Jolliet's journey reflects a lot of the practical realities of French exploration in the 17th century. The journey combined the desire to expand French control on the continent, to develop new sources of furs from more distant peoples, and to convert Indians to Christianity. Success required courage, planning, and hard work. Since the Europeans were also greatly outnumbered, it also required diplomatic skills to avoid violent confrontations and misunderstandings.

EARLY FRENCH EXPLORATIONS

In the years between the death of Samuel de Champlain in 1635 and Marquette and Jolliet's journey in 1673, French coureurs de bois, adventurers, Jesuit priests, and governors of the colony had expanded French interests in North America from the St. Lawrence River valley to Lake Superior. Their exploration was made easier by the terrain. A network of rivers and lakes made their travels deep into the continent easier. Even when rivers did not conveniently lead into one another, local Indians were often able to lead and assist them to good portages where they might find the shortest or most easily traveled point between two waterways. By these means, the French had made contact with a wide range of peoples. They had met and traded with the Anishinabe around Lake Superior; the Cree to the north of that lake; the Illinois, on the river that now bears their name; and the Mascoutens on the Fox River. Pierre Radisson, a French explorer and fur trader, noted they had even met "ambassadors from the nations of Nadoneseronons," probably the Dakota people, who wore buffalo skins. And Jesuit priest Jean de Quen wrote in his annual report of a great lake "as large as the Caspian Sea" called "Ouinipeg."

Much of the information about these discoveries was in colonial and Jesuit reports. However, the system of forts and missions also provided places where travelers could exchange information. For example, in 1665, Jesuit priest Claude Allouez founded a mission at Chequamegon Bay on Lake Superior, near present-day Ashland, Wisconsin, and explored around the lakeshore. In 1668, Jacques Marquette, who had recently arrived in New France, also came out to Chequamegon Bay. Later, Allouez moved to a mission at Green Bay, in the northern part of Lake Michigan. At the same time, young fur trader Louis Jolliet was also in the neighborhood, traveling with his brother Adrien. Adrien then went to join another Jesuit, Jean Peré, who was searching for copper mines on the shores of Lake Superior. It was in this area that Louis Jolliet met Marquette for the first time.

In 1669, when Jolliet was making his way home to Quebec by way of Lake Ontario, he met another fur trader, René-Robert Cavelier, sieur de La Salle. La Salle was very interested in exploring the land to the west and was traveling with two Sulpician missionaries, Fathers François Dollier de Casson and René de Bréhant de Galinée. The Sulpicians were a recently established order that trained men for the priesthood. Jolliet told the men about a new route to Lake Huron. La Salle turned back due to illness, but the two priests pressed on, following Jolliet's directions. By the time Dollier and Galinée returned to Montreal the fol-

lowing year, they had proved that Lakes Huron, Erie, and Ontario were all connected, and they were able to produce the most accurate map to date of the region. These few examples indicate the informal ways in which these explorers and others had the opportunity to gain and share knowledge.

The influence of the French extended broadly into the interior of the continent, but at the same time the European population of New France stayed very small, only 3,000 in 1663. So, while the Spanish Empire used its military power to subjugate Native peoples, and the more numerous English settlers regularly fought Indians over land use, the outnumbered French used commercial, diplomatic, and social relationships to secure their interests in North America.

Some adventures of the Jesuits show how much the French relied on Native goodwill. Claude Dablon and Gabriel Druillettes set off in May 1661 to try to establish a mission to the Cree Indians who occupied territory to the south of Hudson Bay. They planned to go up the Saguenay River from Tadoussac, the settlement at the confluence of the Saguenay and St. Lawrence Rivers, into the hills and then find a river that flowed down the other side into Hudson Bay. Huron Indians were to be their guides on the first part of their journey to Lake Nekouba (Nikaubau), which was a trading center for many Native peoples. The priests relied on Indian diplomacy to smooth their path. The previous year, Huron guides had gone ahead to arrange meetings there with other Indian nations.

The report of their difficult journey to Lake Nekouba, probably written by Dablon, appeared in the *Jesuit Relations*. He reported that they had relied heavily on Indian labor and that, day after day, the party had to carry everything, as many as 40 canoes and all their baggage, around waterfalls and rapids. One day they had to "shoulder our baggage four times and twice on the day after." It took them a month to reach the lake and required 64 portages. Exhausted, they turned back.

Still, they had gained useful knowledge and connections for the next explorers. Dablon noted that they had met "people from eight or ten nations, some of whom had never beheld a Frenchman" and built a body of knowledge about the region. A decade later, in 1672, another expedition, led by Jesuit Charles Albanel, successfully crossed the hills and found a route along what is now known as Rupert River, which flowed into James Bay at the southern tip of Hudson Bay.

The journey of Father Jean de Quen was also dependent on Native labor and goodwill. After spending several years with the Montagnais in Tadoussac, he went with them in 1647 to travel to the Porcupine nation, who lived on Lake Piékouagami (now Lake Saint-Jean). Led and aided by Montagnais guides, the party traveled up the Saguenay River and then followed a variety of lakes and waterways. The journey, de Quen wrote, involved "constant rowing against the current" and many portages. But Lake Piékouagami, when they got there, was worth the hard work. It was large, "deep and full of fish . . . [and] surrounded by flat land," but with "high mountains" in the distance. Cooperation and diplomacy were essential to successful exploration.

THE ENGLISH EXPERIENCE

While the French presence in New France stayed small, English men and women were arriving in large numbers on the Atlantic coast and, by 1660, more than 70,000 were there. More than half this population was concentrated in New England and around the Chesapeake Bay, where there were also about 3,000 African slaves. Settlement was still largely clustered along the coast and easily navigable waterways, but the desire for good farmland was steadily drawing colonists into the backcountry. As they settled new communities, ordinary farmers and their families became explorers as they surveyed their towns so property lines could be drawn accurately.

In New England, other groups of English people were exploring. One group was men who were interested in harvesting the beautiful, tall white pine trees that made good masts for sailing ships. These lumbermen explored and mapped the area that is now New Hampshire and Maine to search for the best trees. Along the rivers near the forests, they built

New England colonists harvested Eastern white pines for ship masts. *(Facts On File)*

White Pines Make Great Masts

English colonists were thrilled when they saw the forests of New England because so much of their woodland at home had already been depleted. They enjoyed harvesting the New England forests to provide fires for warmth, to build homes and ships, to make barrels and many other items they needed. The white pine (*Pinus strobus*) they found in Maine and New Hampshire proved especially valuable. These trees, which grew to be 120 to 200 feet tall and up to six feet in diameter, were large enough that a single trunk could serve as a mast for a ship. Usually European trees, which were smaller and thinner, had to be spliced together to make masts. (The American white pine would be introduced into England, but it has never grown much more than 100 feet tall there.) The single, straight white pine tree made a strong mast and was immediately in high demand for shipbuilding. The English government especially wanted them for use in Royal Navy ships. By the end of the 1600s, the white pine had become so valuable that, apart from those trees on private land, it was a crime to cut any of a diameter of 24 inches or more without a royal license. In 1704 royal surveyors began to go through the forests marking the trees that they wanted for masts to ensure no one else would take them. With the American Revolution, the British lost their right to take the white pine of the eastern United States, but by the 1850s most of the great white pines of New England had been cut.

lumber mills to process the felled trees, and they charted rivers and settled towns such as Kittery, Wells, and Portland in Maine.

Another group of English people became explorers unintentionally. These were the people who were banished from the Massachusetts and Plymouth colonies for religious reasons. Puritan leaders who had settled there were not tolerant of anyone who disagreed with their way of doing things. In 1635, they banished one young minister, Roger Williams, who challenged their authority. He spent the winter sheltering with the Narragansett Indians and then, with a few followers, settled a town they called Providence in what became a few years later the separate colony of Rhode Island. Thomas Hooker, another defiant minister, took his whole congregation through the

backcountry to establish a town on the Connecticut River they called Hartford.

In these ways, the English settlements expanded slowly but steadily inland. In the 1670s, these new farming communities again brought the English into conflict with Indians. In New England, in the summer of 1675, a loose coalition of Native peoples led by Metacom of the Wampanoag, whom the English called King Philip, led an uprising against the English. Metacom attacked and destroyed many outlying villages. Even though what became known as King Philip's War ultimately failed, it did temporarily drive back English settlement. It would be the next century before settlers inched their way back into the territory that they had occupied before the war.

Still, conflicts over land did not bring the Indian trade to a halt and, through it, Englishmen continued to extend their knowledge of the west. The first known European to journey west of the Blue Ridge Mountains of Virginia was actually a German immigrant, John Lederer. He made two journeys, building his knowledge of the region and then, traveling with Indian guides and an Englishman, he journeyed in 1670 from the falls of the Rappahannock River (now Fredericksburg, Virginia) to the top of the mountains. The following year, Virginian Abraham Wood, who himself knew western Virginia well through his trade with Indians, recruited Thomas Batts, Robert Fallam, and an Indian guide, Perecute of the local Appomattox people, to lead a party west. The journal of the expedition, probably written by either Batts or Fallam, noted that the party's mission was "for the finding out the ebbing and flowing Water on the other side of the Mountains." The journal is vague, but they appear to have followed the North Fork of the Roanoke River and reached as far as present-day Union, West Virginia. The trip, the journal recorded, "cost us hard labour," and finally, fearing bad weather and running short of food, the party turned back.

In 1674 Wood sponsored another journey west, though in this case the young explorers he recruited saw more of the land beyond the mountains than they had intended. Wood wrote that he sent out "two Englishmen and eight Indians" with three months of supplies to travel through the Piedmont and mountains of North Carolina to trade with the

In this painting, English soldiers and American Indians are smoking pipes and trading goods. The American Indian standing and facing the soldier sitting on a stump holds wampum, a woven belt of shells, in his outstretched hand. Wampum became quite important to American Indians for trade after the arrival of the English and the French settlers and traders. *(National Archives, Courtesy of the Franklin D. Roosevelt Library, NLR-PHOCO-A-521114[2])*

Cherokee. Unfortunately, one of the Englishmen, James Needham, was killed, and the other, Gabriel Arthur, was taken prisoner by Ohio Indians. On his way home, Arthur became the first European to see what would become known as the Cumberland Gap in Tennessee and related his travels to Wood. Wood also found that those in power gave "no encouragement at all" for these kinds of enterprises, but he hoped for better days.

Alas, these days did not come quickly. Open conflict with Indians over land now slowed westward exploration and settlement in Virginia. As poorer farmers pursued cheaper property inland, their settlements created tensions with local Indians and that interfered with the Indian trade controlled by the governor and his friends along the eastern coast. This conflict had two dimensions. One was between colonists and Indians concerning competition for land. The other found wealthy planters and those who traded with Indians on one side and poorer farmers and some wealthy men who had been shut out of the Indian trade on the other. Nathaniel Bacon was one such embittered, wealthy man shut out from Indian trade, and he encouraged poor men and settlers in the backcountry to join him in a rebellion against the governor. What began in 1675 as a war between the Susquehannock Indians, who lived north of the Potomac River, and the settlers became a larger conflict known as Bacon's Rebellion. The governor was able to crush it, but the episode slowed westward exploration and settlement.

Despite these tensions between Indians and settlers in Virginia and New England, England was creating and exploring other colonies on the East Coast. In 1663 the British king, Charles II, gave a colonial charter for the Carolinas to a group of wealthy men, and these new colonial proprietors wanted to know where the best place might be to establish a town. They commissioned English sea captain Robert Sandford to explore and report on the coast; he did so, including a detailed account of the Savannah River. The owners also sent with him Henry Woodward, who was left in the Carolinas to establish relations with local Cusabo Indians, to learn their language, and to gain knowledge of the region. After the founding of Charles Town, Woodward expanded the Indian trade, this time with the Westo people.

An English aristocrat who settled in Virginia in his late 20s, Nathaniel Bacon led a rebellion against Virginia's governor to express his and other small farmers' displeasure at being denied trading rights with American Indians. *(Library of Congress, Prints and Photographs Division [LC-USZ62-91133])*

THE DUTCH PRESENCE

Meanwhile, on the Hudson River, Dutch fur traders were successful by staying relatively

After exploring much of the area of New Netherland, Father Isaac Jogues wrote a descriptive account of the colony. *(Library of Congress, Prints and Photographs Division [LC-USZ62-100823])*

than ten and twenty days journey" to trade with the Dutch.

Ironically, it is a French Jesuit explorer who has left one of the best surviving descriptions of this Dutch colony: Father Isaac Jogues traveled extensively around the upper Great Lakes with Father Charles Raymbaud in 1641. The following year, Jogues returned to the east and to Iroquois territory. He was captured and tortured by them before managing to escape to the Dutch at Albany. Jogues was impressed by the kindness the Dutch showed him even though they could not easily communicate and they had religious differences (they were Protestant and he Catholic).

The politics of the region were transformed when, in 1664, the Dutch colony fell into English hands and was renamed New York. This change meant that the fur trading rivalry between what was now called Albany and Quebec became part of a larger imperial contest between the French and English that kept the two countries at war with each other for much of the next 100 years. The Five Nations of the Iroquois Confederacy tried to maneuver this situation to their advantage and formed an alliance with the English that became known as the Covenant Chain. This was a metaphor for the friendship between the two. The English supported and encouraged the Iroquois to dominate other Indians in the Northeast. This made the Iroquois more powerful, but it also kept the English colonists safe from attack and allowed economic growth. The English thus confined themselves, for the moment, behind the natural barrier of the Appalachian Mountains and the military power of the Iroquois.

HUDSON BAY AND THE FUR TRADE

While the English were slowly securing and settling colonies on the coast to the south and

close to their trading posts and doing little inland exploring. The Indians of the powerful Iroquois Confederacy with whom they traded did not want the Dutch trading directly with peoples farther inland and preferred to be the middlemen. The town of Beverwyck (formerly Fort Orange), which became Albany, had a significant number of fur traders among its small population, but many of these men were also farmers. One Dutch colonist, Adriaen Van Der Donck, wrote an *Account of the New Netherlands* that showed that the Dutch organized their trade very differently from the French. He wrote that few Dutchmen had been "more than seventy or eighty miles from the river." Rather, it was the Indians who came "more

Father Jean de Brébeuf Learns New Languages ⤳

Both Indians and Europeans had to learn new languages as they encountered each other. Unfortunately, for the first centuries of contact there are accounts only from Europeans of how they coped with this. Each community had individuals with a facility for languages who came to act as translators. The French priest Jean de Brébeuf had a particular facility for languages; he spoke Huron fluently and was able to communicate in several other Native languages. The Jesuits, formally the Society of Jesus, to which Brébeuf belonged, were a religious order founded by Ignatius of Loyola in 1534. The Jesuits were trained in Latin and Greek, and that made them observant about the structure of language when they encountered new ones. When he arrived in Quebec in 1625, Brébeuf first lived among the Montagnais for about a year and learned something of their language. Then, for some 15 years, he lived among the Huron, and he gave their language particular thought. He noted that the Huron used compound words a lot and that they had different verbs for animate and inanimate things. He also began to realize the different cultural values in language. For example, he was trying to teach the Christian prayer that begins "Our Father who art in heaven" but discovered that it was very insulting to the Huron to speak of a dead parent. So Brébeuf had to substitute another word for father in order not to give offense. Before he died at the hands of the Huron's enemy, the Iroquois, he had compiled a Catholic catechism in Huron and a French-Huron dictionary.

east of the French, they did manage to secure a claim to a vast expanse of territory to the north. This claim was around Hudson Bay, the sea route to which lay above 60°N and was only open to shipping for two months of the year. London merchants provided the finance to establish trading posts, but the men who first explored the region and understood its potential as a trading center were two Frenchmen. Their actions transformed the struggle to control the continent.

The two men who led this journey of exploration in 1658 to 1660 were two French-born fur traders, Pierre-Esprit Radisson and his brother-in-law, Médard Chouart, sieur des Groseilliers. Individually, the two men already had extensive experience in the interior of the country prior to their journey. Groseilliers,

born in 1618, had traveled extensively around the Great Lakes both as a lay worker with the Jesuits and as a fur trader. It was while on a journey to Green Bay that he heard stories from local Indians about the rich fur territory that lay north of Lake Superior.

For his next journey, he chose as his traveling partner Radisson, who was probably around 21 in 1659. They set out with Frenchmen and Huron Indians and made their way to Green Bay. At first they were in familiar territory. As Radisson noted, "We mett several sorts of people. We conversed wth them, being in longtime alliance wth them." There they heard of a great river that forked with one branch going to the west and the other to the south. Radisson and Groseilliers believed that the great river to the south they heard of

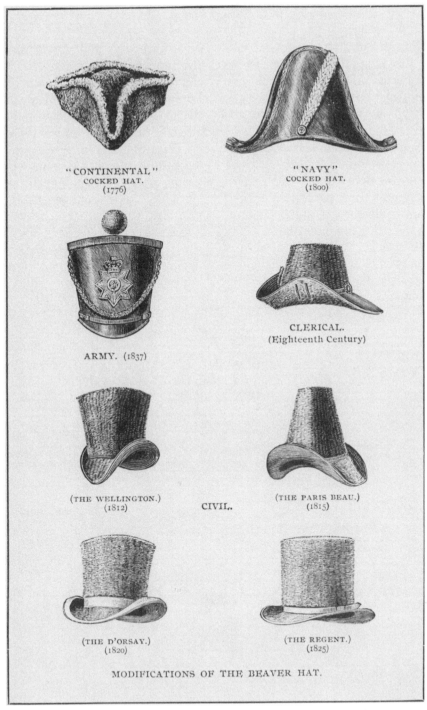

"CONTINENTAL"
COCKED HAT.
(1776)

"NAVY"
COCKED HAT.
(1800)

ARMY. (1837)

CLERICAL.
(Eighteenth Century)

(THE WELLINGTON.)
(1812)

CIVIL.

(THE PARIS BEAU.)
(1815)

(THE D'ORSAY.)
(1820)

(THE REGENT.)
(1825)

MODIFICATIONS OF THE BEAVER HAT.

Popular from the late 16th century through the late 18th century, beaver hats were fashioned into the many different styles shown here. The popularity of the hats motivated fur traders to collect great quantities of pelts. *(National Archives of Canada)* "runns towards Mexico from the tokens they gave us." By "tokens," Radisson meant that the gifts the Indians gave them were in fact trade goods of European, probably Spanish, origin. The river they were hearing about was the Mississippi.

However, the traders' interests lay not to the south but to the north, in which climate animals produce richer furs. The rest of the Frenchmen in their party had turned back, but the two adventurers still had Huron and other local guides and interpreters. Along Lake Superior's shores they were accompanied by as many as 20 boats of the Anishinabe (Chippewa) people. Radisson recorded, "they keepe us company, in hopes to gett knives from us," an important trade item. Radisson

and Groseilliers built a makeshift fort when they got to Chequamegon Bay and enjoyed the fact that they were the first Europeans to see the area. This was probably the same spot where Father Claude Allouez built his mission when he arrived there a few years later.

The two men enjoyed the freedom their adventures offered. As Radisson wrote, "We weare Cesars, being nobody to contradict us." However, this sometimes meant they were also free to suffer. One winter they were reduced to eating the dogs that traveled with them. Another time, when their sleds were laden down with "a great store of booty," Radisson's sled broke through some thin ice. In his efforts to save the load, he injured himself and became soaked with icy water. Gro-

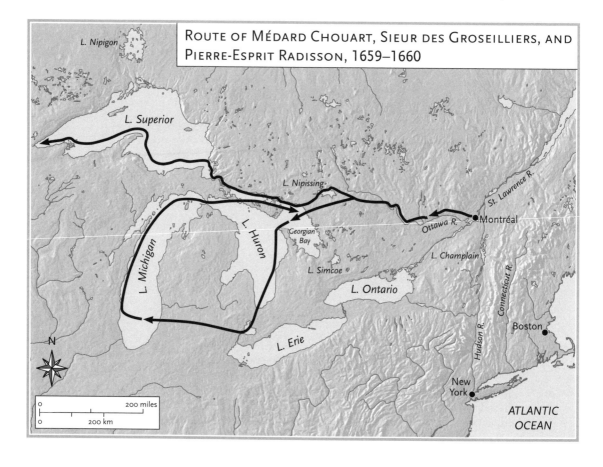

ROUTE OF MÉDARD CHOUART, SIEUR DES GROSEILLIERS, AND PIERRE-ESPRIT RADISSON, 1659–1660

seilliers left him wrapped warmly and rushed off to get help and send back local Indians to get Radisson "and the slids [sleds]." After running a fever for a week, Radisson slowly regained his strength.

Aided by Indian guides and interpreters, the men ranged into what is now the Mille Lacs region of Minnesota and met the Dakota. Moving north they met the Cree who occupied territory between Lake Superior and Hudson Bay. All along the way, they not only were able to trade for luxurious glossy furs but heard stories of yet greater riches to the north. They realized the possibility that, given the distance from Montreal, this source of furs might be better tapped from the sea. They returned to Quebec elated and laden with high-quality furs.

Unfortunately, the governor of New France, although delighted at their haul, did not greet them or their plan with open arms. In fact, the two men's plan interfered with his tight control of fur trade routes. He not only had no interest in sponsoring a sea journey, he fined them for trading without a license.

Radisson and Groseilliers turned to the English. In London, they found merchants willing to sponsor a sea voyage to Hudson Bay. The cargo the ship brought back was so lucrative that their backers immediately formed the Hudson's Bay Company, created by royal charter in 1670. The British king, Charles II, gave the company a monopoly over trade and also gave it the right to govern not only the bay but also all the land draining into it, an area covering 3,036,000 square miles (7,770,000 square kilometers). Unfortunately, the two Frenchmen did not get to share the wealth their actions generated. The company employed them for five years after its founding, but they ultimately left and returned to New France.

The English, now with posts on Hudson Bay and at Albany, saw the chance to extend their influence into the Ohio River valley and possibly interfere with French trading networks there. Into this potentially volatile situation, two new figures came to political power in New France. The first of these was a new intendant, Jean Talon, who arrived in Quebec in 1665. The intendant was an official who was responsible for the administration of justice and economic growth. The other, who arrived seven years later, was a new governor, Count Frontenac. In the French imperial system, the governor's primary responsibility was colonial defense.

Frontenac and Talon wanted to secure and add to French claims to the continent. The first important journey of exploration they sponsored was that of Father Jacques Marquette and Louis Jolliet. In the commission that Frontenac and Talon gave them, they expressed hope that the great river they had heard about from the Indians might prove to be the elusive route to China or might lead to nations where there were "said to be numerous gold mines." Old dreams die slowly.

Commission in hand, Jolliet now set out to meet Marquette, who had now established a mission on the north shore of the Straits of Mackinac, between Lake Huron and Lake Michigan. It was there that Jolliet joined him, and they spent winter 1672 planning their journey. They set off in May 1673, accompanied by five *voyageurs*, canoe men who worked for a wage.

The party succeeded in reaching the Mississippi, but as noted earlier, they decided to end their journey before they reached its mouth. They returned to Lake Michigan by way of the Illinois River, to which Native guides had directed them. Later, Marquette was anxious to return to the Illinois River region to establish a mission, and he set off the following year. By 1675 he was almost there but unfortunately in declining health; he died before reaching his goal. Jolliet returned

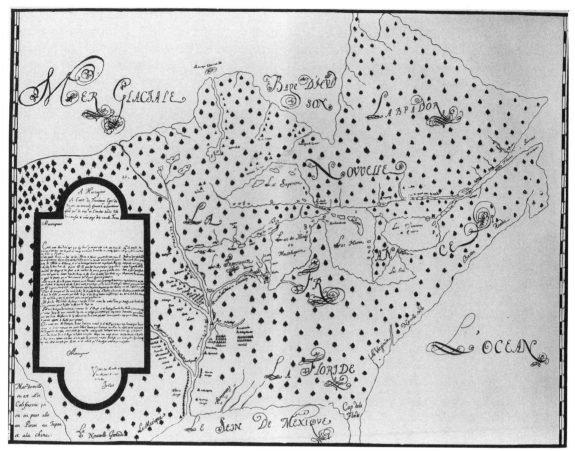

Louis Jolliet drew this map of eastern North America to replace the one he created, and then lost, during his and Jacques Marquette's journey down the Mississippi River and back. The Great Lakes occupy the map's center. *(Library of Congress, Prints and Photographs Division [LC-USZ62-77103])*

to the St. Lawrence River Valley and never traveled west again.

With Marquette and Jolliet's journey, French claims to the interior of the continent seemed secure. Still, the French knew that the English colonies on the coast were becoming more populous and more economically and militarily secure. A small English presence had arrived around the southern part of Hudson Bay but had yet to make serious inroads into either French fur trading interests or Native societies. Native peoples continued to adapt to the new economic, political, and cultural world in which they found themselves and, where possible, tried to shape tumultuous events to their own advantage. From the perspective of the English and the French, however, the opening up of new markets around Hudson Bay and along the Illinois and Mississippi Rivers just raised the stakes of the competition between them, and both were anxious to explore the territory quickly.

9

LA SALLE'S ADVENTURES AND WARTIME MISERY

1673–1715

 In 1675 René-Robert Cavelier, sieur de La Salle, set sail from France to travel to Quebec, capital of New France. La Salle had received royal support for his plan to establish forts all around the Great Lakes and to become governor of all the territory he might discover between New France and the Spanish-claimed territory of Mexico and Florida. Traveling with him was Father Louis Hennepin, a Récollet priest from Belgium. Hennepin's official duty was to establish a mission in the new territory, but the journey also satisfied his long-time desire to travel. In the book that Hennepin later wrote about his journey, *A New Discovery of a Vast Country in America,* he remembered that, as a young man, he had been so drawn to travel that he used to frequent "victualling-houses [eating places] to hear the seamen give an account of their adventures."

La Salle's expedition gave Hennepin the great adventure he had longed for. In 1678,

Hennepin passed Niagara Falls, which he thought the "most terrifying waterfall in the universe." Below the falls, Hennepin watched the construction of a ship, the *Griffon,* that La Salle was having built. In 1679, it was the first sailing ship to navigate the Great Lakes, and it took the expedition to the new French post at Michilimackinac, on the Straits of Mackinac, where Lakes Huron and Michigan meet. From there, La Salle sent the *Griffon* back with a load of furs, but unfortunately it was never heard from again.

The expedition pressed on. La Salle's second in command, Henri Tonti (sometimes spelled Tonty), located the Chicago River and the portage to the Illinois River, which he knew was the route by which Marquette and Jolliet had returned to Lake Michigan from the Mississippi. La Salle's party now followed the route down the Illinois River to near present-day Peoria, Illinois, where they stopped and

A Franciscan friar, Louis Hennepin accompanied La Salle on his expedition in the first large ship to sail across the Great Lakes. In this painting, Hennepin discovers St. Anthony Falls, present-day Minneapolis. *(Library of Congress, Prints and Photographs Division [LC-USZ62-114954])*

built Fort Crèvecoeur. La Salle then returned to Quebec to sell the furs they had acquired. While he was gone, he instructed Hennepin and two other Frenchmen to go to the Mississippi River and head north to explore the river's headwaters.

At this point, Hennepin's adventure became more than he had bargained for. Six weeks into their journey, the group was captured by a Dakota war party on its way to attack the Miami and the Illinois Indians. The war party turned around and, with its prisoners, headed home to what is now the Mille Lacs region of Minnesota. It was an arduous journey upstream to near present-day St. Paul. From there, the party walked overland for five days. The captives stayed with the Dakota for four months until finally rescued by Daniel Greysolon, sieur Du Luth, a French explorer and a cousin of Henri Tonti's who was exploring west of Lake Superior. After lengthy negotiations between Du Luth and the Dakota, Hennepin and his group were released. Du Luth and his party escorted them

Captivity Narratives

Some explorers, such as Father Louis Hennepin, were taken prisoner by Indians as they traveled. As prisoners, they came to discover even more places that were unknown to Europeans. Settlers, too, sometimes found themselves captives when they got caught up in wars either between Native peoples or between the French and English and their Native allies. However, most of these did not see territory new to Europeans. They were mostly taken along routes already well worn by trade and diplomacy. Perhaps as many as 1,600 white settlers were captured in New England alone before the American Revolution. Many of them are known about because they later wrote about their experiences. In contrast, very little is known about the thousands of Indians who were taken captive by the English because they were unable to tell their stories; it is known that some were sold into slavery in the southern colonies or the sugar islands of the Caribbean.

Those English captives who were weak or injured might be killed, but more commonly Native communities in the Northeast took prisoners either to adopt into their own societies or to ransom. Some settlers taken captive, especially those taken young—such as Eunice Williams, who was seven when she was taken from Deerfield in 1704—chose to make their lives with their adoptive families and never returned to live in English society. Others returned when they were ransomed and wrote about their experiences. Most of their books, popularly known as captivity narratives, were, on the surface, about their religious experiences while captives. They wrote about how their faith in God sustained them. However, many people at the time enjoyed the books because they were great adventure stories about life in a world that seemed to the English strange and fascinating. A few of them are still read today because they provide accurate descriptions of Native life, and they tell a lot about the way English people of the time thought and felt. While most take the perspective of wanting to return to their homes, some—such as *A Narrative of the Life of Mrs. Mary Jemison* (1824)—favor the Indians. (Jemison refused to be "rescued," married a Seneca Indian, and went on to become an important woman in the community.) Some accounts, such as that by Mary Rowlandson who was taken captive from Lancaster, Massachusetts, in 1675, which was published in 1682 titled *A Narrative of the Captivity, Sufferings and Removes of Mrs. Mary Rowlandson,* and Eunice Williams's experiences, written about by her father in 1707, are still used in college classrooms today.

back to Michilimackinac, where Hennepin was pleasantly surprised to find a Jesuit priest from his home town of Ath, Belgium.

EUROPEAN RIVALRIES IN NORTH AMERICA

It was a small European world around the Great Lakes of North America. Throughout the late 17th and early 18th centuries, a number of traders, explorers, coureurs de bois, and priests passed through the trading centers at Forts Frontenac (modern Kingston, Ontario) and Michilimackinac on their way to and from the west. At this time, there were probably only a few hundred Frenchmen in the back-country, but since many of them passed through these trading centers at one time or another, they came to know each other.

These small centers of activity were becoming key parts of great imperial struggles. The journeys of exploration in this period brought Europeans not only new information and alliances with Native trading partners but also into direct contact with each other in the interior of the continent. Coincidentally, they began bumping into each other at exactly the time their countrymen were coming to blows in Europe. The result was a new anxiety about international competition and more blood-shed when the European wars became North American ones.

La Salle's discoveries during the 1680s were an important part of the increased tension between the French and English over who controlled what land in North America. La Salle returned to the west in 1681 and the following year traveled with Tonti and a large party down the Mississippi all the way to the Gulf of Mexico. Tonti had had a grueling time in the Illinois country while waiting for La Salle to return. In his report of the expedition to his patron, Abbé Renaudot, Tonti told him

that the party had been so hungry in winter 1680, they were reduced to eating "acorns which we found under the snow" and had been glad to "feast" on the remains of a deer "which had just been devoured by wolves." On the journey down the Mississippi with La Salle, however, food was plentiful. La Salle wrote in his later book that they found "roes [deer], bears not savage and very good to eat, turkeys and all sorts of game."

LA SALLE'S FATEFUL EXPEDITION

On a successful journey down to the mouth of the Mississippi, La Salle claimed all the terri-tory of the river valley for France and extended French interests to the edge of the Spanish Empire. Despite this great accom-plishment, those who knew him remembered him as unstable. Father René Bréhant de Ga-linée, who had met La Salle in 1669, described him in his journal as acting "almost in a daze," and others thought him incompetent and bad tempered. However, he was ambitious and driven by the desire to find a route to China, which he never found, but having made the discoveries he had, he was determined to ben-efit from them. He wanted to found a settle-ment at the mouth of the Mississippi and govern it. He would not succeed in doing that either, but his actions set in motion another string of related journeys of exploration.

La Salle needed King Louis XIV's approval for this new settlement at the mouth of the Mississippi that would be called Louisiana. He returned to Quebec by retracing his route via the French post at Michilimackinac and then went on to France to get the approval. After receiving permission, he set sail from France in 1684 in four ships and with 320 people to found the colony. Sailing along the coast of the Gulf of Mexico, he could not locate the Missis-

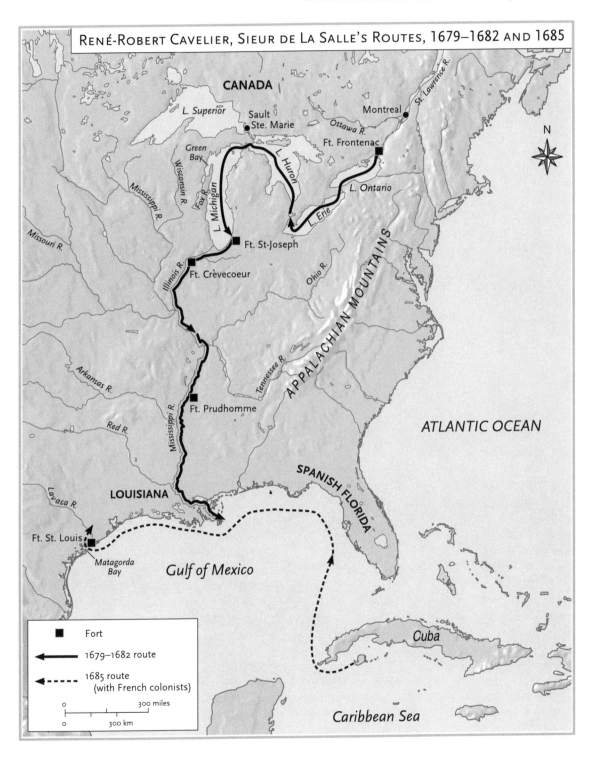

RENÉ-ROBERT CAVELIER, SIEUR DE LA SALLE'S ROUTES, 1679–1682 AND 1685

CANADA

L. Superior

Sault Ste. Marie

Montreal

Ottawa R.

St. Lawrence R.

Ft. Frontenac

Green Bay

Wisconsin R.

Fox R.

Mississippi R.

L. Michigan

L. Huron

L. Ontario

L. Erie

Missouri R.

Illinois R.

Ft. St-Joseph

Ft. Crèvecoeur

Ohio R.

APPALACHIAN MOUNTAINS

Arkansas R.

Tennessee R.

Ft. Prudhomme

ATLANTIC OCEAN

Red R.

Mississippi R.

LOUISIANA

SPANISH FLORIDA

Lavaca R.

Ft. St. Louis

Matagorda Bay

Gulf of Mexico

Cuba

Caribbean Sea

N

■ Fort

→ 1679–1682 route

◀---- 1685 route (with French colonists)

0   300 miles

0   300 km

In this engraving, La Salle and his expedition continue their unsuccessful expedition to found a colony named Louisiana at the mouth of the Mississippi River. Eventually, La Salle would be killed by those accompanying him. *(National Archives of Canada)*

sippi from the sea. Instead, he landed at Matagorda Bay, off the Texas coast, and built a fort at Garcitas Creek. However, by 1687, sickness, desertion, death, and hunger reduced the party to about 36 people.

Setting off overland in search of the Mississippi, he located the Rio Grande and then proceeded across south-central Texas, reaching perhaps as far as the Trinity River. Finally, the party's frustration with La Salle's incompetence, bad temper, and poor planning turned violent. Intrigue and mystery surround the subsequent events, but apparently, in March 1687, the party set upon each other, and La Salle was one of those killed.

Meanwhile, Tonti had heard of La Salle's expedition by sea and, in 1686, led a party from the Great Lakes region down the Mississippi to look for him. Upon reaching the Gulf Coast, he sent search crews out 60 to 70 miles in each direction, but they had no luck. Tonti returned to New France and in 1688 was on the Illinois River when he met five men who had been part of La Salle's party, one of whom was La Salle's brother, Abbé Jean Cavelier. The men concealed the fact that La Salle was dead, and Abbé Cavelier asked Tonti for a loan to pay for his passage home. The following year, Tonti led another party south to search for rumored survivors but found none. Before returning to New France, he made extensive journeys of exploration up the Red River, often traveling with Jean Couture, a coureur de bois, reaching what is today northeastern Texas.

Abbé Cavelier and the rest of the survivors from the La Salle expedition were making their way back to Canada through Michilimackinac when they met another traveler, Louis-Armand de Lom d'Arce, baron de Lahontan. The previous year, Lahontan had traveled with Du Luth to Fort Saint Joseph, which Du Luth had earlier established at the entrance to Lake Huron from Lake Erie. That fort was running short of supplies, and it was a quest for provisions that brought Lahontan to Michilimackinac in 1688. Lahontan later became famous as an explorer largely by writing popular books about his adventures. Ironically, he became most famous for a journey he probably made up. He wrote that he started "another journey because I cannot stand to mope around here [Fort St. Joseph] all winter" and left with five "good Ottawa hunters" and some others. Years later, he described at length a "long river" he had found and the peoples who lived along it. No one else ever found the "long river." The popular books he wrote about his travels were a mixture of interesting fact, cultural and geographical detail, and imagination.

EUROPEAN CONFLICTS SPREAD TO NORTH AMERICA

Adventurers now routinely traveled along the corridor between Michilimackinac and the Mississippi River. Their activities intensified as war broke out in Europe in 1689. That war concerned the European balance of power and, while it involved other nations, primarily pitted Britain and France against each other. In North America, it was called King William's War and lasted from 1689 to 1697. A second European war, also concerning the balance of power among the leading European states, broke out in 1702. This second war was known in North America as Queen Anne's War and was ended by the Treaty of Utrecht in 1713.

When the first of these wars broke out in 1689, the French decided to attack the English trading posts on Hudson Bay. The French chose Pierre Le Moyne, sieur d'Iberville, a Montreal-born naval officer, to lead the raid. He returned to New France with a large haul of furs and English prisoners and repeated his success the following year. At the end of the war, Iberville moved on to a warmer climate. In 1698, he led an expedition from France to Louisiana by sea, found the mouth of the Mississippi, and explored the delta region. He returned with reinforcements the following year and sent out parties, including one led by his brother Jean-Baptiste Le Moyne, sieur de Bienville, to explore the Pearl River in Mississippi and the Red River in Louisiana. For the moment, Spain and France were allies, and Iberville received assistance from the Spanish in settling colonists on Mobile Bay. With these expeditions, Iberville broke the Spanish monopoly of the Gulf of Mexico.

Joining the Louisiana explorers were some old hands from the Great Lakes. Tonti arrived in 1700, and Iberville used him as a negotiator with the Choctaw and Chickasaw peoples. Pierre Charles Le Sueur, a coureur de bois who had become wealthy trading on Lake Superior and who was related to Iberville by marriage, also joined him. Le Sueur had already found a route from Lake Superior to the Mississippi. Now, in 1700, Le Sueur led a large party up the Mississippi from the coast all the way to just below the St. Anthony Falls (now Minneapolis). They then traveled up the Minnesota River to the Blue Earth River before arriving at a post already established by Nicolas Perrot, a fur trader who was influential in expanding trade, near Lake Pepin, a broad section of the Mississippi where the Chippewa River flows into it. One member of the expedition, André Penicaut, kept a journal. He noted that the French were trading in "pelts and other merchandise" and that "game is very plentiful in the prairies." The party traded with the "Cioux" (Sioux), Penicault wrote, and had found St. Anthony's Falls, which "one can hear two leagues [about six miles] away."

Another experienced Great Lakes explorer and fur trader arrived in 1713 to be the new governor of Louisiana. He was Antoine de la Mothe Cadillac. He had earlier commanded Fort Michilimackinac and had established Fort Pontchartrain (now Detroit). As governor of Louisiana, he sent out a large number of exploring parties in search of extractable resources such as lead and copper. One of these parties was led by Francois Guyon Des Prés Derbanne, who claimed to have already traveled up the Missouri River. He and Louis Juchereau de Saint-Denis, who had come with Iberville, explored many parts of East Texas and reached the Spanish community at San Juan Bautista across the Rio Grande.

THE ENGLISH ROLE

While French government energies were directed toward the Great Lakes, the Mississippi River valley, and Louisiana, the Englishmen of the Hudson's Bay Company were extending their influence west at higher latitudes. As a rule, the English were reluctant to leave their posts, preferring that the Indians brought furs to them. In 1690 Henry Kelsey, a skilled linguist and company employee, was sent off, not to explore specifically, but to make new contacts and encourage western Native peoples to bring their furs into the company post. His journey took him overland farther west than any European had yet gone in the region.

Kelsey set off from Hudson Bay and probably traveled down the Hayes and Fox Rivers and eventually reached the Saskatchewan River near what is now The Pas, Manitoba. He spent the winter there with the Assiniboine and then continued west the following year to present-day Saskatoon. He probably met Sioux (Dakota, Lakota, Nakota) or Atsina (Gros Ventre) Indians on the prairie, traveled with them on bison hunts, and saw a grizzly bear. Little evidence of his exploits survives except a journal that he kept. He wrote it in rhyme, probably to entertain himself. For example, he wrote: "This wood is poplo ridges with small ponds of water / There is beavour in abundance but no otter." He returned to the company post called York Factory leading "a good fleet of Indians." He had been gone for two years. Decades would pass before another Hudson's Bay Company man went so far west again.

Meanwhile, in the English colonies on the east coast of the Atlantic, population and economic growth was rapid. By 1700 there were about a quarter of a million people living in the colonies. Of this total, about 10 percent were enslaved Africans, most of whom lived around Chesapeake Bay and in the Carolinas. In all of the English colonies, most people still lived close to the coast or near navigable rivers, although the farming frontier was moving slowly inland.

Enterprising souls still vigorously pursued trade with Indians and that activity led them to map new territory. In 1683, Henry Woodward, an agent of the Carolina proprietors, explored westward from coastal South Carolina. He traveled to what is now western Georgia,

As more English colonists settled in North America, they developed particular styles of homes. This *half-house*, or half–Cape Cod, known as the Rowell House and located in Barnstable County, Massachusetts, was built around 1730. This distinctive American home, a one-room cottage, is the smallest type of Cape Cod home traditionally built. *(Library of Congress, Prints and Photographs Division, HABS [HABS, MASS, 1-WEL, 14-2])*

The Hudson's Bay Company established many trading posts, such as the one shown in this 1896 photograph at Lake Temiskaming, Ontario. *(National Archives of Canada)*

established trading posts on the middle Chattahoochee River, and began trading with the Creek. He also ran into some opposition from the Spanish, who went looking for him, but Woodward quickly returned to Charleston.

Another enterprising man was Thomas Dongan of New York, who was appointed governor in 1683. He was eager to divert the French fur trade to New York and sponsored a number of journeys west. The first of these, in 1685, was led by Johannes Roseboom (Rooseboom), a Dutch Albany fur trader. Guided by a French-army deserter, Abel Merrion, Roseboom led a large party in 10 canoes laden with trade goods. He naturally headed for the place where Indians and fur traders congregated, the French fort at Michilimackinac. He traveled down Lake Ontario, portaged to Lake Erie, then on to Lake Huron, where the Ottawa and Huron were eager to trade. French governor Jacques René de Brisay, marquis de Denonville, was outraged when he heard about Roseboom's actions. "Missilimakinak is theirs," he wrote. "They have taken its latitude, have been to trade there with our Outawa and Huron Indians, who received them cordially on account of the bargains they gave." He lamented that there had not been enough Frenchmen at the fort at the time to drive them off. Dongan, on the other hand, was thrilled with the party's success and sent Roseboom out again the following year.

In 1687 Dongan sponsored another venture, this time by Arnold (Arnout) Viele, another Dutch fur trader from Albany and a skilled linguist. He, too, headed for Michilimackinac, but unfortunately the French took him prisoner and held him at Quebec before he finally escaped. In 1692, traveling with Lenni Lenape (Delaware) and Shawnee guides, he went to the Ohio River valley to trade, probably by way of the Delaware, Susquehanna, and Allegheny Rivers.

These trips, the English success in breaking into the French fur trade, and a nasty exchange of letters between the governors of New France and New York happened before the outbreak of King William's War in 1689. This tense environment did not bode well for restraint in war. The stakes for the Europeans were high. France and England saw an opportunity to drive the other from the continent, and Spain was anxious to defend its imperial interests. New England troops and their Iroquois allies fought the French and their Algonquian allies. During the war, French and Indian troops sacked Schenectady, New York, in 1690, and New England troops seized Port Royal, which was the principal town in Acadia,

modern-day Nova Scotia. The Treaty of Ryswick that ended the war in 1697 returned all the territory that either side had captured in North America.

The next war broke out just as Iberville was establishing his settlement in Louisiana. This time there was fighting in many parts of the colonies. The English attacked the Spanish at St. Augustine and their other missions in Florida. A joint Spanish and French force attacked Charleston, South Carolina. In 1704, an Abenaki and Mohawk force attacked the Massachusetts town of Deerfield on the Connecticut River. New England troops again took Port Royal and kept it under the final peace treaty, the Treaty of Utrecht, in 1713. The war

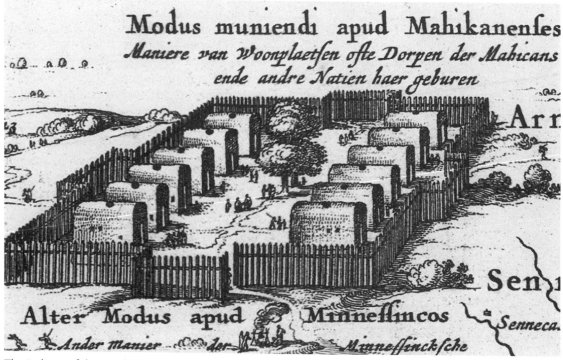

The Indians of the Northeast developed distinctive houses. This detail of a 1685 map by Nicolaes Visscher based on the explorations of Henry Hudson shows longhouses, which were divided into apartments and housed many families. The stockade around the village's perimeter provided defense from intruders. *(Library of Congress)*

The *Voyageurs*

Voyageurs were canoe men who worked for a wage and were the force on which the French fur trade rested. They learned their craft from Indians. Samuel de Champlain greatly admired the skill of the Native guides as his party navigated falls where there were dangerous "eddies and surf." He noted that the Indians navigated these "with the greatest possible dexterity, winding about and going by the easiest places, which they recognize at a glance." The French voyageurs had to learn this skill and build up stamina. Men paddled for hours at a time, setting the pace with songs, and paddling at about 45 strokes per minute. Heavily laden as they were with trade goods or furs, portages were arduous. Everything had to be removed from the canoes and carried past rapids, a waterfall, or to another waterway, and then the canoes had to be carried. Occasionally, the voyageurs might run rapids, letting the turbulent, fast-moving water carry them, but that meant risking the precious cargo of furs if they should spill and, possibly, their lives. When they were traveling against the flow of a river, the going was tough. Sometimes, in difficult terrain, to avoid a portage, the men towed their canoes, either wading in the cold water or walking along the river's edge. It was a hard life, but the men who did it enjoyed their independence and celebrated their strength and endurance in their own stories and songs.

prompted the Spanish to reinforce its military presence in Florida, and in 1718 it established permanent settlements at the outer edge of its empire in Texas at San Antonio.

In the midst of this warring, the Iroquois carved out a diplomatic solution to protect themselves. In 1701, still powerful but weakened by repeated epidemics, they developed a policy of neutrality. This policy, combined with their military strength, meant that for the next few decades the Iroquois were able to play the two major European powers against each other. This worked because both Britain and France had a vested interest in keeping the Iroquois neutral, at least to prevent them from allying with the other side and to keep trade goods flowing.

All this activity provided a backdrop for English exploration at the end of the 17th century. War gave an extra motive to Englishmen anxious to break into the French fur trade. To that end, in 1698, Thomas Welch of South Carolina set off from Charleston for the Arkansas River. The following year, William Bond wanted to get to the Gulf Coast and set off with a large party from Charleston overland to the Mississippi, guided by Jean Couture, who had explored Texas with Tonti in 1686 in the search for the La Salle party. Bond then traveled downriver to the Gulf of Mexico and explored the coastline of Florida.

The next year, Couture was instrumental in helping other Carolinian traders break the French hold on the fur trade on the Mississippi. Few Europeans knew more about the region than Couture. After Couture's previous travel with Tonti, he traveled on the Ohio and Tennessee Rivers, traded with the Cherokee, and traveled to Spanish posts in Florida before arriving in Charleston. He was thus able to lead Carolinian traders along the Savannah, Tennessee, and Ohio Rivers to the Mississippi.

Couture was not the only French fur trader to work and settle with the English. Others were instrumental in extending English influence in the fur trade in the new English colony of Pennsylvania. Wealthy English Quaker William Penn founded the colony in 1681 and its European population soared, reaching almost 20,000 within 20 years. Most of its settlers farmed, but a number, including Penn's agent James Logan, wanted to break into the French fur trade. They did not explore themselves but simply hired French fur traders who knew the region. Pierre Bisaillon was one of them. He, too, had been with Tonti on the 1686 search party. Now with Martin Chartier and Jacques Le Tort, he provided most of the furs for Logan, bringing them in to posts established on the Susquehanna River. Of course, being French during wars against France sometimes meant that Bisaillon was harassed by local English officials. Logan came to his defense, writing that Bisaillon "though a Frenchman, he had been very faithful."

In Virginia, the lieutenant governor, Alexander Spotswood, was also eager to enter the fur trade and promote westward settlement. He sponsored journeys to the Blue Ridge range searching for a route to the Great Lakes. In 1716 he led a group of gentlemen, their servants, rangers, and Indian guides along the Rapidan River in northern Virginia and then overland to the Shenandoah River. He formally claimed the Shenandoah Valley of northwestern Virginia for England and returned home and promoted it as a perfect place for Englishmen to settle.

Some explorers were anxious to observe the natural world as they surveyed land. In South Carolina, John Lawson set off with six Englishmen, three Indian men, and one Indian woman. He first traveled territory

familiar to the colonists up the Santee River. He met the Congaree people and thought the Congaree women very pretty. "Every step present[s] some new Object," Lawson

After receiving a charter from King Charles, William Penn informed Native Americans inhabiting the area that would become Pennsylvania of his intentions to establish an English colony there. *(Library of Congress, Prints and Photographs Division [LC-USZ62-2583])*

enthused, "which still adds Invitation to the Traveller in these Parts." Then he went overland as far as present-day Hillsborough, North Carolina, carefully noting the different peoples he met and the landscape. In Virginia, Englishman Mark Catesby, another traveler with an interest in the natural world, set off to satisfy his "passionate Desire" to see the plants and flowers of the region. Between 1712 and 1719 he traveled in the Blue Ridge Mountains and later in the Caribbean.

CONFLICTS WITH NATIVE AMERICANS

English exploration and expanding settlement led to a new round of battles with Native peoples. By 1710 there were so many English settlers along the South Carolina coast down to the Savannah River that tensions rose with the local Yamassee and Creek Indians. War broke out in 1716, and both groups were defeated by the English and their Cherokee allies.

Earlier, in North Carolina, tensions between mostly Swiss and German settlers and the Tuscarora had also led to the Tuscarora War of 1711–13. The plight of the Tuscarora demonstrates some of the complications Native peoples faced as they encountered Europeans. Once powerful, their numbers had declined from disease, and they had suffered at the hands of their more powerful Indian neighbors who were allied with Virginian and Carolinian traders. Finally, the Tuscarora struck back, killing John Lawson and then attacking a European settlement. The colonists responded with a devastating attack that killed hundreds of Tuscarora. Others were captured and sold into slavery. The remainder, perhaps about 2,000, moved north and sought protection from the powerful Iroquois and, in 1722, were admitted as the sixth nation in the Iroquois Confederacy, although not on equal terms with the original five nations.

THE FRENCH REASSERT THEMSELVES

This flurry of English competition on the Mississippi and its tributary rivers did not distract the French from exploring new territory. In fact, it gave their explorations a new urgency. Additionally, the peace treaty that marked the end of Queen Anne's War specifically required France to acknowledge Britain's right to Hudson Bay, which meant there could be no more attacks against the English there to drive them out of the market.

However, if the French were to remain dominant in the fur trade, they had to make new contacts with people who trapped the animals that bore the luxuriant furs found in cold climates. So the French government authorized the governor of New France, Philippe de Rigaud, marquis de Vaudreuil, to send expeditions westward from the Great Lakes and the Mississippi River valley. Vaudreuil was eager to comply. He was a military officer who had been involved in campaigns against the Iroquois and was experienced in working with Native allies. He thought it critical to increase French control of the western fur trade. The new French plan was for the government to pay for the expeditions, but the forts established would be self-supporting from their fur-trading activities. With this plan, the French government explicitly linked the fur trade to its national interests. And, by the end of the decade, a new wave of explorers were heading into what is today Minnesota and Manitoba.

By the end of this period, the French laid claim to the Ohio and Mississippi River valleys by means of a system of forts and missions but with a scant population. The Spanish, too, maintained a tenuous hold on Florida and Texas, the outposts of its empire. Meanwhile, the population of the English colonies was rising rapidly, and adventurers and traders from the middle and southern colonies were now regular visitors to the Mississippi. The stage was set for another century of new discoveries and new conflicts for Europeans and Native peoples.

10

GAINING KNOWLEDGE— COMING TO BLOWS

1715–1756

In 1749 the French Jesuit priest, Father Joseph-Pierre de Bonnecamps, was on an expedition to what he called "La Belle Rivière," the Beautiful River. This was one of the names the French gave to the Upper Ohio River. The expedition was led by Pierre Joseph Céleron [Céloron] de Blainville, an army officer whom Bonnecamps greatly admired. In his account of the journey, he described Céleron as "attentive, clear sighted, and active; firm, but pliant when necessary; fertile in resources, and full of resolution."

Céleron would need all those skills on this expedition, the goal of which was to map and secure French claims to the Ohio River valley. The party of about 200 Frenchmen, Native guides, and interpreters set off in 23 canoes from Montreal. On their journey, they had some exhausting portages, and Bonnecamps noted that Céleron regularly needed "to give his people a breathing space." The party was traveling in late July, so the rivers had low water levels, which caused them even more hard work. Bonnecamps was so despondent about it that, when they encountered low water on the Chautauqua River, he even noted the exact time in his journal: 10.30 A.M. on July 28 was, he wrote, "a fatal hour, which plunged us again into our former miseries." They were forced to "the sad necessity" of dragging the canoes over the stones in the riverbed.

Despite this occasional misery, Bonnecamps was a keen observer of the world around him. He measured the latitude regularly and carefully noted the flora and fauna— that is, the plant and animal life—that he saw. He was excited to see his first rattlesnake. He had heard that, if a person was bitten, a "sovereign remedy" was to apply a mixture of saliva and sea salt. He was pleased to note, though, that the party had not had "any occasion to put this antidote to the test."

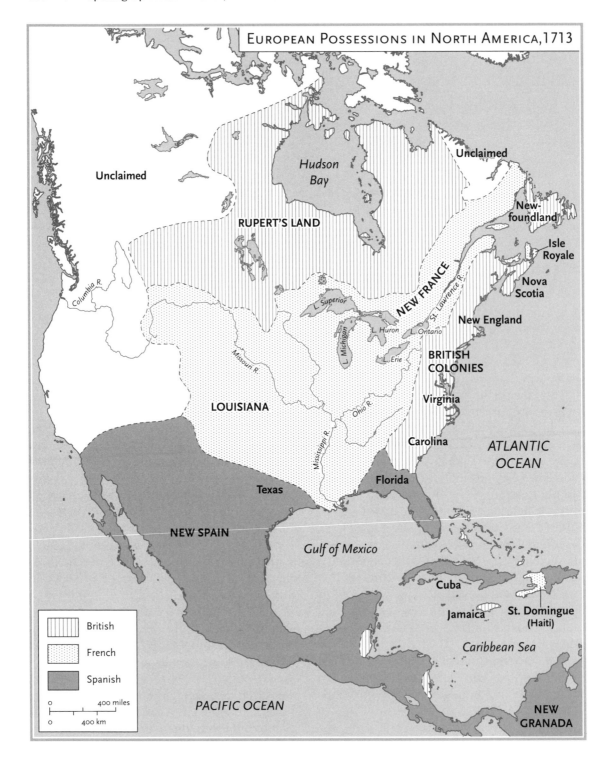

EUROPEAN POSSESSIONS IN NORTH AMERICA, 1713

Unclaimed

Hudson
Bay

Unclaimed

New-
foundland

RUPERT'S LAND

Isle
Royale

NEW FRANCE

Nova
Scotia

Columbia R.

L. Superior

St. Lawrence R.

New England

L. Huron

L. Ontario

BRITISH
COLONIES

Missouri R.

L. Michigan

L. Erie

Virginia

LOUISIANA

Ohio R.

Carolina

ATLANTIC
OCEAN

Mississippi R.

Florida

Texas

NEW SPAIN

Gulf of Mexico

Cuba

Jamaica

St. Domingue
(Haiti)

Caribbean Sea

British

French

Spanish

0   400 miles

0   400 km

PACIFIC OCEAN

NEW
GRANADA

The expedition staked its claim to the region by making a large circuit around it. The party traveled out by way of Lake Ontario and Lake Erie, portaged over to the Allegheny River, traveled along the Ohio to the Great Miami River near what is now Cincinnati, and returned to Montreal by Fort des Miamis (Fort Wayne, Indiana, today). Along the route, Céleron buried lead plates. These plates signified "the renewal of possession which we [the French] have taken of the said river Ohio and of all those [rivers] which fall into it, of all lands on both sides of it as far as the sources of said streams."

At first glance, the expedition appeared to have been a success. It helped the French understand the geography of the region more fully. Additionally, Céleron had ordered some Englishmen who were trading with the Indians to leave the area, and they did. Since trading and military relationships were closely connected, the French were particularly anxious to prevent the British from making these trade connections. Having sent the Englishmen away, Céleron tried to arrange alliances with the Native peoples he met to secure their loyalty to France.

But the expedition ultimately failed. The English traders, who were primarily trading for bear, otter, and deer skins, came back as soon as Céleron's party left and succeeded in drawing Native communities into their trading networks. And despite Céleron's efforts to reinforce loyalty, French fur traders were often not very interested in trading there, as they could make much more money in colder climates far to the north and west, where more luxuriant furs were to be found. So even though the French knew the military importance of the Ohio River valley, they did not do enough to strengthen their trading networks there. Tension increased in the region between the British and French, with Native Americans caught in the middle, and the Beautiful River became a scene of terrible bloodshed.

However, for most of the first half of the 18th century, British and French explorers usually managed to stay out of each other's way. The French explored the rich fur trading territory west of the Great Lakes and the territory west of Louisiana that is present-day Texas. British explorers and settlers moved steadily inland from their coastal communities toward the Appalachians. In the 40 years between signing the Treaty of Utrecht that ended Queen Anne's War in 1713 until conflict began in the Ohio River valley in 1754, British and French traders greatly added to European knowledge of North America.

THE FRENCH PUSH WESTWARD

The first focus of the French explorers was the area immediately to the west of Lake Superior, particularly Rainy Lake, in present-day southwestern Ontario, on the border with Minnesota. In 1717 the governor of New France, Philippe de Rigaud, marquis de Vaudreuil, sponsored an expedition there led by Zacharie Robutel de la Noüe. The cold climate in the region promised good quality furs, a French presence would help encourage western Indians not to trade with the Hudson's Bay Company, and the west still seemed to be where they would find a river route to the western sea and China.

Robutel was not the first Frenchman in the region. French coureurs de bois had been west of the Great Lakes since 1688. That year, one fur trader, Jacques de Noyon, had led a group from Thunder Bay on Lake Superior as far west as Rainy Lake. Noyon apparently heard from local Indians, probably Assiniboine, of a large lake farther west, possibly the Lake of the

Woods. It is not known exactly where Noyon got to, but it is clear that a few other coureurs de bois followed him into the area.

Almost 30 years later, in 1717, Robutel set out with a large party to establish posts in the region. He managed to establish a post on the Kaministikwia River, which flows into the north side of Lake Superior at Thunder Bay, but he probably got no farther west. Unfortunately, his expedition found itself in the middle of hostilities between the Dakota and the Cree; after four years, he returned home to Montreal.

The French government also sponsored secret journeys to find a route to the Pacific. In 1721 Jesuit priest Pierre-François-Xavier de Charlevoix was sent to find such a route under the pretext of inspecting all the Jesuit missions in the west. However, after an arduous journey through the Great Lakes, he turned south and went down the Mississippi to the French fort and trading post at New Orleans, which had been established in 1718. After this burst of activity, the enthusiasm for western exploration temporarily waned.

THE LA VÉRENDRYE FAMILY

The driving energy for the next push came from Pierre Gaultier de Varennes, sieur de La Vérendrye, and his family. La Vérendrye, an enthusiastic adventurer, had met Father Nicolas de Gonnor, a Jesuit missionary to the Dakota, at Michilimackinac. There Gonnor told him about a great river he had heard about leading to the western sea. In 1731 La Vérendrye set off with his sons, a nephew, and 50 men. By the following year, they had built a fort at the Lake of the Woods, at the border of present-day Ontario, Minnesota, and Manitoba, and another at Lake Winnipeg. Relations between the Dakota and the Cree were still

tense, but La Vérendrye was able to avoid getting involved for a while. However, in 1736, about 21 of his men, including one of his sons, were killed on an island in the Lake of the Woods, probably by the Dakota, who were concerned about the French establishing good relations with the Cree. La Vérendrye was determined to stay and devoted the next few years to diplomacy as much as exploration.

By 1738 he had ventured farther west and had built Fort La Reine on the Assiniboine River (present-day Portage La Prairie, Manitoba). There La Vérendrye had met the western Cree. He wrote in his report to the governor that he had encouraged them "to be faithful to the French" and not make the arduous journey to Hudson Bay to sell their furs to the English any more. La Vérendrye and his party pressed on, traveling now with a large community of the Assiniboine, who guided him across the prairies. He was impressed by these "magnificent plains of three or four leagues in extent." He was also impressed by the Assiniboine, who moved in a column with advance scouts, guards on the wings and rear, and with the weakest members of the community in the middle.

The party journeyed across the plains to the headwaters of the Missouri River, where they met the Mandan people, who greeted them cordially. Once there, the party's Assiniboine escort left them and moved on. But their departure also meant that La Vérendrye was forced to turn back for a surprising reason. La Vérendrye had been eager to question the Mandan about a river route to the western sea. However, he was dependent on a complicated communication system. One of La Vérendrye's sons spoke Cree, enabling the son to communicate with a Cree interpreter who spoke Assiniboine. Some Mandan spoke Assiniboine, so communication was possible.

Pierre Gaultier de Varennes, sieur de La Vérendrye, and his two sons explored the area constituting present-day North and South Dakota. In this painting, La Vérendrye stands over a lake, with Native Americans below, offering food to one of his expedition members. *(National Archives of Canada)*

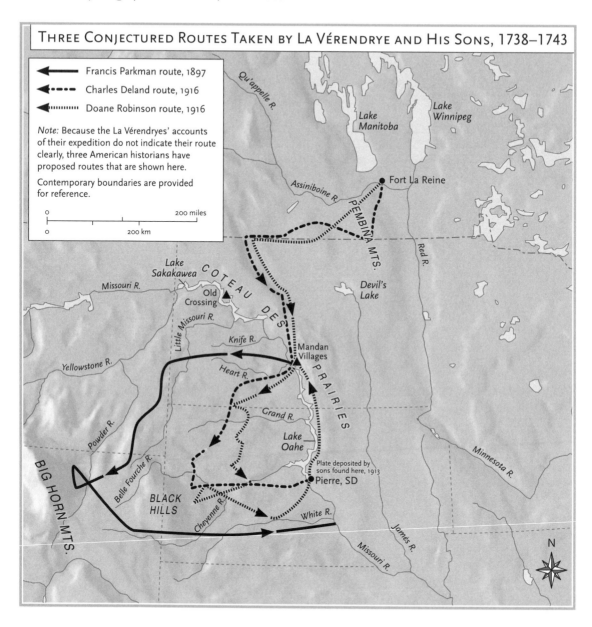

THREE CONJECTURED ROUTES TAKEN BY LA VÉRENDRYE AND HIS SONS, 1738–1743

← ▬▬ Francis Parkman route, 1897
←- - - - Charles Deland route, 1916
←·········· Doane Robinson route, 1916

Note: Because the La Vérendryes' accounts of their expedition do not indicate their route clearly, three American historians have proposed routes that are shown here.

Contemporary boundaries are provided for reference.

Unfortunately, as La Vérendrye told the governor, the system broke down when the Cree interpreter left suddenly "to follow an Assiniboine woman of whom he was enamored." This left the party "reduced to trying to make ourselves understood by signs and gestures."

Unable to learn which direction to head in, the expedition returned home.

Four years later, in 1742, two of La Vérendrye's sons set off again. The historical records are unclear about which sons went, and there is even more confusion over where exactly they went. However, the party did meet the Mandan again and this time set off to the west with Mandan guides. By January 1743, they reached mountains, probably the Big Horn Mountains in northern Wyoming, and met Cheyenne and Pawnee peoples along the way. As with Céleron, these explorers also buried a lead plate to stake French territorial claim to what is today Pierre, South Dakota.

THE HUDSON'S BAY COMPANY ON THE MOVE

While the French were exploring toward the west, so were the English traders from the Hudson's Bay Company. For a long time the English had been content to stay at their posts on the bay and let the Native hunters make the long journey to them to sell their furs. The increased activities of La Vérendrye and his family and the coureurs de bois who followed them changed their minds. The company now wanted to make direct contact with the nations to the west of the Cree, principally the Atsina (Gros Ventre) and nations of the Blackfoot confederacy.

The man chosen to explore and forge these new relationships was Anthony Henday. He set off in June 1754 from York Factory, the Hudson's Bay Company trading post on the western side of the bay at the mouth of the Nelson River. He was traveling with a party of Cree who were returning west, having sold their furs at the post. When they got to the prairies, the expedition left their canoes and the rivers behind and went by land, crossing Saskatchewan and reaching what is today the Battleford area.

Historians are unsure about exactly which route the explorers followed after this; they probably followed the Battle River from western Saskatchewan and reached what is now central Alberta. On his journey, Henday

traded with Assiniboine people. On October 18, 1754, he arrived in a Blackfoot village near present-day Red Deer, Alberta, with the Cree fur trader Ateesh-Ka-sees, Henday's guide and interpreter. Even though the Blackfoot greeted them warmly, the community's leaders were not willing to make the difficult journey to Hudson Bay to sell their furs. In fact, the Cree themselves preferred to act as middlemen between the Blackfoot and the English. Also, French traders were in the region, and Henday knew that they had two big advantages over the Hudson's Bay Company. The French Fort Pasquia (now The Pas, Manitoba) was easier for these far-western Indians to get to than Hudson Bay and, Henday observed in his journal, French traders "talk several languages to perfection." Thus he felt that the French "have the advantage of us in every shape."

Henday pushed farther west and may have been the first European to see the Rocky Mountains. In spring 1755 he and his Cree guides built canoes on the North Saskatchewan River for the journey home. On his way, he came across another French trading post, and Henday noted that he and the Frenchmen met each other with "a good deal of Bowing and Scraping, but neither he understood me nor I him." Still, the group shared "brandy and half a bisket" before parting. In the next five years, Henday made several more trips to the west before he left the company's service.

FRENCH AND BRITISH IN THE WEST

French and British explorers also continued to be active west and east of the Mississippi River. In 1714 French officer Claude Charles Dutisné traveled through Illinois country to the Kaskaskia River, which flows to the Mississippi. He then traveled south to Louisiana and, two years later, he traveled up the Red River, establishing a post named for the Native peoples who lived there, the Natchitoches. In 1719 the governor of Louisiana, Jean-Baptiste Le Moyne, sieur de Bienville, sponsored him to travel up the Missouri River to contact Indian nations in the west. On that journey he met the Osage and the Pawnee. Relations with the Pawnee were tense, Dutisné reported to the governor, "as the Osage had made them believe our intentions were to entrap them and make them slaves." However, Dutisné was able to persuade them that was not the case,

and they "consented to make an alliance and treated me very well." There is some speculation that Dutisné was the first European to reach the modern state of Kansas, but he probably was not. If he did get there, it was only barely into the southeastern corner.

Other French explorers were busy in the area, too. François Guyon des Prés Derbanne was on the Red River the same year as Dutisné. Derbanne lived on Dauphin Island on Mobile Bay and he set off with a group of traders by canoe, headed for the Red River, and reached Natchitoches, in northwestern

Tracking Explorers
HISTORIANS BECOME DETECTIVES

Figuring out the routes explorers followed often requires a lot of detective work. Even if historians are lucky and have a detailed account to reference, they still need to draw on their knowledge of local geography, flora, and fauna, Native American culture and history, and any archaeological evidence they can find to place the explorers exactly.

Many explorers' descriptions were vague. Few traveled with any instruments that enabled them to measure their latitude. If the explorers did not immediately establish a settlement of some kind, it is sometimes hard to know exactly where they had been. It is also difficult to place them by the Native peoples they met, as some of these peoples either controlled large areas or moved around a lot.

As a result, much of modern knowledge of explorers' journeys is the result of educated guesswork. For example, little is known about where René-Robert Cavelier, sieur de La Salle, traveled as he repeatedly left Matagorda Bay to search for the Mississippi. But more is known about his last journey because one of his lieutenants, Henri Joutel, was, on this occasion, traveling with him, and Joutel kept a very detailed diary. Joutel did not witness La Salle's murder but was one of the group of survivors of the expedition who eventually found the French post where the Arkansas River flows into the Mississippi.

Even with Joutel's journal, it is hard to reconstruct their exact route, but he does provide clues. He wrote that they often followed Indian trading routes and that trade flourished as "each tribe trades according to their skill." He recorded in great detail different styles of home building, canoes, and food among the peoples they met. Joutel also enjoyed the fruit "piaquiminia"—probably persimmon—from which some communities made bread. Joutel noted that the

Louisiana. From there, they went by land on mules heading west to what is now eastern Texas. They spent two months trading with the Hasinai (Tejas) Indians while traveling to the Texas Colorado River and, escorted by a Spanish captain, crossed the Rio Grande to the Spanish *presidio* (fort) and mission at San Juan Bautista, Mexico (present-day Guerrero in the state of Coahuila). Ultimately, Derbanne decided there was not enough money to be made trading there, and he finally settled in Natchitoches with his wife Jeanne, who was probably a Natchitoches Indian.

Despite Derbanne's low expectations for profit, other French traders and explorers were drawn to the region to trade with the Indians in the areas under Spanish control. Joseph Blancpain (Blanpain) was one. He traveled around western Louisiana trading with the Atákapa and Opelousa peoples. He then used Natchitoches as his base and traveled around the upper Trinity and San Jacinto Rivers in Texas. However, the Spanish were not pleased by these French efforts to trade in territory they claimed. In 1754 the Spanish caught Blancpain trading at a French post on

bread from this fruit "is similar to gingerbread in appearance, but it does not taste the same." Knowing where persimmon grows and which peoples used it for bread helps to trace the explorers' path.

Sometimes historians just need luck to help them discover a route. The journey of the sons of Pierre Gaultier de Verennes, sieur de La Vérendrye, in 1742 would probably be better known if scholars could actually be sure of where they had been. Their route was shrouded in mystery for a long time. In their journal, they noted simply that they passed "plenty of wild beasts" and met people they called "Bow men" who may have been Kiowa, Arapaho, or Lakota. They turned back when they reached mountains, but these were impossible to locate by their description. However, they buried a lead plate as a way to claim French rights to the region and noted in their journal that they had buried one at the point where they had turned around. In 1913 some schoolchildren playing on a hillside in Pierre, South Dakota, on the Missouri River, found it. That find allowed historians to identify the mountains they reached as the Big Horn Mountains.

There is also plenty of confusion about the journey of Claude Charles Dutisné and whether he was the first European in the modern state of Kansas. Early books about his journey probably exaggerated how far west he had managed to get. Today, by carefully working with his original report of his trip, historians have been able to piece together his descriptions. He wrote the direction he wanted to travel as being "south, one-quarter west" and mentions the distances between Pawnee villages that no longer exist. So, with archaeology, geography, and Dutisné's journal, scholars can reconstruct his path. Good detective work and luck help historians piece together explorers' journeys, but some parts of them will probably always remain mysteries.

Jean-Baptiste Le Moyne, sieur de Bienville, helped establish and governed the French colony of Louisiana. *(Library of Congress, Prints and Photographs Division [LC-USZ62-113863])*

Galveston Bay with the Orcoquiza Indians. When they saw from Blancpain's records that he had been selling guns, they imprisoned him and his trading partners and took them to Mexico City. Blancpain died there two years later, and his partners were taken to Spain, where they were imprisoned for life. The king of Spain, Ferdinand VI, issued a warning that any other Frenchmen found trading in Spanish territory would also be imprisoned.

The British colonists did not sit idly while the French made journeys expanding their geographic knowledge and trading relations with Native peoples on either side of the Mississippi. Naturalists continued to explore because of their interest in discovering the flora and fauna of northeastern North America. Mark Catesby, who previously explored Virginia, traveled extensively in South Carolina beginning in 1722. He made detailed notes and drawings of plants as he explored along the Savannah River through Georgia and into northern Florida. John Brickell, an Irishman traveling in North Carolina, was looking as much for economic opportunity as

Buffalo were plentiful in North America, but their numbers dwindled east of the Mississippi River by about 1760 as a result of exploration and colonization. *(Library of Congress, Prints and Photographs Division [PAN SUBJECT-Miscellaneous, no. 5 (E size)])*

he was for plant and animal life when he set off with 10 other people to travel west through North Carolina to Tennessee. He was as interested in what he called the small "rotten-wood worm" as he was in the large polecat and buffalo, which he drew in detail in his 1737 book, *The Natural History of North Carolina.* Unlike Catesby, he was also interested in Native culture and made detailed records of local medical practices.

THE BRITISH INCREASE ACTIVITY

The end of another war between the British and the French brought new energy to exploration in North America. The war, known in the colonies as King George's War, had lasted from 1744 to 1748 and, like the earlier wars, it was mainly fought in Europe with only small battles in North America. After the war, the British Crown granted charters to new land companies in the Ohio River valley and in Kentucky. This was territory the French also claimed and which the Native peoples still controlled. The stage was set for renewed exploration and conflict.

One of the earliest explorers in Kentucky was John Findley (Finlay/Findlay), a British trader who had gone there in 1744. Findley had traded and lived among the Shawnee for many years, spoke their language, and had heard from them about the abundant land of Kanta-Ke. The land there had natural salt springs that attracted grazing animals and, consequently, many groups of Native peoples, such as the Shawnee, Lenni Lenape, Kickapoo, and Miami, among others, hunted there. It was a perfect place, Findley thought, to establish a trading post, which he did.

In 1748 he returned to Virginia and told Thomas Walker, a wealthy doctor and adventurer, about the rich land to the west. Walker

and other wealthy Virginians were intrigued. Accompanied by James Patton, a former British navy officer with interests in western land, and others and guided by Findley, Walker crossed the Holston, Clinch, and Powell Rivers. He then went through a gap in the Allegheny Mountains in what is today eastern Tennessee. He named it the Cumberland Gap after the duke of Cumberland, a famous British military leader of the time for whom he also named the Cumberland River. He circled back to Virginia through southeastern Kentucky by way of the Licking River and the Big Sandy River. This route and the rich hunting grounds were densely forested, and so his overall impression of the region was that it was not suitable for farming. It was about 15 years later before he discovered the fertile lowlands of central Kentucky. However, Walker's report was glowing enough to send many traders into the region and for Virginian investors to organize the Loyal Land Company. In 1749 the company received a royal charter to 800,000 acres in the area that is today southwestern Virginia and southeastern Kentucky.

The real focus of British exploration in this period was the Ohio River valley. Pennsylvanian traders had been active in the area since the beginning of the century, building geographic knowledge and establishing important trading and political ties. One trader Irish immigrant was Thomas McKee. He was married to a Shawnee woman, Tecumspah, and lived on the south bend of the Susquehanna River in the 1740s and on the Ohio River in the 1750s; McKee sometimes worked for the Pennsylvania authorities as an interpreter. Other Pennsylvania traders were *métis*, such as Andrew Montour, whose mother was an Iroquois woman. Montour also was multilingual and used that and his political influence with Native communities to the benefit of the

Flintlock Muskets

Few explorers, adventurers, or traders would have set off on a journey without a flintlock musket. The flintlock musket was the most important weapon used in warfare and hunting in the 18th century and thus was a desirable trade item. (Rifles differ from muskets in having "rifled," or spirally grooved, bores.) Muskets had been around since the 16th century, but in the 18th century the invention of the new flintlock firing mechanism made the musket safer to use, faster to load, and more reliable in wet or windy weather. To fire it, users had to complete a sequence of actions. They had to put a small amount of powder in the small "priming pan" near the barrel of the musket and click a steel plate in place to cover it. Then they had to use a ramrod to push more powder, wadded paper, and the musket ball down the barrel. After removing the ramrod, they could pull the trigger. If this was all done correctly, pulling the trigger would strike the cock containing flint against the steel cover of the pan, which ignited the powder in the pan, which then ignited the main charge, sending the musket ball down and out the barrel.

Needless to say, a lot could go wrong. The charge might not have been rammed home tightly enough, the powder might be damp, or there might be a "flash in the pan" where the powder in the pan would spark but not ignite the main charge. Still, a well-trained soldier could carry out the sequence quickly, firing up to four times a minute. This improved firing mechanism made the musket easier to use but not more accurate. The user could still not be sure of hitting any target more than 100 yards away.

Explorers relied on flintlock muskets for protection. *(Catalog of Francis Bannerman Sons, New York, N.Y.)*

English. Over time he worked with George Croghan, Conrad Weiser, and William Trent, traders themselves and agents for the colony of Pennsylvania, as they negotiated with Ohio Indians.

The next great British journey of exploration in the Ohio River valley was only one year after the French explorer Blainville had buried

lead plates to secure France's claim to it. In 1750 Christopher Gist, a trader, was hired to survey land for the newly organized Ohio Company, another land company owned by wealthy Virginians, including the governor of the colony and the family of young George Washington, the future American president. The company had received its royal charter to about 200,000

In his late 20s, George Washington courted Martha Washington. Around Martha in this painting of their courtship are her two young children from a previous marriage. *(Library of Congress, Prints and Photographs Division [LC-USZ62-113387])*

acres of land between the Blue Ridge Mountains and the Ohio River the year before.

Gist's mission was to determine the best route for settlers, describe the best lands, and observe Indian trading patterns. He traveled from Shannopin's Town (named after a famous Delaware Indian chief and located in or near present-day Pittsburgh, Pennsylvania), to the falls of the Ohio at what is today Louisville, Kentucky, with many sidetrips up rivers that flow into the Ohio, such as the Scotio and the Muskingum. In his report to the Ohio Company, Gist made useful observations about the landscape. On the Muskingum

River, for example, he noted that there were "Meadows upon the Creek, [and] fine Runs for Mills." In another place he noted where the party was in "broken country" and found themselves "cutting our Way thro' a Laurel Thicket." But mostly, Gist found the land fertile and the hunting good.

FRENCH-BRITISH CONFLICT

This was not territory that the French were going to give up without a fight. In fact, it was new British interest in the region that prompted the governor of New France, Roland-Michel Barrin, marquis de La Galissonière, to sponsor Blainville's expedition in 1749. The same year, the governor ordered another expedition, this time by Gaspard-Joseph Chaussegros de Léry, a military engineer. His mission was to gather strategic information about the route between Montreal and Detroit. In his journal, Chaussegros noted that, once at Detroit, he "began surveying" and noted a place "where the clay is good for making brick," which water routes were good for transporting lumber, where "beautiful stone" could be quarried, and where the channel of the Detroit River was deepest. Continuing his military mission, the following year he went eastward and explored the Chignecto Isthmus (an isthmus is a narrow neck of land that connects two larger parts). The Chignecto Isthmus links Nova Scotia to the rest of Canada. In 1754 Chaussegros worked on building forts on the Allegheny River and surveyed the route between Detroit and the newly built Fort Duquesne (in present-day Pittsburgh).

As the British and the French were set to challenge each other in the Ohio River valley, Native peoples were forced to choose sides. The Iroquois chose the British because of their long-standing diplomatic and trading connections with them. Most other Native peoples sided with the French because the French only wanted to trade and did not come with settlers who wanted to compete for land. The crisis escalated in 1754 when the governor of Virginia sent a military force under a young George Washington into the region to challenge the French. Washington quickly built Fort Necessity near the French Fort Du-

quesne. After Washington led an unsuccessful attack on Fort Duquesne, the French responded and destroyed Fort Necessity, killing one third of Washington's men. These attacks began the French and Indian War, which in 1756 merged into a larger war between the British and French, called the Seven Years' War. Unlike earlier wars, this one would be mostly fought in northeastern North America, and at stake was control of the northeast of the continent.

It was, perhaps, inevitable that these two great European powers should come to blows over their interests in northeastern North America. The first half of the 18th century saw great gains in geographic knowledge by French and British explorers. These activities took on great military and political importance in the late 1740s and early 1750s as both focused on the Ohio River valley and explored and mapped the region so they could outmaneuver each other. After returning from western Pennsylvania—where he had been sent by the British governor of Virginia to warn the French—George Washington reported to the governor that the Ohio Indians were feeling caught in the middle of this European struggle for control. In his report, Washington stated that one leader of the Ohio Seneca, called Tanaghrisson, also known to the English as Half King, had told him they felt trapped "in a country between." Little exploration took place during the costly and terrible war. When it formally ended in 1763, France had lost and Britain was the sole imperial power in the region. A number of British colonists and traders were excited by the opportunities this presented and turned their sights again westward.

11

WARTIME AND EXPLORATION
1754–1783

 In 1769, the Pennsylvania born Daniel Boone, a hunter and frontiersman, led a hunting party from his home on the Upper Yadkin River in North Carolina to look around Kentucky, where he thought he might settle. He had tried to get there before on a 1767 trip when he crossed the Appalachians to hunt with his brother, Squire, and a friend. The hunting had been good, but they were unable to reach the fertile part of Kentucky they had heard about because—as Boone's son Nathan later reported in an interview—"they ware ketched in a snow storm." But Boone was inspired by stories from an old acquaintance, the trader John Findley, and he set off again accompanied by Findley, his brother-in-law John Stewart, and three other neighbors from the Upper Yadkin.

The three leaders of the group had a lot of backcountry experience. Findley was the oldest and had been trading for years in *Kante-Ke*. Boone, about 35 years old, was already an experienced frontiersman who supported himself and his young family by hunting. In addition to his hunting experience, he had fought in a war against the Cherokee in 1761 and, a few years year later in 1765, had gone on an expedition with Squire and others through the Carolinas and down to northern Florida in search of new land to settle. John Stewart had also been on the Florida expedition and had hunted west of the Appalachians.

The party made their way quickly over the Appalachians to the Clinch and Powell Rivers. They then passed through the Cumberland Gap and finally made their camp at what is today Irvine, Kentucky. After successful hunting, Boone and Stewart were taken prisoner by the Shawnee, who were appalled to find them hunting on their land. Fortunately, the Shawnee wanted only to warn them off. Boone's nephew, Daniel Boone Bryan, later told an interviewer that the Shawnee treated his uncles in "the most friendly manner." The group escaped and made their way back to camp.

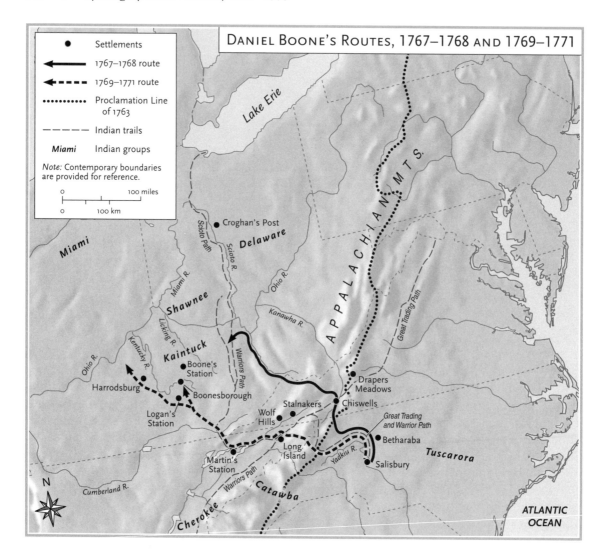

DANIEL BOONE'S ROUTES, 1767–1768 AND 1769–1771

Despite the warning from the Shawnee, Boone had seen enough of the potential of Kentucky to keep him in the region. In 1770, he and Stewart were joined by Squire and friend Alexander Neeley, and the four camped near the present-day town of Blue Lick. Stewart, unfortunately, went missing after he went out to check his hunting traps; he was presumed dead. Others found his remains five years later. Neeley returned home, leaving Daniel and

Squire Boone to continue to hunt. As Daniel later told the writer John Filson, they were soon in a "dangerous, helpless, situation." Short of food and ammunition, Squire went home to get more supplies, leaving Daniel alone for three months. During that time, Daniel wandered Kentucky, becoming more familiar with the terrain than any other European.

Daniel Boone's adventures were the subject of books even in his lifetime. Tales of his

Daniel Boone explored much of present-day Kentucky with acquaintances and relatives (and sometimes alone) from 1769 until 1770. This portrait of Boone much later in life was completed in 1819, the year before his death. *(Library of Congress, Prints and Photographs Division [LC-USZ62-112549])*

adventures and the abundant land, often exaggerated by biographers and promoters of the Kentucky country, helped entice thousands of settlers to follow him through the Cumberland Gap to settle in the west. Boone's expeditions remind us that success often depended on teams of people and relied on the knowledge of others. Boone knew that other Europeans had been there before him. He rarely set off alone, and there was often someone who could act as an interpreter. Findley spoke Shawnee, and the leader of the Shawnee group who captured Boone, known to the English as Will Emery, spoke English.

Boone also had a variety of motives. He was restless and adventurous and that drew him beyond his known world. He was also motivated to seek new economic opportunities in trading and hunting.

PONTIAC'S REBELLION AND THE OHIO RIVER VALLEY

While Boone was making his journeys, the international landscape was dramatically changing. France had been defeated in the Seven Years' War—in North America, this was known as the French and Indian War—which ended in 1763, and France was no longer a power on the continent. By the terms of the Treaty of Paris that ended the war, Britain was the uncontested European power in northeastern North America. British people in the colonies as well as at home in Britain celebrated the success and power of their empire. With French authority removed, British colonists began to head across the Appalachians.

However, the war made the Ohio and Kentucky regions less safe for explorers and settlers, as it brought a dramatic change in relations with Native peoples. Some Native peoples had long-standing relationships with the French that had now ended. The Iroquois Confederacy had previously enjoyed a powerful position, playing the French and British off against each other, but now, with the French gone, they were in a significantly weaker position. As these diplomatic patterns broke down, violence increased, especially in areas where settlers began arriving in increasing numbers.

No one felt this change more keenly than Pontiac, the leader of the Ottawa and a former French ally, who lived in western Ohio. In 1763 he led a loose coalition of Ohio peoples against the British in the west, destroying a

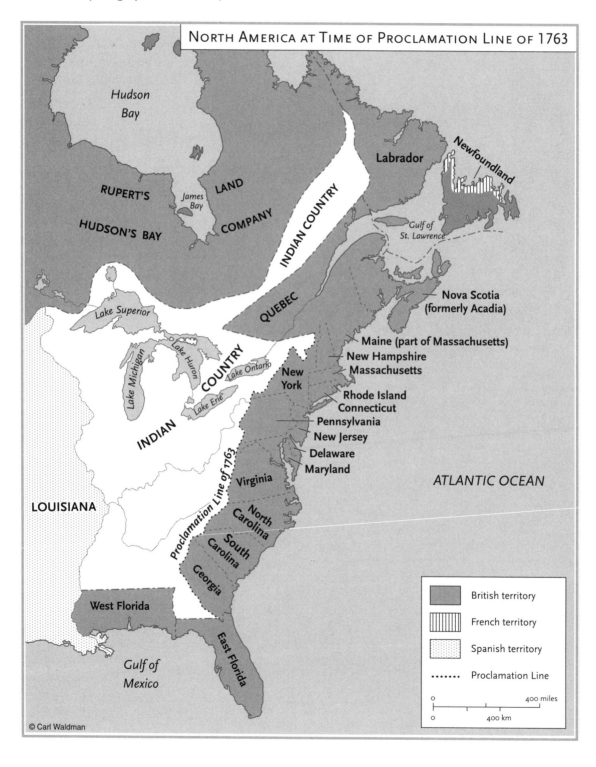

NORTH AMERICA AT TIME OF PROCLAMATION LINE OF 1763

Hudson Bay

RUPERT'S LAND

James Bay

HUDSON'S BAY COMPANY

Labrador

Newfoundland

INDIAN COUNTRY

QUEBEC

Gulf of St. Lawrence

Nova Scotia (formerly Acadia)

Lake Superior

Lake Michigan

Lake Huron

Lake Ontario

Lake Erie

INDIAN COUNTRY

Maine (part of Massachusetts)

New Hampshire

Massachusetts

New York

Rhode Island

Connecticut

Pennsylvania

New Jersey

Delaware

Maryland

Proclamation Line of 1763

Virginia

North Carolina

South Carolina

Georgia

LOUISIANA

ATLANTIC OCEAN

West Florida

East Florida

Gulf of Mexico

British territory

French territory

Spanish territory

Proclamation Line

0   400 miles

0   400 km

© Carl Waldman

number of forts and besieging the British at Detroit and Fort Pitt, the British name for the rebuilt Fort Duquesne (in present-day Pittsburgh). The British were able to defeat Pontiac, whose forces were weakened by military losses and disease, but were shocked at what it had cost in lives and money. To calm the situation, the British government in London issued a proclamation, forbidding colonists to settle west of the Appalachians. Its goal was to slow down the westward flow of settlers while British authorities purchased Indian lands. This legal barrier, which the colonists called the Proclamation Line, was often disregarded, but it was one of the colonists' many grievances against British authority as they moved toward independence.

Meanwhile, Daniel Boone and other traders such as Simon Kenton, Michael Stoner, and William Bush explored the Kentucky country, thinking of settling there. In 1774 Boone was hired by Richard Henderson

Leader of the Ottawa, Pontiac organized attacks on English forts and settlements in the area surrounding Fort Detroit. In an attempt to reach a compromise, he met with Major Henry Gladwin, commander of the fort. Not pleased with the results of their meetings, Pontiac led an attack on the fort but was ultimately defeated. *(National Archives of Canada)*

of North Carolina to survey land in Kentucky for his new land company called the Transylvania Company. He then asked Boone to lead a group of settlers there, which he did, founding the settlement of Boonesborough in 1775.

ACTIVITY IN THE GREAT LAKES REGION

While the Ohio River valley and the Kentucky country were the focus of eastern exploration, settlement, and conflict, the fort at Michilimackinac (at the tip of Michigan where Lake Huron joined Lake Michigan) was again becoming a center of exploring activity. The British fort had been attacked during Pontiac's uprising but now the region was quiet, and three veterans of colonial military service arrived there. The first was Robert Rogers, a New Hampshire man who had achieved fame during the war as the head of a ranger company known as Rogers' Rangers and who had seen action at Detroit and Fort Pitt. The second man was James Tute, who had been one of Rogers' Rangers. And the third was Jonathan Carver, who had served in the Massachusetts militia.

In 1766 Rogers was put in command of the fort at Michilimackinac. He was still convinced, as were others, that there was an inland northwest passage, the elusive river route to the Pacific. Rogers sponsored two expeditions to search for it. The first, in 1766, was led by Tute. The plan was that Tute would make his way to the Saskatchewan River and search for the connecting river from there. However, he traveled no farther than the Grand Portage at the northwestern edge of Lake Superior, in the present-day northeastern corner of Minnesota. At nine miles, the Grand Portage was the longest portage fur traders had to make in their journey westward. It connected the Great Lakes to the

Robert Rogers is best known for leading a group called Rogers' Rangers in the fight against the French and their Native American allies in the French and Indian War. *(National Archives of Canada)*

river networks of the Far West. At Grand Portage, Tute heard from Rogers that he had no money to buy supplies for him, so Tute turned back.

Jonathan Carver led the second expedition Rogers sponsored that year. Rogers commissioned Carver to map the territory the British now controlled in the region. French fur traders led Carver to Green Bay, after which he was guided by Winnebago people along the Fox and Wisconsin Rivers to the Mississippi. He then traveled up the Mississippi to St. Anthony's Falls, modern-day Minneapolis, which was territory previously known only to Native people and the French. He spent the winter with the Dakota Sioux at their camp on the Minnesota River. Carver wrote in his later book of his travels that this was a region that "exceeds for pleasantness and richness of soil all the places that ever I have seen." He was struck by the vegetation, which included nettles and vines and "all sorts of herbs of a most aromatick smell."

The following year, 1767, Carver met Tute and his party on the Mississippi. Tute had been sent out again to find a river to the Pacific. Together they searched through what is now Wisconsin. They followed the Chippewa River to Lac Court Oreilles, made a portage over to the Namekagon to St. Croix Lake, then to the Bois Brulé River, which led to Lake Superior. At Grand Portage, they again learned that Rogers had no money to supply them and so they made their way back to Michilimackinac. Although Carver did not find an inland northwest passage, he later published popular accounts of his travels, and as a cartographer, a mapmaker, he was successful in trying to clarify the location of places known by their English, French, and Native names. He also was perhaps the first to speculate about "the river Oregan, or the River of the West"—what would become known as

Fort Michilimackinac ～◠

The fort at Michilimackinac had a long and distinguished history from its time as a location of Indian trade through the French and British colonial periods. By the time the British took over the fort from the French in 1761, it was an active fur-trading center, and a few years later the British decided to require traders to have licenses. In 1765 one of the first went to Alexander Henry, who was given a monopoly to trade on Lake Superior and who joined in a partnership with the Frenchman Jean Baptiste Cadotte. But the rich history of Michilimackinac soon came to an end. The British abandoned the fort in 1781, preferring the nearby, better defended Mackinac Island, located in the Straits of Mackinac between Lakes Huron and Michigan. Traders who wanted the security of a fort and who always approached by water anyway followed the British, and the old fort fell into disrepair.

Today archaeologists work at the site of the old fort to try to discover as much as they can about the fur-trading era. They have reconstructed sections of the fort and have searched for abandoned tools and artifacts so they can understand how traders and their families lived. Colonial Michilimackinac, the name of the site today, is run by Michigan State Historic Parks, and it is one of the longest ongoing archaeological digs in the United States.

In the late 19th century, the region became the second national park in the country (the first was Yellowstone), but in 1895 it was transferred to the state of Michigan. Today there are four living-history museums in and around the Straits of Mackinac to celebrate and remember the region's fur-trading history. Almost 1 million people visit the park each year.

the Columbia River—becoming the link to trade with China and the East Indies.

THE RISE OF ST. LOUIS

Southward on the Mississippi, the end of the Seven Years' War also brought changes. By the terms of the Treaty of Paris, Britain acquired the Spanish territory of Florida (Spain had been a French ally), but Spain received New Orleans and Louisiana. The Spanish hoped Louisiana would be a buffer for their empire's northeastern frontier.

In 1763, just as this legal change was taking place, a New Orleans merchant, Pierre de Laclède, and his stepson, Auguste Chouteau, embarked on a bold new venture. They founded a new trading settlement on the Mississippi River that they called St. Louis. The site they chose was one from which the Missouri and the Illinois Rivers could be easily reached. Chouteau later wrote in his "Narrative of the Settlement of St. Louis" that they thought their site so perfect that it would become "one of the finest cities of America." Following Laclède's death, the driving force behind the community was Auguste's mother, Marie-Thérèse Chouteau, who with Auguste and her other sons made the family rich as the city became a fur-trading center.

Farther south, some merchants saw a trading opportunity if they could connect Natchitoches with other parts of the northern Spanish Empire, particularly Santa Fe. Diplomacy was going to be critical to success as any possible route had to go through regions populated by warring Native communities. Lack of geographical knowledge compounded the problem. Athanase de Mézières, a French-born nobleman who lived in Natchitoches, led five expeditions to try to negotiate alliances with various peoples of the region. On one of these, in 1770, he traveled up the Red River;

the following year he was on the Trinity and Brazos Rivers. On another, in 1772, he went even farther up the Trinity River, crossed to the Brazos and then went on to San Antonio. Unfortunately, he was unsuccessful in his efforts either to negotiate peace or to find a route to Santa Fe, but he did add much to geographic knowledge.

THE FOUNDING OF THE NORTH WEST COMPANY

In northern latitudes, the departure of French authority changed the political and practical world of fur trading, which led to new journeys of exploration. Before 1763, British fur traders had coveted the trade in luxurious furs that the French enjoyed in northwest North

Joseph Frobisher was one of the fur traders who formed the North West Company to challenge the Hudson's Bay Company. *(National Archives of Canada)*

Simon McTavish helped lead the effort to establish the North West Company. *(National Archives of Canada)*

America. The British Hudson's Bay Company dominated part of this market, but the company was a privately held monopoly. Only company employees could trade on its land, and only shareholders profited.

After the Seven Years' War ended in 1763, individual British traders wanted to get in on the opportunities the region offered, and they joined French and Métis fur traders in the Far West. James Findley, Thomas Corry, William Bruce, Barthélemi and Maurice Blondeau, and Thomas, Joseph, and Benjamin Frobisher were all trading farther and farther west and north by the early 1770s. A few men from the colonies joined them. James Tute was trading in Saskatchewan by 1774. Alexander Henry was there the following year before settling in Montreal to run his business from there. Simon McTavish, an Albany-based fur trader who had traded around Detroit in the 1770s, also moved to Montreal to run his business. Peter Pond of Connecticut went too. A veteran of the Seven Years' War, Pond had traded in the Detroit area but, as with the others, he was beginning to find it difficult to make money south of the Great Lakes because of competition from traders at St. Louis. Exploring new lands to the far west and north as well as finding new sources of fur was appealing for all of them.

These men, with their Native guides and trading associates, dramatically extended geographic knowledge of northwestern North America. The Hudson's Bay Company derided them as peddlers, that is traveling salesmen who went from place to place buying and selling (peddling) goods. The company, of course, preferred to have its employees stay in a couple of important posts and have Native hunters come to them with furs. The French had established posts across a broad region, but they still expected Indians to come to them. In contrast, the peddlers exchanged their trade goods for furs in Native villages. Initially, they traded independently, but they soon realized that if they pooled their resources, they could offer more goods at better prices. At first, they did this informally, but, in 1783, they organized themselves into the North West Company. Led by Simon McTavish, Alexander Henry, and others, it would challenge the Hudson's Bay Company at every step.

The group made many important journeys, gaining geographic knowledge as they opened new markets. One of their greatest journeys was made by Peter Pond. In 1778 he traveled through the extensive waterways of the Saskatchewan and Churchill Rivers to the Athabasca region, which stretches across the northernmost parts of modern Saskatchewan and Alberta. At its southern edge, Pond discovered an important new portage, longer than the Grand Portage at Lake Superior. This one, 13 miles long, went from Lac La Loche (Methy Lake today) over to the Clearwater River and was a link between the northwestward-flowing watershed of the Athabasca region and the eastward-flowing one that led to Hudson Bay. This new portage, known as the La Loche or Methy [Methye] Portage, opened up a whole new section of the continent to European traders. Years later, Scottish explorer Alexander MacKenzie, in his account of his travels, wrote of the view near the end of this portage of the plains below and thought it "a most extensive, romantic, and ravishing prospect." Pond established his base just south of Lake Athabasca and traded with Cree and Chipewyan hunters. He had intercepted the source of the Hudson's Bay Company's supply of prime furs.

THE HUDSON'S BAY COMPANY RESPONDS

The Hudson's Bay Company was not sitting idly while the North West Company stole their business. It saw the need to expand its operations. At first it set its sights to the north. In 1765 it established a whaling base at Marble Island at the Chesterfield Inlet, at a latitude just above 62° north. The company was also intrigued by new stories of northern copper deposits, still richer furs, and a possible northwest passage. The man commissioned to find these things was 24-year-old Samuel Hearne, and he made three journeys between 1769 and 1772. The first ended quickly when his Native guides left him, taking his supplies with them. In 1770 he set off again with a large Chipewyan group, and they reached Yathkyed Lake, but again his guides left him. Hearne spent three days alone before being rescued by the Chipewyan leader,

The Hudson's Bay Company employed young Samuel Hearne to find a "northwest passage" and compete with the North West Company to find furs and establish claims. *(National Archives of Canada)*

Matonabbee, and his band. Matonabbee, who in addition to his own language spoke Cree and a little English, took Hearne back safely to the company's Prince of Wales's Fort on Hudson Bay. This was the beginning of a lifelong friendship between them.

In 1771 Hearne set off for his third expedition with Matonabbee and his extended family of wives and children. Among them was a young Chipewyan man, known as Nestabeck, who would later become a famous guide and leader. Hearne took no supplies with him. He lived entirely with, and was dependent on, Matonabbee and his group. Their journey took them to the Coppermine River, which they followed to the Arctic Ocean. In July, in a snowstorm, Hearne looked down on Coronation Gulf, as it is known today, and realized that no ship would ever be able to get through the ice floes that he saw before him. If there was a northwest passage, this was not it. His return journey took him a year. On the way he saw the Great Slave Lake and part of the river system that today bears the name of Mackenzie. When they returned home, the group had covered approximately 3,500 miles, an extraordinary accomplishment by any measure. Hearne's assessment of his discoveries was modest. He wrote in his journal that, "Though my discoveries are not likely to prove of any material advantage to the Nation at large, or indeed to the Hudson's Bay Company, yet I have the pleasure to think that I fully complied with the orders of my Masters."

Despite these great journeys, the Hudson's Bay Company and its employees, such as Hearne, still resisted the idea that they should take goods out and peddle them. After Hearne went on to establish the company's first post inland, Cumberland House on the Saskatchewan River in 1773, he was quite clear that Indians had to come to him to trade. He wrote in his journal that Indians from "Buffalow Country," who had brought in wolf skins, tried to get him to come into their territory, as there were people there who were "desirous of having goods brought as near their own doors as Possable." Hearne told them that his intent

The Great Chipewyan Guides
MATONABBEE AND NESTABECK

Matonabbee and Nestabeck were two Chipewyan leaders and guides of the latter part of the 18th century. Matonabbee was an imposing figure, standing six feet tall, a large man by the standards of the time. He had been born at the Hudson's Bay Company Fort Prince of Wales to a Chipewyan father and Cree mother and had lived around the fort for much of his young life. Consequently, he gained knowledge of the fur trade and picked up some English in addition to his two Native languages. As an adult, he lived among the Chipewyan but seemed to move easily between the English and Chipewyan worlds. By 1775, he was a recognized leader of his people and was renowned for his ability to negotiate good trading deals.

Nestabeck, sometimes known as Mis-ta-poose, was probably a younger man. He traveled with Matonabbee on his expedition with Samuel Hearne. By the 1790s, he was the central figure in an extensive network of traders and explorers and was often simply referred to in explorers' journals as the "English Chief." He was well known to many of the most famous British explorers and fur traders of the period, including Alexander MacKenzie, David Thompson, Peter Pond, and the Hudson's Bay Company surveyor, Philip Turnor. All valued his skills as a guide and his ability to navigate between the Native and European worlds. Many years later, Alexander MacKenzie wrote about Nestabeck in a letter to a young man who was organizing an expedition: "I wish you could fall in with my old friend . . . he would be invaluable."

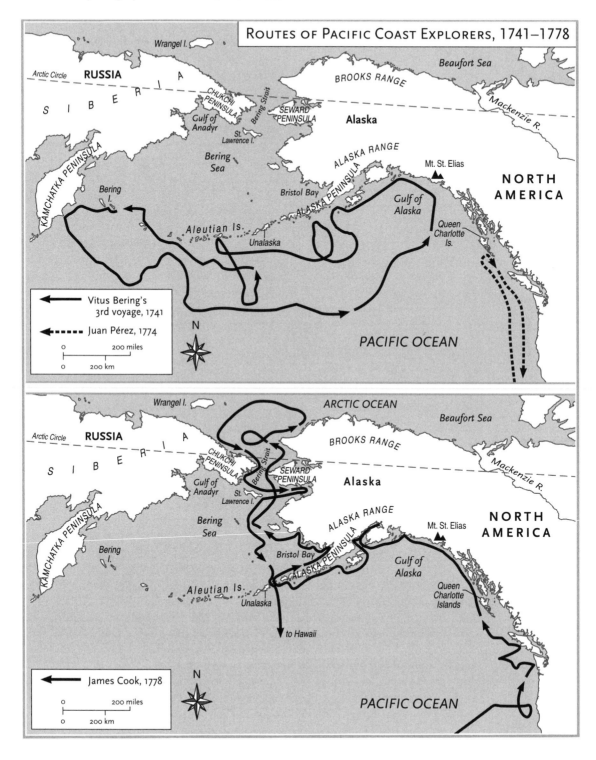

ROUTES OF PACIFIC COAST EXPLORERS, 1741–1778

was to have the post serve a large community and that policy was "firmly fixed."

Even though Hearne was modest, his travels made him well known. Indeed his fame helped him on one occasion during the American Revolution. In 1782 France, an ally of the United States during the war, seized the Hudson's Bay Company Fort Prince of Wales, where Samuel Hearne was then commander. The French admiral, Jean François de Galaup, comte de La Pérouse, and Hearne came to be friendly even though Hearne was his prisoner. La Pérouse read some of Hearne's journal and encouraged him to publish it before releasing him.

THE PACIFIC NORTHWEST COAST

By the 1770s there was a better understanding of the size of North America and a steadily growing interest in its western coast. Vitus Bering, a Danish-born explorer working for the Russians, had trekked across Siberia, and in 1728 sailed into the strait that now bears his name. On a second expedition, in 1741, he traded for furs in Alaska and the Aleutian Islands. Following this, Russian fur traders established posts on the Alaskan coast and traded down what is today the coast of British Columbia.

The Spanish also began to take an interest in the northwestern outpost of their empire. In 1769 Gaspar de Portolá sailed up the coast of California to establish a post at Monterey. In 1774 Juan José Pérez Hernandez with the pilot Francisco Antonio Mourelle de la Rua among his crew sailed as far north as the Queen Charlotte Islands off what is today northern British Columbia. The following year Bruno de Heceta sailed north and traded with the Coast Salish Indians in present-day Washington State. In 1779 Juan Francisco de la Bodega y Quadra,

accompanied by Mourelle, also navigated the coast.

The Spanish were keeping a close eye on British activities in the region and the British were returning the favor. In 1776 British naval captain James Cook's third great journey of exploration took him to this part of the coast. On Cook's first two voyages, he had circumnavigated the earth, mapped parts of the coast of New Zealand and Australia, and encountered the people of what he called the Sandwich Islands (modern Hawaii). In 1776 Cook was intrigued by what he knew of Spanish activities in the Northwest and officials in the British government still dreamed that he might find a northwest passage. Cook crossed the Pacific and made landfall on the Oregon coast and then traveled north to what is today Vancouver Island, where he and his crew met the Nootka people. He traveled up to Alaska, went through the Bering Strait to the Bering Sea, which comprises the southwestern part of the Arctic Ocean, until ice forced him to turn back. As a result of this Russian, Spanish, and British activity, the geography of the west coast of the continent was now more completely understood, but they did not agree on who controlled it.

A REVOLUTION'S IMPACT ON EXPLORATION

In 1775 war broke out between Britain and the colonists in the thirteen colonies along the east coast of North America from what is now Maine down to Georgia. From 1775 to 1783, during the American Revolution, settlement in the west was slow, but the war brought a great many men into the region when the Americans were fighting Indians who were British allies. Many Native peoples, especially the Iroquois, allied themselves with the British during the Revolution, feeling that the British were the only force holding back American settlement. Consequently, in 1779, Patriot general John Sullivan led a campaign against the Iroquois in upstate New York. One soldier on the campaign, Sergeant Thomas Roberts of New Jersey, wrote in his journal that he saw "the Back Woods" for the first time. As he marched with the army, he was struck by the good timber he saw and "a piece of Meddo [meadow]" that was very fertile. A number of Revolutionary War soldiers saw opportunity and settled on the frontier after the war.

Exploration continued while the war was going on. Thomas Walker, who had explored Kentucky in 1750, made another journey in 1779 and 1780 to survey the boundary between the new states of Virginia and North Carolina. At the time, both states claimed all territory to the west of them as far as the Mississippi. Walker was unable to get all the way there and had to estimate the last part, but did reach the Tennessee River.

The result of the American Revolution would be the emergence of a new power on the continent, the United States of America. The 29 years between the beginning of the French and Indian War and the end of the American Revolution had witnessed many important journeys of exploration. These were closely connected to the changes in the political landscape and the opportunities that resulted from them. As the century came to a close, the international stakes stayed high. Britain, Spain, and the United States were the leading powers in North America. Russia was also taking an interest in the continent. The commercial stakes were equally high as American traders and land speculators looked west while the Hudson's Bay Company and the new North West Company tried to out do each other. Under these circumstances, the search to find a route to the Pacific could only intensify.

12

IN THE FOOTSTEPS OF MACKENZIE

1783–1800

 The year 1797 was extraordinary for David Thompson. That year, he decided to leave his long-time employer, the Hudson's Bay Company, and go to work for its rival fur-trading firm, the North West Company. He wanted to have more opportunity to explore and, as he was already a seasoned traveler and navigator, his new company was glad to let him do it. After spending the summer at Grand Portage on the western end of Lake Superior, he set off into the west determined to take exact measurements of familiar places, locate shortcuts for known routes, and find new groups of Native hunters with whom to do business.

Thompson was well prepared for this trip. Born in 1770 in England, he had been apprenticed to the Hudson's Bay Company at age 14. After a few years in Canada, he had traveled on the North Saskatchewan River, wintered with Piegan Indians on the Bow River, been tutored in navigation by Philip Turnor, the company's chief surveyor, and survived a life-threatening injury. When his apprenticeship was over at age 21, he was a seasoned backwoodsman. In 1796 he had found a more direct route to Lake Athabasca from Sisipuk Lake. In his journals, Thompson wrote that this was a journey "attended with much danger, toil, and suffering." On his return from Lake Athabasca through Black Lake, he had intended to portage around a 12-foot high waterfall, but an accident caused his canoe, with him and his baggage in it, to go over it. He remembered being first "buried under the waves" and then buried under the weight of the canoe before getting himself, bedraggled and bleeding, to the shore.

Thompson set off on another remarkable journey of exploration in 1797. He traveled from Grand Portage through Rainy Lake, Lake of the Woods, Lake Winnipeg, and Lake

153

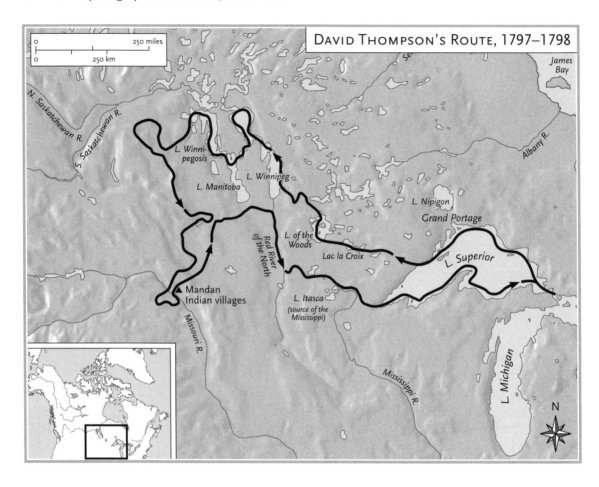

DAVID THOMPSON'S ROUTE, 1797–1798

Winnipegosis. He then followed a series of smaller rivers and lakes that eventually took him to the source of the Assiniboine River, then to the Red Deer River and its source. He finally reached a friend's house on the Souris River in present-day North Dakota, where he could have stayed the winter. Instead, he decided to press on. He wanted to meet the Mandan people who lived on the Missouri River to encourage them to trade with him.

In early December, he set off across the plains to the section of the Missouri River known as Lake Sakakawea, also in North Dakota. He now traveled with nine men, one of whom spoke Mandan fluently, and 30 sled dogs that Thompson thought were "half dog, half wolf." Early in their journey, the daily temperature readings Thompson took were –36°F, that is 67 degrees Fahrenheit below freezing, "too cold to proceed," he observed, and they stayed in their tents. Moving again, they found themselves in "a perfect storm" with snow blinding them. In the confusion, one man and his team of dogs went missing. After some time, they heard the man calling, and they finally found him crawling in the snow. His dogs and sled were never seen again. The group endured periods when they were all "very hungry, and the dogs getting weak," but they eventually reached the Mandan at the end of December. Although they were received cordially, the Mandan did not want to travel north through the territory of their enemy, the Dakota, just to trade, and so Thompson and his party returned home after a couple of weeks.

THE FUR TRADE HEATS UP

Thompson's journeys in 1793 and 1797 were just the beginning of a long and distinguished career as a trader and explorer that took him over much of the northern part of North America. He was one of a dynamic group of fur traders, Hudson's Bay Company men, North West Company traders, and independents who mapped and remapped much of the northwest at the end of the 18th century.

Traders explored to find new sources of furs because competition between them was increasing. Fur-bearing animals were becoming fewer in regions closer to eastern markets, so traders had to go continually farther and farther west or north to make new contacts with Native hunters from whom they obtained the furs.

At the same time that competition was increasing and furs were getting harder to find, the market was expanding. News of the travels of British, Spanish, and Russian seamen in what is now Oregon and British Columbia sparked interest in trading furs, especially sea otter skins, between the west coast of North America and China. British, Spanish, and U.S. traders participated in this by sailing around Cape Horn—the tip of South America—sailing up the west coast and then crossing the Pacific. The Russians traded in the northwest from their posts in Alaska and the Kamchatka Peninsula on the western side of the Bering Sea.

It was becoming clear that the region would be a source of wealth for European traders, but it was not clear which European nation would control it. Spain claimed sovereignty over all territory between the Mississippi and the Pacific and wanted to include in that the territory north of California and south of Alaska. However, the Spanish claim was weak because the Russians and the British were already there. At the time, geographic knowledge and a trading presence were key to making territorial claims and so the race was on to explore and claim the Far West.

THE OHIO RIVER VALLEY IN THE NEW REPUBLIC

By the end of the 18th century, the U.S. government had not yet participated in exploration. The Treaty of Paris that ended the American Revolution gave the United States sovereignty over all the territory between the Appalachians and the Mississippi, but no more. The new government then focused on securing that land and creating a stable economy. It wanted to be sure that the territory east of the Mississippi came into the Union and was sold to settlers quickly to pay off the national war debt. In 1784, 1785, and 1787, Congress passed three acts that were called Northwest Ordinances—the "northwest" in this instance referring to the territory that would eventually become Ohio, Indiana, Illinois, Michigan, Wisconsin, and part of Minnesota. They provided for the orderly settlement of the land and set out a procedure that would allow a territory to become a state and be admitted to the Union. Exploration of the Far West could wait.

Native peoples, of course, had not been part of the peace negotiations ending the Revolutionary War and had not agreed to their land becoming part of the United States. As the trickle of U.S. settlers became a flood, violent conflict increased in what was by now designated as the Ohio, Indiana, and Illinois Territories. In 1790 and 1791, a loose confederation of Indians led by Little Turtle of the Shawnee defeated U.S. military forces in the region. In fact, at what is today Fort Recovery in western Ohio, on the banks of the Wabash River, they inflicted on General Arthur St. Clair one of the heaviest military defeats in U.S. history. There 900 men out of St. Clair's force of about 1,500 were either killed or wounded. The United States sent out a new larger force under General Anthony Wayne, a hero of the American Revolution, and in 1794 he defeated Little Turtle's forces at the Battle of Fallen Timbers near present-day Toledo, Ohio. The following year, under the Treaty of Greenville, the Indians ceded two-thirds of what is now the state of Ohio and part of Indiana. In return, they were promised a lasting boundary between the United States and their lands.

Farther south, in the 1780s, settlers moved into the land west of Georgia and the Carolinas controlled by the Creek, Cherokee,

The British and the newly independent United States finally compromised when they signed the Treaty of Paris of 1783. *(Library of Congress, Prints and Photographs Division [LC-USZ6-279])*

Pemmican

Pemmican was the "fast food" of the plains and the Northwest. It was easily carried, could be kept for a long time, and was a great high-energy food. Native peoples all over the region had used it for many years. Voyageurs, traders, and other European travelers quickly learned to use it too. Sometimes traders learned to make their own. More commonly, they traded with Native peoples for pemmican at the same time they traded for furs.

Although the recipe for pemmican varied from community to community, its basic ingredient was meat that was first dried and then ground into a powder. The meat would usually be buffalo, deer, or moose. The powdered meat was then made into a paste, with fat from the animal and marrow taken from inside its bones. For flavor, some kind of fruit was added, such as cranberries, cherries, or blueberries. It was then shaped into small cakes for easy carrying.

Pemmican is still made today. Some hikers carry it for a fast, high-energy food source. Modern recipes reflect popular tastes and use spices from all over the world. Some recipes include nuts and sweeten the pemmican with sugar or honey. Other recipes make it more savory and add cayenne pepper or Worcestershire sauce. Some people prefer not to use animal fat as a paste and instead use peanut butter to bind the ingredients. Whatever the exact mixture, it makes an easily carried, nutritious food. Robert Peary, U.S. naval officer and great explorer of the Arctic, wrote in *The Secrets of Polar Travel,* "Of all items which go to make up the list of supplies for a polar expedition, the one which ranks first in importance is pemmican."

Choctaw, and Chickasaw. Those peoples negotiated treaties with the United States to cede land in exchange for a guarantee of their boundaries. However, settlement there moved at a slower pace than in the north, and many U.S. settlers moved west only after cotton became an important crop at the end of the century.

At this time, few in the United States focused on new explorations in the Far West. Some men, such as Jedediah Morse, who wrote a popular textbook called *American Geography* in 1789, thought that the United States would ultimately extend its territory to the west. Morse wrote in his book, "The Mississippi was never designed as the western boundary of the American empire." Most, however, saw plenty of opportunity in the new territory between the Appalachians and the Mississippi, about which a great deal was already known. Men such as John Sevier, who had been a trader in Tennessee, found opportunity for leadership. He sat on the council that served the newly organized territory south of the Ohio River and was the first governor of the state of Tennessee after it was admitted to the Union in 1796.

Others such as Daniel Boone preferred the opportunities of the frontier. Boone had served two terms in the Virginia legislature, but he was restless. Even though he had led parties of settlers to Kentucky, he never wanted to live surrounded by other families. After the American Revolution, he lived in western Virginia, then on the Ohio River, and later back in Kentucky. Finally, in 1799, he relocated his family to the Missouri River, which was Spanish-controlled territory. He moved to Femme Osage about 70 miles up the Missouri from the trading center of St. Louis, which was located on the Mississippi. There he was able to renew his old hunting life.

THE MISSISSIPPI VALLEY AND THE MISSOURI RIVER

St. Louis was attracting settlers who wanted to participate in the vigorous trading life of the town. By 1800 there were just under 2,500 people in and around the town. And, as suited a town at the junction of three rivers—the Mississippi, the Missouri, and the Illinois—it was a diverse community that included French, Spanish, Métis, Indian, and slowly a few U.S. farmers and traders. They were all expanding their activities farther and farther up the Missouri River, weaving the Kansas, the powerful Osages, and other Native peoples into the fur-trading network.

Rumors that traders from Canada were already trading with the Mandan on the Upper Missouri encouraged some traders to push even farther up the river. One of the earliest traders to do so was Jacques d'Église in 1792. He was followed a year later by Jean-Baptiste Truteau, who had been hired by a group of St. Louis merchants who had formed the Company of Explorers of the Upper Missouri. Truteau probably reached the point on the Missouri where the Grand River flows into it and traded with the Arikara people. Truteau passed the Niobrara River and wrote in his account of his travels that the river might be "the most abundant one in the entire conti-

nent of beaver and otter." Unfortunately, the river's raging waters prevented him from ascending it. The next explorer on the Missouri was James MacKay, a former North West Company trader now working for the Spanish who was traveling with John Evans, a young Welshman. They set off in 1795 and established the trading post of Fort Charles, near present-day Homer, Nebraska. Evans continued up the Missouri and contacted the Mandan, but since he found the Canadian traders already established there, he turned back. All these journeys added significantly to the geographic knowledge of the Missouri by the end of the century.

Farther south, New Orleans, now a Spanish-controlled city, was also attracting some U.S. traders interested in exploring the land to the west. The Irish-born Philip Nolan moved there about 1790 to represent the businessman and former Revolutionary War officer James Wilkinson. Nolan went on four journeys to trade and explore Texas. He traveled to the Comanches and lived among them for two years. From 1794–96 his travels took him to San Antonio. In 1797 he went to the Rio Grande and on to near present-day Austin, Texas. Nolan had become an enthusiastic horse trader, but the Spanish, who rightly suspected him of political intrigue, revoked his trading license, and he was killed in a skirmish with Spanish troops. Before his death, he passed on to Wilkinson much information about the region.

Naturalists, as well as traders, continued to take the lead in building geographic knowledge. In 1785 the French government commissioned André Michaux, a French botanist, to travel to North America to find trees that would be useful for French shipbuilding and furniture making. After traveling down the east coast, describing and categorizing plants, he met with leading scientific figures

of the day, such as Benjamin Franklin. In 1792 he made a proposal to the American Philosophical Society for an expedition to the Pacific by way of the Missouri River. Thomas Jefferson, then secretary of state, supported the venture and wrote instructions for the expedition similar to those he would give to explorers Meriwether Lewis and William Clark a decade later. The project was abandoned when Michaux became embroiled in a political scandal, but he did make a 1,100-mile journey through Illinois country to the Mississippi, collecting botanical samples and publishing a book, *North American Sylva,* with his findings.

The French government also sponsored a secret mission to explore the West. The Directory, the rulers who had come to power in the years following the French Revolution, had ambitions of regaining former French territory in North America. To that end, the French ambassador to the United States recruited a Frenchman in Philadelphia, Georges-Henri-Victor Collot, to make a strategic survey of the region west of the Appalachians. In 1796 Collot began what would ultimately be a 7,600-mile odyssey on the Ohio and Mississippi Rivers and some of their major tributaries. Although at different times he was detained for spying by both the U.S. and Spanish authorities, he was able to complete his remarkable journey. He did not explore territory new to Europeans, but he did correct maps, detail natural resources, and note trade patterns. In 1800 Napoleon forced Spain to return Louisiana to France but, since he was distracted by military crises elsewhere, he was never able to act on Collot's information or his American ambitions. Finally, pressing financial needs forced Napoleon to sell the territory to the United States in 1803—what is known as the Louisiana Purchase.

EXPLORING THE PACIFIC NORTHWEST BY SEA

Even though Americans were not exploring the Far West by land, they were going by sea, inspired by the accounts of British captain James Cook's voyages, which had been published in 1784. During 1787 a group of Boston merchants funded Robert Gray and John Kendrick, Boston sea captains, to take two ships to the Pacific Northwest to trade for furs and to take those furs on to China. Two years later the hold of one ship was full, and Gray set off for China, leaving Kendrick trading on what is now Vancouver Island. Having sold his cargo in China, Gray sailed on to Boston, becoming the first American to circumnavigate the earth. After refitting his ship, the *Columbia,* he set off and rejoined Kendrick. Gray now sailed south to trade and, on May 11, 1792, sought a safe anchorage behind the shelter of a sand bar at the mouth of a large river he named Columbia, after his ship. In fact, a Spaniard, Bruno de Hezeta, had probably been the first European to sight the mouth of this river—in 1775—but he did not recognize it as a river. And, if Gray realized he was making a historically important discovery, his ship's log that day does not record it. He was much more concerned with noting the route through the sandbar and the fact that "vast numbers of natives came alongside" to trade. If his log is an indication, it was just another day of work for Gray.

Gray and Kendrick's journey was part of a flurry of exploring and trading activity that was taking place along the Pacific Northwest coast following the publication of Cook's adventures. Former British naval officers Nathaniel Portlock and George Dixon had been with Cook on his journey and, later, funded by the new London-based King George's Sound Company, went out to trade with the coastal peoples.

Smallpox Crosses the Continent

Smallpox was a disease that came to North America with the Europeans. Today it is possible to inoculate people against smallpox. No cases of the disease have been recorded since 1979. However, in earlier centuries, people justifiably feared it. It had existed in Europe and many other parts of the world for hundreds of years, and many people, including Europeans, had built up some resistance to it. Even so, smallpox often killed about 15 percent of the people who contracted it. Those who suffered from it and survived were immune for the rest of their lives. Because the disease was not known in North America until Europeans arrived, Native Americans suffered more severely. Often, more than half of all people who contracted it died, and sometimes whole communities were wiped out.

Between 1775 and 1782, a great smallpox epidemic hit North America. It broke out in the St. Lawrence River valley, in Chesapeake Bay, and then in Mexico. It devastated George Washington's army in the early years of the American Revolution as there were many young soldiers in his army who had never been exposed to the disease. The movement of people during that war helped carry it around the eastern seaboard. Also, the rise of complex networks of inland trade helped spread the disease quickly across the continent. There had been smallpox epidemics before in North America, but now Indians and traders from British Canada, the United States, and the Spanish Empire moved along trade routes that crossed the continent, carrying smallpox with them.

The Native communities in the area of Oregon and British Columbia had had limited trading contact with peoples to the east, and it is not known exactly when smallpox reached them. What is known is that, by 1792, it appeared to have already taken its toll. That year, George Vancouver and his exploring party were surprised to see deserted villages. A young officer traveling with Vancouver, Thomas Manby, noted in his account of the journey that "this country has been considerably depopulated, but from what cause is hard to determine." The cause, it is now known, was smallpox. Historian Elizabeth Fenn has estimated that this epidemic resulted in the death of at least 130,000 people in North America, including 25,000 Indians on the northwest coast.

Dixon quickly wrote a book *A Voyage Round The World,* about their experiences trading as far north as Alaska, and the book in turn raised more interest in the region.

This increased activity attracted the attention of the Spanish, who claimed the region by right of discovery, which led to an incident that almost caused a war. Another former

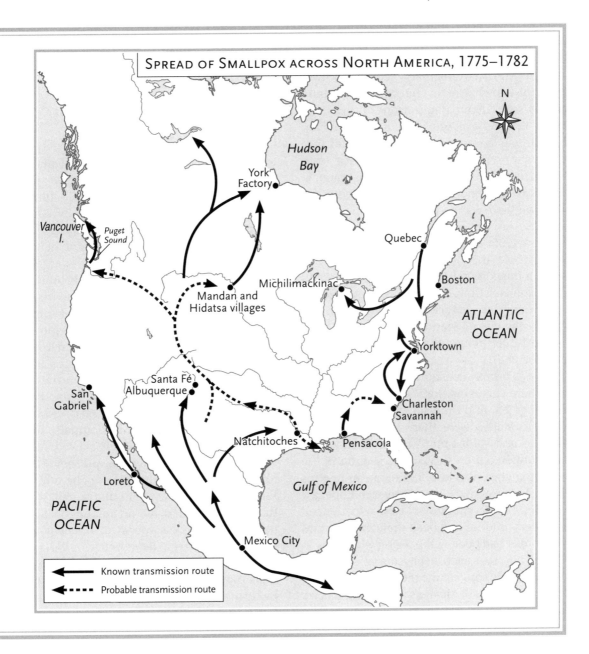

SPREAD OF SMALLPOX ACROSS NORTH AMERICA, 1775–1782

Known transmission route
Probable transmission route

British naval officer, John Meares, had founded a trading post on Nootka Sound, located on the west coast of Vancouver Island. In 1789 he had launched the first sailing ship to be built in the region. While Meares was away, the Spanish seized his post and three of his ships and arrested the crews. The British government made a formal protest to the

Spanish and, after much warlike talk, they reached an agreement in 1790 that enabled them to use the area jointly.

The Nootka Agreement led to another flurry of expeditions in the far west by land and by sea. The most important of these was led by British naval officer George Vancouver. The British government commissioned him to survey the coast of North America from California to Alaska, to fill in the gaps in Cook's charts, and to confirm—once and for all—that there was no possible northwest passage by sea. His detailed survey lasted from 1791 to 1795. His strategy was that his large ships would anchor in a sheltered spot while smaller boats from his ships would go out and chart the coastline. In this way, they charted such complex waterways as Puget Sound (where the city of Seattle is now located) and Burrard Inlet (where the city of Vancouver is now located).

It was a busy coastline. The Spanish were also there surveying. José Maria Narváez was there in 1791, and Dionisio Alcala Galiano and Cayento Valdes were there in 1792. In fact, Galiano and Valdes met Vancouver that year and cooperated on surveying a section of the coast together. Also in 1792 Vancouver met his Spanish counterpart, Juan Francisco Bodega y Quadra. Both commanders were experienced explorers. Bodega had been there in 1775, and Vancouver had been in the region with Cook in 1778. They had each been commissioned to meet to settle some of the remaining problems from the seizure of Meares's ships, a subject on which they could not agree. However, the two men became friendly and cooperated on their surveys. When Vancouver left the area for the winter, he went to California and his was the first non-Spanish sailing vessel to enter San Francisco Bay. He then sailed on to Monterey to meet Bodega before heading out to winter in Hawaii. Vancouver made one more survey of the coast before returning home. On that journey, he confirmed that Vancouver Island was indeed an island and concluded that there was no northwest passage.

EXPLORING THE PACIFIC NORTHWEST BY LAND

Fur traders in western Canada also wanted to participate in the new trade between the Pacific Northwest and China. So the flurry of coastal exploration was matched by equally vigorous efforts to reach the coast by land. The most famous and most successful of these journeys were the two by Alexander Mackenzie in 1789 and 1793 described at the outset of this book. His journey of 1789 was his first attempt to lead a party to find a river route to the Pacific. Instead he found the river system that now bears his name, the Mackenzie River, that flows to the Arctic Ocean. In 1793 he made a second attempt. This time traveling with a small group, he crossed the Rocky Mountains and, by a sequence of portages across lakes and rivers, he eventually found one, the Bella Coola, which flowed to the Pacific. With that momentous journey, he fulfilled the hopes and dreams of generations of European explorers. For almost 300 years, they had searched for an inland northwest passage. Mackenzie found it, but it was no shortcut. However, his discovery did mean that traders from Canada could now extend their trade networks from coast to coast and in turn make a connection with the already lively trade that was taking place across the Pacific Ocean.

The 18th century ended with great journeys of exploration that altered and clarified the map of North America. The dream of an ocean northwest passage was halted but in its place came a vast array of knowledge about the Pacific Northwest. The dream of an easy inland passage had also died. But that search, too, had resulted in an extensive understanding of the waterways of North America. From the Arctic Ocean to the Gulf of Mexico, many of the great waterways of the continent had been mapped. Trade and international rivalry still drove exploring activities. Mackenzie's journey to the coast by land, Gray's discovery of the mouth of the Columbia River, and Vancouver's mapping of the northwest coastline led many U.S. traders and adventurers to believe that there were more rivers and many more riches to be found in the west. The century to follow would prove them right.

13

NORTH AMERICA IN 1800

 Many factors had drawn Europeans to explore northeastern North America from 1497 to 1800. At first, European explorers sought precious metals and a passage to China to gain access to the silk and spice trade. Despite their initial failures to find either of these, other motives continued to draw them. Fishing along the Atlantic coast provided what appeared to be an inexhaustible supply of cod. Forests provided abundant supplies of wood. Trading European manufactured goods with Native peoples for luxurious beaver furs drew explorers further inland each year.

Other Europeans crossed the Atlantic for religious reasons, either to found their own colonial refuges or to spread the faith among those they considered savages. Eventually, permanent settlements provided economic opportunities as the North American coast grew in population and wealth and increasingly came to resemble Europe itself, with bustling seaports and large public buildings. (By the late 18th century, Philadelphia would be the second-largest English-speaking city in the world, outranked only by London.) As the years passed,

many of the inhabitants of these cities and towns chose to move on, constantly pushing westward as they sought both more land for farming and more opportunities to make a profit.

Competing European nations continued to sponsor expeditions in the hope of finding a new trade route to Asia. Increasingly, European wars were played out on the frontiers of colonial empires as well. English, French, and Spanish spheres of influence gradually closed in on any remaining space. However, individual Europeans, motivated by the prospect of finding new lands to settle and exploit, embarked on daring enterprises into what was, for them, the unknown. Through exploration, they might profit from securing new natural resources and trading with new Native communities.

THE FUR TRADE AT 1800

Across the northern tier of North America, the fur trade in particular did indeed generate immense wealth for some European traders. However, by the end of the 18th century, the fur trade was in trouble. Supplies of furs were

John Jacob Astor emigrated to America at the age of 20 and became quite wealthy from the fur trade. *(National Archives of Canada)*

exhausted in eastern regions due to over-hunting and were being rapidly depleted around the Great Lakes and even farther west. Native communities, on whose hunting skills the trade depended, were reeling from the smallpox epidemic that swept the continent in the early 1780s. Only steady exploration into new territory where furs had not yet been commercially harvested kept the trade profitable.

The declining fur supply led to fierce competition between the two great British fur-trading companies, the Hudson's Bay Company and the North West Company. As each company raced to set up trading posts to cement relationships with Native hunters, costs rose dramatically. The rivalry between the two companies was not friendly, even though prominent traders moved between the two organizations. The competition occasionally became violent, especially when rival trading posts were located near each other.

As the century came to an end, disagreements within the North West Company itself were undermining the organization. Company partners fell out over how to develop the business in the future. Some, such as Alexander Mackenzie, thought they should merge with their archrival, but few agreed. In 1798 a group of partners broke away to form a new company, popularly known as the XY Company, and in 1800 Mackenzie joined them. Although the XY Company merged back into the North West Company in 1804, this corporate turmoil reflected the tense and contentious state of the fur trade at the dawn of the 19th century.

THE MEN OF THE TRADE

Despite all this corporate maneuvering, exploring activity continued unceasingly. Peter Fidler, who had been trained by the Hudson's Bay Company's chief surveyor, Philip Turnor, mapped terrain in great detail, particularly in Southern Alberta. Malcolm Ross, Alexander MacKay (who had traveled with Mackenzie in 1793), Duncan McGillivray, and Alexander Henry (the nephew of the trader by the same name who was at Michilimackinac after the French and Indian War), all traveled extensively along the rivers and mountains of the west through the 1790s. Traveling with them were experienced voyageurs, mostly French Canadian, Métis, and Native young men, with skills any expedition could use. So, between the Hudson's Bay Company, the North West Company, and independent traders, there were a large number of men whose skills led to the dramatic expansion of geographic knowledge. However, it should also be said that the rivalry between these firms led to their originally keeping much of this knowledge secret from the scientific community as well as from the general public.

By the closing years of the 18th century, the most active explorer was David Thompson. The pace of his traveling and surveying did not let up after his great journeys earlier in the 1790s. In 1798 and 1799, he crossed the northern interior of the continent, traveling around what is today northern Alberta and along the Saskatchewan and Churchill Rivers. Thompson's career as an explorer was already remarkable, but he was still only 30 years old. By 1812, when he left the North-

west to return east to Montreal, he had logged more than 55,000 miles, surveying 13,000 of them, and the detailed maps he had made ranged from latitude 40°N to latitude 60°N.

Thompson's life mirrored the lives of some of the great explorers who had preceded him, as well as those of some of his contemporaries. He was a diligent surveyor, anxious to make his measurements as accurate as possible. He was prepared to listen to those around him and learn from them. He had started in the trade at a young age and had come to speak the Cree language fluently, which helped him navigate his way through Native diplomacy and trade. As with many other men in the fur trade, Thompson

African Americans in the Fur Trade

One group who found greater freedom in the West were the few people of African descent who worked in the fur trade. Africans, free and enslaved, had been part of the fur trade since settlers had arrived in North America. One of the first was Mattias de Sousa, who had arrived in North America as an indentured servant—that is, someone who agreed to labor for a set period (usually five years) in exchange for his or her passage and food and shelter. When Sousa's servitude was over, he had traded furs on Chesapeake Bay in the 1640s. Jean-Baptiste Pointe du Sable, a free man who was born in Haiti in the Caribbean and was the son of an African slave mother and a French father, arrived in New Orleans in 1779. He entered the fur trade and lived for 16 years at the mouth of the Chicago River on Lake Michigan. As had other French fur traders, he married a Potawatomi woman named Catherine, and together they ran a trading post for many years. Although slave labor was more commonly used on plantations, a few slaves found themselves in the fur trade. Pierre Bonga was owned by a North West Company trader and was frequently left to run the post while his master was gone on long journeys. Bonga became a skilled linguist, married a Chippewa woman, and, since the status of children followed from the mother, their children were free. As the 19th century dawned, the fur trade in the Far West offered opportunities for many people from many walks of life.

had a wife, Charlotte Small, who was mixed race, the daughter of British partner in the North West Company and a Cree woman. Thompson married Charlotte in a civil ceremony in summer 1799, and the two were together until their deaths more than 57 years later.

The fur trade offered men a variety of opportunities. For a few, especially those who were of British origin, there were fortunes to be made. Thompson and Mackenzie, for example, came from humble, though not poor, backgrounds and had the advantage of education to prepare them for the trade and for surveying. Through their driving ambition and hard work, they became rich. Other North West Company partners could count on becoming at least prosperous, if not wealthy, as could the salaried traders of the Hudson's Bay Company.

For many other men, such as the voyageurs, the trade offered a steady job, if a physically demanding one. There was little opportunity for voyageurs to move up to becoming traders, separated as they were not only by ethnicity but also often by language, literacy, and religion. (The mostly British or U.S.-born traders were Protestant, with a few exceptions, and the French Canadian and Métis voyageurs were Catholic.) For many men, despite the hardships of the life, whether working as employees or as small independents, the trade offered freedom from supervision.

NATIVE PEOPLES AND EXPLORATION

Many journeys of exploration within the continent and some that charted the coastline had depended for success on assistance from Native people. Jacques Cartier's exploration of the St. Lawrence River, for example, was only possible because he had Native guides. Often it was with the help of these guides that Europeans discovered portages that were links between different watersheds and found well-worn Native routes along which there were already long-standing networks of trade and diplomacy.

The arrival of Europeans transformed these trading networks. Native connections tended to be local, that is, with people with whom they had direct contact, and trade items passed along a chain of trading relationships. Europeans created a larger market and connected Native peoples to a global network. In doing so, Native diplomatic and military relationships were changed as nations in strategic locations were able to exploit their position and become middlemen as the Cree did between Native communities in the Far West and the Hudson's Bay Company.

From the Native Americans whom the Corte-Reals encountered early in the 16th century to individuals such as Squanto, who showed the Puritan settlers from the *Mayflower* around Massachusetts Bay, to the great Chipewyan leaders such as Matonabbee, who guided Samuel Hearne to the Arctic Ocean, Native leadership, language, and diplomatic skills were essential to an expedition's success. Additionally, European explorers were generally unprepared for the hard life of northeastern North America and needed Native assistance to cope with it. This was a role particularly played by Native women when they married fur traders as part of diplomatic and commercial ties and helped introduce European traders to the customs of the region.

The arrival of Europeans had transformed the Native landscape in other profound ways.

Photographed in 1878, this Haida house, located on one of the Queen Charlotte Islands, is one of the ways Native Americans preserved their culture in the face of the losses caused by European exploration and settlement in North America. *(National Archives of Canada)*

They cleared forests for agriculture, they introduced foreign species that often devastated local flora and fauna, and most important they introduced new diseases to which Native peoples had no resistance. This resulted in catastrophic population decline in the first three centuries of contact and consequent social upheaval as communities merged and language and culture were lost.

The thrust of Europeans across North America brought other kinds of upheaval to Native peoples. Hunting became a year-round activity instead of a seasonal one. Communities became dependent on trade goods such as firearms, kettles, and cloth. Military alliances shifted as European power struggles had a direct impact on the Native world. As the 18th century ended, Native peoples had to continue to face the ambi-

NORTH AMERICA, 1800

ARCTIC OCEAN

RUSSIAN

Baffin Bay

Hudson Bay

BRITISH NORTH AMERICA

PACIFIC OCEAN

Columbia R.

Missouri R.

Mississippi R.

L. Superior

St. Lawrence R.

St. Croix R.

L. Huron

L. Michigan

L. Ontario

L. Erie

FRENCH LOUISIANA

Ohio R.

UNITED STATES

ATLANTIC OCEAN

SPANISH NORTH AMERICA

West Florida

East Florida

SPANISH FLORIDA

N

Gulf of Mexico

Disputed by Russia, Spain, Britain, and the United States

0   500 miles

0   500 km

tions of European powers and the new United States of America. With its rapidly growing population, settlers from the United States were already farming in what had recently been Indian land west of the Appalachians and some of its citizens were already looking to discover more of the resources of the Far West.

THE UNITED STATES LOOKS WEST

European powers had been intrigued by the possibility of finding an inland northwest passage across North America and participating in the lucrative China trade. Some in the United States shared that goal. In 1792, when U.S. captain Robert Gray had found the broad mouth of the Columbia River, traders felt that this might be the navigable trade route to the Pacific they had been searching for if they could just locate it inland. Mackenzie, on his 1793 expedition, thought he had briefly been on it before turbulent waters drove him to seek a more navigable route. In fact, he had been on the Fraser River. So, while Mackenzie had reached the Pacific, he had not found an easily navigable trade route and explorers still searched for the Columbia River.

The search would be completed early in the next century. It would be the 1804–06 journey of a U.S.-government-sponsored expedition led by Meriwether Lewis and

Located in San Francisco, this mission, shown in a 20th-century photograph, was built in the 1780s, shortly after San Francisco was founded. *(Library of Congress, Prints and Photographs Division [HABS, CAL,38-SANFRA,1-])*

William Clark that located the Columbia by an inland route. It would be five years after that, in 1811, before David Thompson would lead a party that traveled the length of the river to the Pacific. Gray, Lewis and Clark, and Thompson had found a great river to the Pacific, but not an easily navigable one. There was no equivalent of the Mississippi that would provide easy access to the Pacific. Although San Francisco had been founded as early as 1776, it would be some time before dynamic commercial cities such as New Orleans and St. Louis—neither of which at that time belonged to the United States in 1800—would appear in the land west of the Mississippi.

Such developments lay in the future. At the end of the 18th century, Thomas Jefferson was among those Americans intrigued by the opportunities of the West. He had been interested in the West long before he was to sponsor the Lewis and Clark expedition. He had been an architect of the Northwest Ordinances of the 1780s, writing the first ordinance in 1784, which laid out the way in which territories would be admitted to the Union. While secretary of state under President George Washington, Jefferson had already been interested in the proposal of André Michaux, the French botanist, to explore the Far West, though little came of that project.

Part of Jefferson's interest in exploration was linked to his political philosophy, in which he thought that security for the future of the new nation would come from widespread property ownership. At the time, in most states only white men who owned property could vote. Jefferson believed that the more property owners, the greater the number of men who would have a stake in the future of the country and the government. To this end, he envisioned a nation of small, independent farmers. That vision of the future required land, and he saw the territory to the west of the Appalachians and east of the Mississippi as available to fulfill that vision. The Northwest Ordinances and the later Southwest Ordinance of 1790 laid out plans for mapping the territory, surveying the land, and selling it off to settlers and speculators. (The "Northwest" and "Southwest" referred at the time to land east of the Mississippi.)

Jefferson did not, at this time, think the land in the Far West was suitable for settlement. This view was confirmed after the land was acquired from France in the Louisiana Purchase in 1803 and explored by Lewis and Clark. Lewis later wrote in his 1806 report of the expedition that the upper Missouri and the Far West were "richer in beaver and otter than any country on earth." Jefferson and others were sure that the fur trade and participation in the China trade were the keys to extracting the wealth of the West and laying claim to the region.

THE END OF A QUEST

For 300 years, European explorers had searched for a northwest passage to Asia, either by ocean to the north of the continent or by an inland passage by river through it. Their quest had led them from the Arctic Circle all the way south to Florida. From there they headed inland across North America, steadily farther west by rivers and lakes, until they were finally successful in finding the last piece of the puzzle, a river that led to the Pacific. There had been many failures along the way. When there were great successes, they often involved strong leadership, good planning, skilled teams or crews, active cooperation of Native peoples, and a good deal of luck.

The economic opportunities of exploiting North America's many natural resources, the skill and talent of the men of all races and nationalities who were involved in this, and intense competition among European nations for control of the continent had encouraged exploration. The years since John Cabot landed on the Newfoundland coast in 1497 had seen changes in which European nations were involved in this contest. The Portuguese and the Dutch, for example, had managed to find what everyone was looking for in the first place: a sea route to Asia—in their case, around Africa and India—and with their footholds along that route, they thus forgot about North America. And few Europeans could have suspected that Russia would join the cast of players from the Pacific side. War and economic changes shifted the balance of power between European nations, and that in turn altered their role in North America. With their loss of the final French and Indian war, France ceased to have a significant presence on the continent it had done so much to map and explore.

By the end of the 18th century, the new United States—now proudly building its capital in Washington, D.C.—joined European powers in staking a claim to North

Sitka, Alaska, was founded by the Russians in 1799 as a base for the Russian-American Company, which was chartered by Russia to oversee the growing fur trade with Native peoples. This photograph shows the old harbor as it looked in the early part of the 1900s, with the mountain peaks known as the Three Sisters in the background. *(Library of Congress, Prints and Photographs Division [LOT 11453-1, no. 501])*

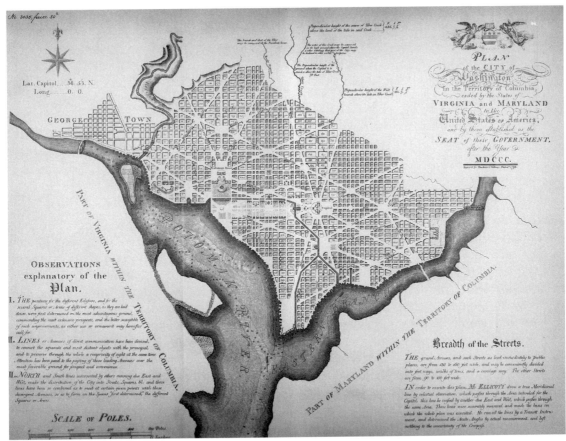

Located where the Potomac and Anacostia Rivers meet, Washington, D.C., was initially planned by Pierre L'Enfant. In the midst of construction, L'Enfant was replaced by Andrew Ellicott, who redrew L'Enfant's existing plans. Ellicott's plans for the capital city are shown here. *(Library of Congress, Prints and Photographs Division [LC-USZ62-120270])*

American territory. It was still entirely uncertain, though, who would control the continent as the 19th century dawned. Geographic knowledge would be as critical in the 19th century as it had been in the preceding years. Discovery and exploration would continue to determine the future of North America.

GLOSSARY

adelantado This title of a Spanish administrative position roughly translates as "military governor" in the period of initial conquest of the New World. The early adelantados were granted almost absolute power to conquer, settle, and exploit the land and people they were assigned. Once colonization efforts were underway by the 1530s, this position was systematically replaced by other officials appointed by the viceroy in Mexico or Peru, or, as in the case of Florida and the Philippines, with a captain-general answerable directly to the king and the Council of the Indies in Spain.

America This term, which only gradually supplanted the name New World, was created in 1507 by obscure German mapmaker Martin Waldseemüller to match the other feminine names of continents (Europa, Africa, and Asia). It was created from the name of Florentine explorer Amerigo Vespucci, who claimed to have been the first European to set foot on the continent.

astrolabe A metal disc that hangs from a frame; precisely measured marks and grooves allow the navigator to sight stars or the sun and determine the degrees of elevation. From ancient times on it was used in navigation, along with charts accounting for seasonal variation. Mariners could thus figure out where they were north or south on the earth (latitude), but it would be the 18th century before other instruments allowed them to determine their location east or west (longitude). The astrolabe itself was replaced by more modern instruments, such as the sextant.

Basques An ethnically distinct people inhabiting northern Spain and southwest France whose language is unrelated to any other in the Indo-European language group. The Basques were noted fishermen, having made numerous trips to North Atlantic waters in the early 1500s and possibly even before major voyages of exploration.

Bretons A Celtic people from the far northwest coast of France in the province of Brittany. This region was only incorporated into France in the 16th century and kept its own language and culture as well as its seafaring traditions. Bretons were long involved in North Atlantic fishing.

cannibalism Derived from the early Spaniards' pronunciation of the Carib people —from which the Caribbean Sea also takes its name—the eating of human flesh. In fact, few Native peoples on the North American continent practiced it, and ironically it is among desperate starving Europeans that the practice is recorded most frequently.

cartographer   Derived from Greek words, a maker of maps or charts.

civilization   According to European standards, a mode of conduct and level of material culture by which they judged Native American peoples, usually considering them "savage" or in a wild state. But such "uncivilized" people were sometimes, conversely, thought to be in a pure and innocent state of nature, "civilization" itself being tainted by warfare, greed, and hatred. More frequently, however, it was taken as a justification for exploiting and changing Native American cultures to suit European norms.

cod   A species of fish, *Gadus morrhua,* found in abundance in the North Atlantic, usually salted as *bacalao* or dried as stockfish and in great demand in Europe, particularly in Catholic countries, where dietary restrictions during Lent and every Friday forbade eating of meat or animal products.

colony   A territorial possession permanently occupied by settlers and ruled directly by the mother country or indirectly by appointed officials. Colonies were usually exploited for their natural resources or commercially grown crops, provided a market for European goods, and could be used as a base for trade.

coureurs de bois   French phrase literally meaning "runners of the woods." *Coureurs de bois* was the name given to independent French fur traders who went into the interior of the country to trade. Since there was an official trading monopoly early in the history of New France, these men were outlaws, so the term was not a compliment. Later, when there was no longer a trading monopoly, it was simply descriptive.

Covenant Chain   A metaphor for the various councils and treaties intended to maintain good relations between the Iroquois and various European settlers—Dutch, English, and French. The Iroquois themselves used the term and were alleged to have a wampum (bead) belt that portrayed this relationship by two boats symbolizing the two peoples moving along separately but in peace. The English in particular tried to exploit this "covenant" by supporting and encouraging the Iroquois to dominate other Indians in the Northeast and thereby gaining security that allowed for economic growth.

dyewood   A number of plants and exotic woods used to dye cloth. Although no major source of these was found in North America, it was often a stated objective of explorers to find such dyes and provide competition for the very lucrative trade in Brazil Wood from South America.

empire   A series of colonies, trading posts, or subject states held by a nation-state or sometimes a corporate body and usually ruled over by the mother country. The term refers to the total sum of such holdings and often assumes a concerted policy for governing or exploiting such possessions in the interest of the mother country and often to the detriment of the Native populations.

ethnohistorians   This is the name (based on the Greek *ethno,* referring to a people) given to those who study the history and culture of a particular ethnic group and view events from its perspective.

fiefdom   A noble estate on which tenants worked the land, paid a proportion of their crop or rent to their lord, and performed services on his personal property or estate. By the 16th century it was a significantly altered variant of medieval feudalism. Many explorers hoped to create fiefdoms in the Americas modeled after European estates though using Native American labor. The use of Native labor never came to pass but English plantations and even the Dutch patroonships (land patrons or owners) in the Hudson Valley resembled European fiefdoms.

flora and fauna Latin words meaning "plants" and "animals." The phrase is generally used to refer to all plant and animal life in a given region or time period.

fool's gold Technically, iron pyrite, a mineral with a brass coloring that has often led people to believe they have found ore with gold.

galley A long flat ship powered by either sail or oar typically used in Mediterranean trade and often manned by captive slaves taken in combat or prisoners. The term later came to refer to the kitchen facilities on a ship.

Great Khan The emperor of China whom many early explorers hoped to meet at the end of their journey. The term is of Turkic origin, and Europeans probably learned it from Marco Polo, who claimed to have visited China during the Yuan dynasty when Mongols ruled China. The emperors of the Ming dynasty (1368–1644), the period of the search for a route to China, would not have used the term.

immunity Resistance to a disease.

impressment The forcible seizure of men so as to compel them to serve in a military force. This was especially common at sea, where crewmen would be taken to serve on other ships.

indentured servant An individual who has agreed to give his or her labor for a number of years, at the end of which time the individual is granted freedom. In the case of the early period of colonization of North America, indentured servants usually were bound for about five years in exchange for passage to North America and food and board for the period of service.

inland northwest passage A river that Europeans hoped to find that would allow them to navigate across the North American continent easily and would allow traders to travel from the Atlantic to the Pacific Ocean.

intendant A powerful official in New France responsible for the administration of justice and economic growth.

isthmus A narrow neck of land that connects two larger bodies of land.

Jesuits Formally called the Society of Jesus; a religious order of the Catholic Church founded by Ignatius of Loyola in 1534. The order had, and still has, educational and scientific interests in addition to its missionary work.

joint-stock company A financial innovation of the 17th century; usually a temporary association of investors, each of whom owned a certain number of shares or percentage of a specified venture. Eventually, these stocks became negotiable and could be traded as they are today in the stock exchange.

jurisdiction The legal right to control and govern a specified area of land, granted by a king or his appointed official.

league A measure of length of distance that varies considerably in different times and in different countries and whether the measure is on land or sea. It is usually the equivalent of about two and a half to three miles as a land measure, and three to four and a half miles as a sea measure.

letters patent During the European age of exploration, an official decree whereby an individual was granted exclusive rights to explore and exploit a region for a specified number of years. As with a modern patent on an invention or a copyright, it was assumed that the person who bore the expense and whose ideas led to the discovery should be allowed to reap a profit from it without competition.

Loyalists North American colonists who stayed loyal to the British during the American Revolution. Many of them left the United States during and after the war and went to live in Canada, particularly Upper Canada (now Ontario), Nova Scotia, and New Brunswick. Others went to live in England.

mercantile empire A series of overseas possessions strung into a network of fortified posts specifically designed to facilitate and protect trade. These were usually maintained by the state as an object of national interest rather than by private investors. These are contrasted by colonial empires, in which entire regions are held and occupied by settlers.

Métis From the French for "mixed," people of mixed French and Native American ancestry.

monopoly More or less total control over the production and trade of certain products or services. Early modern states often granted exclusive rights to an individual or company to trade or produce a certain commodity. A monopoly to explore a certain region, to import fish, or even produce simple things like soap could be enormously lucrative. The economic benefit, so theorists believed, was that, with such total control, a business was guaranteed success, with which it could compete with foreign businesses and thus bring money into the country. Unlike today, monopolies were not seen as stifling healthy competition and free trade.

nation-state A territorially contiguous area of land that is ruled by one centralized administration; in the early modern period this was usually by a royal dynasty. The nation-state is also assumed to have a common cultural, linguistic, and often ethnic unity that distinguishes it from other nations, though this often has meant ignoring or consciously effacing local identities.

nobles A hereditary and titled aristocratic class in European society that often served military or administrative functions. In some countries, such as France and Spain, nobles were exempt from paying taxes. The base of their power was landholding, so acquiring estates in the New World was a major reason they became investors in overseas exploration.

Normans Derived from the word "Northmen," a reference to their ancestors, the Vikings, who settled in France, these people from the north coast of France—what became known as the province of Normandy—were expert seamen and early became active in fishing North Atlantic waters.

Northwest Passage The sea route to Asia via a strait believed to exist cutting across the North American continent, but in fact the actual passage requires an extremely difficult journey through frozen and iceberg-laden waters some 500 miles above the Arctic Circle in what is now the Northwest Territories of Canada and above Alaska.

peddler This is a general term describing people who go from place to place buying and selling (peddling) goods. It was specifically used by the Hudson's Bay Company to describe traders from the North West Company to belittle them.

Pilgrims A term adopted by the radical Protestant settlers aboard the *Mayflower* who landed in Massachusetts in 1620. The generic (lowercased) form of the term originally is derived from a person who makes a journey, known as a pilgrimage, to a holy site where a miracle had occurred, such as Rome, Jerusalem, or Mecca.

plantation   Although originally referring to any colonial settlement, it eventually came to mean a large estate producing a commercial crop for export, such as tobacco or cotton, and worked by slave labor.

portage   This French word, now also used in English, refers both to the act of carrying canoes and all supplies around an obstacle, such as rapids or a waterfall on a river, and to the places and routes where such an act is required.

portolan chart   From the Latin for "port" or "harbor," charts indicating the distances between ports and along coastlines. These charts directly precede and contribute to the mapmaking techniques in the age of exploration.

privateering   An official license to seize plunder from enemy ships, which in practice differed little from acts of piracy. European rulers found this an effective way to strike their opponents without having to spend money, and for investors it could mean good profits despite the decline in trade caused by war.

Proclamation Line   This was the name given to a British royal proclamation of 1763 that restricted British colonists in North America from settling west of the Appalachians. The goal was to slow down settlement in the West while British authorities negotiated and purchased Indian lands. The colonists almost immediately disregarded this proclamation.

Protestant   A follower of any one of the churches that had "protested" against and broken away from the Roman Catholic Church in the 16th century. These include German Lutherans, the Swiss, Dutch, and Scottish Reformed Churches, the French Huguenots, as well as the Church of En-

gland. Religion became a major point of contention among nations involved in exploration.

Puritan   A term (based on "purify") denoting a Protestant who sought further and more thorough reform of the Church of England, usually along lines specified by French theologian Jean Calvin. The majority of settlers to the Massachusetts Bay colony and New England in the 17th century were Puritans.

quadrant   A navigational instrument consisting of a right angle, an arc inscribed with degrees, and a weighted string or plumb line hanging down. By looking through a sight aimed at a fixed point such as the North Star, the ship's latitude on the earth could be discerned from where the vertical plumb line fell on the arc.

Récollets   The French branch of the Franciscan order of the Catholic Church known for their austerity. Their name is based on the French word for "recollect" and is said to derive from the fact that the friar's hood reminded people of ("recollected") a bird's crest.

rhumb line   The line drawn on a navigator's map to indicate a fixed compass direction for a ship to follow.

sassafras   A tree found in eastern and southeastern North America; its root bark when dried was used as a flavoring for a tea or other drinks, and its oil is used to add scent to soap. Root beer used to be made of sassafras but today is almost always artificially flavored.

scurvy   A potentially fatal illness resulting from a deficiency of vitamin C. Its symptoms include bleeding gums and swollen limbs. The human body can obtain sufficient vitamin C from many foods, but sailors who spent many months at sea with a limited diet were at high risk to get scurvy. It could be cured with citrus juice or with a liquid made by boiling spruce or arborvitae (an evergreen shrub).

slavery Keeping people in servitude and as property. Technically, Europeans would only make slaves out of captives taken in battle; in fact, they often initiated warfare in order to justify taking slaves. In the case of Africa, they often bought slaves from Africans who had captured them. The Spanish enslaved many Native Americans in their New World territories. In North America, Native populations were rarely reduced to slavery because traders and colonists depended on them, but, in the plantation economy of the South, African slaves comprised an overwhelming proportion of the labor force.

social history A kind of historical study that asks questions about what ordinary people were doing rather than just focusing on famous individuals of history and political and military events.

spices A culinary rather than strict botanical term, spices refer to the dried bark, root, fruit, bud, or other part of usually tropical plants imported by Europeans and sold at enormous profit. Among those most in demand were pepper, cloves, nutmeg, and cinnamon from Southeast Asia.

Sulpicians A religious order established in 1642 by Abbé Olier of the parish of St. Sulpice in France. The order trained men for the priesthood.

Treaty of Tordesillas Named after the city in Spain where in 1494 an agreement was made between Spain and Portugal, and given assent by Pope Alexander VI, dividing the entire world into two halves along a line 370 leagues west of the Cape Verde Islands—about 48° west of the Greenwich (Prime) meridian. Spain would have the right to explore and conquer most of the New World; Portugal was given Africa and Asia, and as it turned out Brazil and a claim to Newfoundland as well. These terms became impossible to enforce once other European powers actively engaged in exploration, particularly in North America.

West Indies Due to a geographical misconception, the Caribbean was thought to be adjacent to South Asia, or the "East Indies," and so was regarded as the West Indies. As a result, the term for all Native Americans was "Indians."

FURTHER INFORMATION

NONFICTION

Armstrong, Joe C. *Champlain.* Toronto: Macmillan of Canada, 1987.

Axtell, James. *Beyond 1492: Encounters in Colonial North America.* New York: Oxford University Press, 1992.

———. *The Invasion Within: The Contest of Cultures in Colonial North America.* New York: Oxford University Press, 1985.

Barbour, Philip L. *The Three Worlds of Captain John Smith.* Boston: Houghton Mifflin, 1964.

Bennett, Charles E. *Laudonnière and Fort Caroline; History and Documents.* Gainesville: University of Florida Press, 1964.

Boucher, Philip P. *Les Nouvelles Frances: France in America, 1500–1815, an Imperial Perspective.* Providence, R.I.: John Carter Brown Library, 1989.

Brazão, Eduardo. *The Corte-Real Family and the New World.* Lisbon: Agencia-Geral do Ultramar, 1965.

Buisseret, David. *Mapping the French Empire in North America.* Chicago: Newberry Library, 1991.

Burrage, Henry S., ed. *Early English and French Voyages, Chiefly from Hakluyt, 1534–1608.* New York: Barnes & Noble, 1952.

Calloway, Colin. *First Peoples: A Documentary History of American Indian History.* New York: Bedford St. Martin, 1999.

———. *New Worlds for All: Indians, Europeans, and the Remaking of Early America.* Baltimore: Johns Hopkins University Press, 1997.

Cartier, Jacques. *The Voyages of Jacques Cartier.* Toronto: University of Toronto Press, 1993.

———. *Voyages. Two Navigations to Newe Fraunce.* Amsterdam: *Theatrum Orbis Terrarum;* Norwood, N.J.: W.J. Johnson, 1975.

Cavan, Seamus. *Daniel Boone and the Opening of the Ohio Country.* New York: Chelsea House Publishers, 1991.

Champlain, Samuel de. *Voyages of Samuel de Champlain.* Trans. by Charles Pomeroy Otis. New York: B. Franklin, 1966.

Chiapelli, Fredi, Michael J. B. Allen, and Robert L. Benson, eds. *First Images of America.* Berkeley: University of California Press, 1976.

Codignola, Luca. "Another Look at Verrazzano's Voyage." *Acadiensis* vol. 29, no. 1, 1999: pp. 29–42.

Coulter, Tony. *Jacques Cartier, Samuel Champlain and the Explorers of Canada.* New York: Chelsea House Publishers, 1993.

Crosby, Alfred. *The Columbian Exchange: Biological and Cultural Consequences of 1492.* Westport, Conn.: Greenwood Publishing, 1972.

Crouse, Nellis M. *La Verendrye: Fur Trader and Explorer.* Ithaca, N.Y.: Cornell University Press, 1956.

Delage, Denys. *Bitter Feast: Amerindians and Europeans in Northeastern North America, 1600–64.* Trans. by Jane Brierly. Vancouver: University of British Columbia, 1993.

Demos, John. *The Unredeemed Captive: A Family Story from Early America.* New York: Vintage Books, 1994.

De Vorsey, Louis, et al. *Columbus and the Land of Ayllón: The Exploration and Settlement of the Southeast.* Valona, Ga.: Lower Altamaha Historical Society, 1992.

Dexter, Lincoln A. *The Gosnold Discoveries in the North Part of Virginia, 1602, Now Cape Cod and the Islands, Massachusetts: According to the Relations by Gabriel Archer and John Brereton.* Brookfield, Mass.: L.A. Dexter, 1982.

Durant, David N. *Raleigh's Lost Colony.* New York: Atheneum, 1981.

Eccles, W. J. *The Canadian Frontier, 1534–1760.* New York: Holt, Rinehart and Winston, 1969.

Eckert, Allan W. *That Dark and Bloody River: Chronicles of the Ohio River Valley.* New York: Bantam Books, 1995.

Emerson, Everett H. *Captain John Smith.* New York: Maxwell Macmillan International, 1993.

Faragher, John Mack. *Daniel Boone: The Life and Legend of an American Pioneer.* New York: Henry Holt & Co., 1992.

Faragher, John Mack, and Robert V. Hine. *The American West: A New Interpretive History.* New Haven: Yale University Press, 2000.

Fenn, Elizabeth. *Pox Americana: The Great Smallpox Epidemic of 1775–82.* New York: Hill and Wang, 2002.

Firstbrook, P. L. *The Voyage of the* Matthew: *John Cabot and the Discovery of North America.* London: BBC Books, 1997.

Gleach, Frederic W. *Powhattan's World and Colonial Virginia.* Lincoln: University of Nebraska Press, 1997.

Goetzmann, William H., and Glyndwr Williams. *The Atlas of North American Exploration: From the Norse Voyages to the Race to the Pole.* New York: Prentice Hall, 1992.

Golay, Michael, and John S. Bowman, eds.. *North American Exploration.* Hoboken, N.J.: John Wiley, 2003.

Goodnough, David. *John Cabot and Son.* Mahwah, N.J.: Troll Associates, 1979.

Gookin, Warner Foote. *Bartholomew Gosnold, Discoverer and Planter: New England—1602, Virginia—1607.* Hamden, Conn.: Archion Books, 1963.

———. "Who was Bartholomew Gosnold?" *The William and Mary Quarterly,* 3rd Ser., Vol. 6, No. 3, July 1949: pp. 398–415.

Gordon, Alan. "Heroes, History and Two Nationalisms: Jacques Cartier." *Journal of the Canadian Historical Association,* vol. 10, 1999: pp. 81–102.

Gough, Barry. *First Across the Continent: Sir Alexander Mackenzie.* The Oklahoma Western Biographies, Vol. 14. Norman, Okla.: University of Oklahoma Press, 1997.

Grant, W. L., ed. *Voyages of Samuel de Champlain, 1604–1618.* New York: Charles Scribner's Sons, 1907. Reprint, New York: Barnes & Noble, Inc., 1952.

Greer, Allan. *The Jesuit Relations: Natives and Missionaries in Seventeenth-Century North America.* New York: Bedford/St. Martins, 2000.

Hakluyt, Richard. *Hakluyt's Voyages.* Edited by Irwin R. Blacker. New York: Viking, 1965.

Harisse, Henry. *The Discovery of North America.* Amsterdam: N. Israel, 1961.

Harris, Sherwood. "The Tragic Dream of Jean Ribaut." *American Heritage,* vol. 14, no. 6, 1963: pp. 8–15, 88–90.

Horning, Susan Schmidt. "The Power of Image: Promotional Literature and Its Changing Role in the Settlement of Early Carolina." *North Carolina Historical Review,* vol. 70, no. 4, 1993: pp. 365–400.

Hudson, Charles M. *The Juan Pardo Expeditions: Exploration of the Carolinas and Tennessee, 1566–1568.* Transcribed, translated, and annotated by Paul E. Hoffman. Washington, D.C.: Smithsonian Institution Press, 1990.

Jogues, Father Isaac. "Letter and Narrative of Father Isaac Jogues, 1643, 1645." *Original Narratives of Early American History: Narratives of New Netherlands.* Edited by J. Franklin Jameson. New York: Charles Scribner's Sons, 1909: 235–253.

Johnson, Donald S. *Charting the Sea of Darkness: The Four Voyages of Henry Hudson.* Camden, Me.: International Marine, 1993.

Jones, Phil. *Ralegh's Pirate Colony in America: The Lost Settlement of Roanake 1584–1590.* Charleston, S.C.: Tempus, 2001.

Joutel, Henri. *The La Salle Expedition to Texas: The Journal of Henri Joutel, 1684–1687*. Edited by William C. Foster; translated by Johanna S. Warren. Austin: Texas State Historical Association, 1998.

Katz, William Loren. *The Black West*. Garden City, N.Y.: Doubleday & Company, Inc., 1971.

Kupperman, Karen Ordahl. *Indians and English: Facing off in Early America*. Ithaca, N.Y.: Cornell University Press, 2000.

———. "Roanoke Lost" *American Heritage*, vol. 36, no. 5, 1985: pp. 81–96.

Laudonnière, René Goulaine de. *A Foothold in Florida: The Eye-witness Account of Four Voyages Made by the French to That Region and Their Attempt at Colonisation, 1562–1568, Based on a New Translation of Laudonnière's L'Histoire Notable de la Floride*. Sarah Lawson, ed. with annotations and appendices by W. John Faupel. West Sussex, England: Antique Atlas Publications, 1992.

———. *Three Voyages*. Translated with an introduction and notes by Charles E. Bennett. Gainesville: University Presses of Florida 1975.

Lemay, J. A. Leo. *The American Dream of Captain John Smith*. Charlottesville: University Press of Virginia, 1991.

Lorant, Stefan. *The New World: The First Pictures of America*. New York: Duell, Sloan and Pearce, 1965.

Lyon, Eugene. *The Enterprise of Florida: Pedro Menéndez de Avilés and the Spanish Conquest of 1565–1568*. Gainesville: University Presses of Florida, 1976.

———. *Pedro Menéndez de Avilés*. New York: Garland, 1995.

McConnell, Michael N. *A Country Between: The Upper Ohio River Valley and Its Peoples, 1724–1774*. Lincoln: University of Nebraska Press, 1992.

Merrel, James H. *Into the American Woods: Negotiators on the Pennsylvania Frontier*. New York: Norton, 2000.

Milton, Giles. *Big Chief Elizabeth*. New York: Farrar, Straus and Giroux, 2000.

Morison, Samuel Eliot. *The European Discovery of America: The Northern Voyages*. New York: Oxford University Press, 1971.

———. *Samuel De Champlain: Father of New France*. Boston: Little, Brown and Company, 1972.

Namias, June. *White Captives: Gender and Ethnicity on the American Frontier*. Chapel Hill: University of North Carolina Press, 1993.

Newman, Peter C. *Company of Adventurers*. 2 vols. Ontario: Viking Books, 1985.

Oberg, Michael Leroy. "Gods and Men: The Meeting of Indian and White Worlds on the Carolina Outer Banks, 1584–1586." *North Carolina Historical Review*, vol. 76, no. 4, 1999: pp. 367–390.

Parsons, John. *On the Way to Cipango: John Cabot's Voyage of 1498*. St. John's, Newfoundland: Creative Publishers, 1998.

Pope, Peter Edward. *The Many Landfalls of John Cabot*. Toronto: University of Toronto Press, 1997.

Quinn, David B. *New American World: A Documentary History of North America to 1612*, 5 vols. New York: Arno Press, 1979.

———. *North American Discovery, Circa 1000–1612*. New York: Harper & Row, 1971.

———. *Sir Humphrey Gilbert and Newfoundland: On the Four Hundredth Anniversary of His Annexation of the Island to the Realm of England*. St. John's: Newfoundland Historical Society, 1983.

Quinn, David B. ed. *The Roanoke Voyages, 1584–1590: Documents to Illustrate the English Voyages to North America under the Patent Granted to Walter Raleigh in 1584*. London: Hakluyt Society, 1955.

Quinn, David B., Robert H. Fuson, Olive Patricia Dickason, Cornelius J. Jaenen, Elizabeth A. H. John, and William H. Goetzmann. *Essays on the History of North American Discovery and Exploration*. Edited by Stanley H. Palmer and Dennis Reihartz. College Station: Texas A & M University Press, 1988.

Ribaut, Jean. *The Whole & True Discouerye of Terra Florida. A Facsimile Reproduction*. With introduction by David L. Dowd. Gainesville: University of Florida Press, 1964.

Richter, Daniel K. *Facing East from Indian Country: A Native History of Early America.* Cambridge: Cambridge University Press, 2003.

Shirley, John William. *Thomas Harriot, a Biography.* New York: Oxford University Press, 1983.

Sinclair, Andrew. *Sir Walter Raleigh and the Age of Discovery.* Harmondsworth, New York: Penguin, 1984.

Stannard, David. *American Holocaust: The Conquest of the New World.* New York: Oxford University Press, 1992.

Swagerty, William R. "Indian Trade in the Trans-Mississippi West to 1870." *The Handbook of North American Indians* Vol. 4, *History of Indian White Relations.* Edited by William E. Washburn. Washington, D.C.: Smithsonian Institution Press, 1988, pp. 351–374.

Taylor, Alan. *American Colonies.* New York: Penguin Books, 2001.

Thrower, Norman J. W. "New Light on the 1524 Voyage of Verrazzano." *Terrae Incognitae*, The Journal for the History of Discoveries, vol. 11, 1979, pp. 59–65.

Thwaites, Reuben G. *The Jesuit Relations and Allied Documents: Travels and Explorations of the Jesuit Missionaries in North America.* Toronto: McClelland & Stewart, 1925.

Trevelyan, Raleigh. *Sir Walter Raleigh.* New York: Allen Lane, 2002.

Trudel, Marcel. *The Beginnings of New France, 1524–1663.* Translated by Patricia Claxton. Toronto: McClelland & Stewart, 1973.

Usner, Daniel H. *Indians, Settlers, and Slaves in a Frontier Exchange Economy: The Lower Mississippi Valley Before 1783.* Chapel Hill: University of North Carolina Press, 1992.

Van Der Donck, Adriaen. *A Description of the New Netherlands.* Edited by Thomas F. O'Donnell. Syracuse, N.Y.: Syracuse University Press, 1968.

Van Kirk, Sylvia. *Many Tender Ties: Women in Fur Trade Society, 1670–1870.* Norman: University of Oklahoma Press, 1980.

Viereck, Phillip, ed. *The New Land: Discovery, Exploration, and Early Settlement of Northeastern United States, From Earliest Voyages to 1621, Told in the Words of the Explorers Themselves.* New York: John Day Co., 1967.

White, John. *America, 1585: The Complete Drawings of John White.* Chapel Hill: University of North Carolina Press, 1984.

White, Richard. *The Middle Ground: Indians, Empires, and Republics in the Great Lakes Region, 1650–1815.* Cambridge: Cambridge University Press, 1991.

Winsor, Justin, and George E. Ellis. *Early Spanish, French, and English Encounters with American Indians.* Edited by Anne Paolucci and Henry Paolucci. Whitestone, N.Y.: Council on National Literatures, 1997.

Wroth, Lawrence C. *The Voyages of Giovanni da Verrazzano, 1524–1528.* New Haven, Conn.: Yale University Press, 1970.

FICTION

Aaseng, Nathan. *You are the Explorer.* Minneapolis: Oliver Press Inc., 2000.

Cooper, James Fenimore. *The Deerslayer.* New York: Bantam, Doubleday, Dell, 1982.

———. *The Last of the Mohicans.* New York: Barnes & Noble Books, 2003.

———. *The Pathfinder.* New York: Signet Classics, 1976.

Durbin, William. *The Broken Blade.* Milwaukee: BT Bound, 1997.

———. *Wintering.* New York: Yearling Books, 2000.

Garfield, Henry. *The Lost Voyage of John Cabot.* New York: Simon & Schuster, 2004.

Hesse, Karen. *Stowaway.* New York: Margaret McElderry Books, 2000.

Manson, Ainslie. *A Dog Came, Too: A True Story.* Vancouver, B.C.: Douglas & McIntyre, 2003.

Moore, Brian. *Black Robe.* New York: Plume Reprint, 1997.

Speare, Elizabeth George. *Sign of the Beaver.* New York: Bantam, Doubleday, Dell, 1984.

Stainer, M. L. *The Lyon's Roar*. Circleville, N.Y.: Chicken Soup Press, 1999.

VHS/DVD

Black Robe (1991). MGM, DVD/VHS, 2001.

Cabot (1997). Bristol Film and Video Society, VHS, 1997.

Canada: A People's History (2000). Canadian Broadcasting Corporation, DVD/VHS, 2000.

Empire by the Bay: Ambition, Wealth, and the Hudson's Bay Company (2000). PBS Video, VHS, 2000.

Golden Age of Exploration (1997). Knowledge Unlimited, VHS, 1997.

Ikwe (1986). National Film Board of Canada, VHS, 1986.

Last of the Mohicans (1992). Twentieth Century Fox, DVD/VHS, 2001.

Lost Colony of Roanoke (1999). A&E Home Videos, VHS, 2000.

The Mayflower Pilgrims (1996). Janson Video, VHS, 1996.

Mistress Madeleine (1986). National Film Board of Canada, VHS, 1986.

Sir Walter Raleigh (2002). Cromwell Productions, VHS, 2003.

WEB SITES

General Explorers' Biographies

Enchanted Learning. Explorers of North and Central America. Available online. URL: http://www.enchantedlearning.com/explorers/namerica.shtml. Downloaded on September 17, 2003.

General Exploration of Future Canada

Government of Canada: Canada's Digital Collections. Available online. URL:http://collections.ic.gc.ca/alberta/furtrade. Downloaded on September 17, 2003.

History of Nova Scotia. Available online. URL: http://www.blupete.com/Hist/NovaScotiaBk1/Part1/TOC.htm. Updated in July 1998.

Hudson's Bay Company. Available online. URL: http://www.hbc.com/hbc/e_hi/historic_hbc. Downloaded on September 17, 2003.

National Library of Canada-Bibliothèque Nationale du Canada. Available online. URL: http://www.nlc-bnc.ca. Updated in July 2003.

New France History: Pre-Settlement History To 1599. Available online. URL: http://www.telusplanet.net/public/dgarneau/french1.htm. Updated on April 17, 2003.

Northwest Journal, an online journal of the northwest of North America, especially for re-enactors, teachers, and students. Available online. URL: http://www.northwestjournal.ca. Downloaded on September 17, 2003.

Pathfinders and Pathways: The Exploration of Canada. National Library of Canada. Available online. http://www.nlc-bnc.ca/2/24/index-e.html. Updated on December 7, 2001.

Theresa Ann Wright. "The Winds of Time that Shaped the State." From *Florida Living Magazine,* Vol. 16, No. 11, November 1996. Available online. URL: http://www.geocities.com/SoHo/Bistro/4791/winds.html. Downloaded on September 17, 2003.

Virtual Museum of New France. Available Online. URL: http://www.civilization.ca/vmnf/explor. Downloaded on September 17, 2003.

Voyageurs National Park. Available online. URL: http://www.nps.gov/voya. Downloaded on September 17, 2003.

General Exploration of Future United States

Captain Cook Society. Available online. URL: http://www.captaincooksociety.com. Downloaded on September 17, 2003.

Handbook of Texas Online. Available online. URL: http://www.tsha.utexas.edu/handbook/online/articles. Downloaded on September 17, 2003.

History, geography, and politics of Virginia as taught at George Mason University. Available online. URL: http://www.virginiaplaces.com. Downloaded on September 17, 2003.

History of Detroit. Available online. URL: http://www.historydetroit.com. Downloaded on September 17, 2003.

"I arrived at Detroit" A Presentation of the Clarke Historical Library, Central Michigan University. Available online. URL:http://www.lib.cmich.edu/clarke/detroit. Downloaded on September 17, 2003.

Ohio Historical Society Encyclopedia Online. Available online. URL: http://www.ohiohistorycentral.org. Downloaded on September 17, 2003.

Oregon Bluebook. Available online. URL: http://www.bluebook.state.or.us. Downloaded on September 17, 2003.

Settlement

The Colonization of Newfoundland. Memorial University of Newfoundland. Available online. URL: http://www.heritage.nf.ca/exploration/sponsored.html#gilbert. Downloaded on September 17, 2003.

First English Settlement in the New World. State Library of North Carolina. Available online. URL: http://statelibrary.dcr.state.nc.us/nc/ncsites/english1.htm. Downloaded on September 17, 2003.

Online journal of Early American History: Cities of Early North America. Available online. URL: http://www. commonplace.org/vol-03/no-04. Downloaded on September 17, 2003.

John Cabot

The Avalon Project at Yale Law School. The Letters Patents of King Henry the Seventh Granted unto Iohn Cabot and his Three Sonnes, Lewis, Sebastian and Sancius for the the Discouerie of New and Unknowen Lands. Available online. URL: http://www.yale.edu/lawweb/avalon/cabot01.htm. Downloaded on September 17, 2003.

Derek Croxton. The Cabot Dilemma: John Cabot's 1497 Voyage & the Limits of Historiography. Published by the Corcoran Department of History at the University of Virginia. Essays in History. Volume 33, 1990–91. Available online. URL: http://etext.lib.virginia.edu/journals/EH/EH33/croxto 33. html. Downloaded on September 17, 2003.

Giovanni da Verrazano

Andre Engels. Giovanni da Verrazzano. Available online. URL: http://www.win.tue.nl/~engels/discovery/ verrazzano.html. Downloaded on September 17, 2003.

Jacques Cartier

Jacques Cartier, Explorer. Available online. URL: http://www.publicbookshelf.com/public.html/OurCountryVol_1/jacquesca_cd.html. Downloaded on September 17, 2003.

Jacques Cartier: Explorer of the St. Lawrence. Department of Geography, Concordia University, 1997. Available online. URL: http://collections.ic.gc.ca/stlauren/hist/hi_cartier.htm. Downloaded on September 17, 2003.

Robert La Roque de Roquebrune. Jean-François De LaRocque De Roberval. Available online. URL: http://freepages.genealogy.rootsweb.com/~louislarocque/roberven.htm. Downloaded on September 17, 2003.

Roanoke

John D. Neville and Sir Humphrey Gilbert. Roanoke Revisited Heritage Education Program. Available online. URL: http://www.nps.gov/fora/gilbert.htm. Downloaded on September 17, 2003.

The Lost Colony of Roanoke. Available online. URL: http://muweb.millersville.edu/~columbus/papers/seifarth-shtml. Downloaded on September 17, 2003.

Roanoke Revisited Heritage Education Program. Available online. URL: http://www.nps.gov/fora/roanokerev.htm. Downloaded on September 17, 2003.

Henry Hudson

Henry Hudson. Available online. URL: http://www.ianchadwick.com/hudson. Downloaded on September 17, 2003.

Henry Hudson and Early Hudson River History. Hudson River Maritime Museum. Available

online. URL: http://www.ulster.net/~hrmm/
halfmoon/halfmoon.htm. Downloaded on September 17, 2003.

Medical Impact of Contact

Dean R. Snow and Kim M. Lanphear. "European
Contact and Indian Depopulation in the Northeast: The Timing of the First Epidemics." *Ethno-
history* (Vol. 35:1, Winter 1988, pp.15–33). Available online. URL: http://muweb.millersv.
edu/~columbus//data/ant/SNOWLAN1.ANT.
Downloaded on September 17, 2003.

INDEX

Page numbers in *italic* indicate a photograph. Page numbers followed by *m* indicate maps. Page numbers followed by *g* indicate glossary entries. Page numbers in **boldface** indicate box features.